The Wealth, Walk and Warfare of the Christian

By

RUTH PAXSON

Author of "Life on the Highest Plane"

Fleming H. Revell Company
Old Tappan, New Jersey

To

ELIZABETH HALL PAIGE

my devoted friend and faithful partner
in the stewardship of
the exceeding riches of His grace,
this book is
gratefully and lovingly
dedicated

THE AUTHOR'S NOTE

THIS book does not purport to be an exposition of Ephesians verse by verse, or doctrine by doctrine. Some rich nuggets out of this vast gold mine will not be dug up at all, but left for you to mine for yourself. The book will deal with the *content* of the epistle rather than its *contents*.

The message will be distinctly personal, for it is written of what one's eyes have seen and ears heard, and what has entered into one's own heart of all those wondrous things which God has prepared for them that love Him. If this message stimulates you to dig deep and to dwell deep in Ephesians, then the most fervent prayer for it will have been answered. To that end, will you read Ephesians until you can think through the entire epistle with your Bible closed; will you reread it until it is written on the table of your heart as truly as on the pages of your Bible; will you continue to read it until it permeates the warp and woof of the fabric of your spiritual life, and until you are so saturated with it that you think, talk and live Ephesians.

The message purposely will be practical. It is possible for a Christian to know categorically the doctrinal teachings of this epistle, to believe all of them, and so to be quite orthodox in his creed, while he may never have grasped the vital relationship between truth and life so vividly presented here, and so remain quite heterodox in his conduct. Our desire is to show the essential order in and connection between the first three chapters, which deal with doctrine, and the last three, which deal with experience. We shall see in Ephesians how our wealth is to be manifested in our walk and maintained in our warfare.

You will profit immeasurably by committing to memory 1:4-7; 2:4-7; 6:10-12, and the two inspired prayers 1:15-23 and 3:14-21. Make a few of the key verses your very own, such as 1:3, 21, 23; 2:5, 6; 3:19, 20; 4:1, 22, 24, 30; 5:18, 30; 6:12, 13. To do this will be like having ready cash against the time of spiritual emergency.

For the sake of economizing space sometimes only part of a verse will be quoted; also in giving references from Ephesians the name of the epistle will be omitted, and only the numerals indicating the chapter and verse will be given. Whenever the words, "the Church," are used, the meaning will be that of the Body of Christ as revealed in the epistle, unless otherwise stated. Our purpose will be to let Scripture interpret Scripture, which it will always do if we but search far enough and dig deeply enough. In this way some of the more difficult passages may be understood and errors avoided. After reading Ephesians through several times, study the chart to help in getting the book as a whole before you.

With the prayer that God will use this message to enable some of His children to appropriate more fully their wealth in Christ; to walk worthily of their high calling; and to be victorious wrestlers, this book is now sent forth.

Ruth Paxson.

Tryon,
North Carolina.

CONTENTS

Part III

INTRODUCTION

THE GRAND CANYON OF SCRIPTURE

ONE time when in need of special spiritual inspiration and refreshment I went to the Grand Canyon of Arizona. Of all God's wonders in His natural creation, which He has given me to see, none seems more wonderful than the Grand Canyon. Two never-to-be-forgotten days were spent there.

On the first day I just skirted a bit of the Canyon's rim, getting first-hand impressions of its magnitude, majesty and matchless beauty of colouring. For an hour or two I sat trying to compass in imagination the vast breadth of the gorge which at that point was thirteen miles across. Then I moved on to another spot, where, looking straight down one mile, the sizeable river below looked like a white ribbon. At sunset I went to a distant point where the Canyon stretched itself out over eighty miles before one's eyes, and where it was all ablaze with a veritable orgy of indescribable colour, which left one silent and worshipful in the presence of the Canyon's Creator.

Physically tired, but spiritually renewed, I tumbled into bed for a brief sleep before rising at four to find my way, alone and unaided save by the tiniest ray of light, to the road that led me again to the sunset point, that I might there see the sunrise. On and on I went, until in semi-darkness, standing on the rim of the Canyon, I looked down into an absolutely black abyss. Not even one ray of the sun's light shone upon its rocks to bring out their exquisite beauty. All was unrelieved, awesome darkness in that gaping gorge. As one strained the eye in the vain attempt to discern something to lighten the awful, terrifying blackness, shades of darkness seemed discernible,—the blackness at the bottom seeming to shade off into dark purple and then into lighter purple. Still all was darkness everywhere in the Canyon *before sunrise.* I am not ashamed to admit that, looking into the Canyon devoid of sunlight, I trembled from head to foot.

Soon the sun began to rise, first flashing its glory light upon the heavens above, making them look like the divine painter's palette;

then gradually touching one point after another in the Canyon and lighting it into gorgeous colouring. One stood transfixed in wonder and worship at each transforming touch.

Finally, the sun was fully up, and with all its resplendent, full-orbed light flooded the Canyon and made the thing which was terrifying in the darkness something of transcendent beauty and glory in the light *after sunrise*.

Reluctant to leave this spot, and yet oh! so eager to get still more of the Canyon into my vision and into my heart, I walked rapidly back to the hotel to eat a hasty breakfast before going with a party down the steep, winding trail of the Canyon, seven and one-half miles, to the river below. I rode a burro. At one time the trail was so sharp in its curve that the forefeet of that sure-footed little animal were on the very edge of a sheer precipice, a depth straight down of twelve hundred feet.

After a short time at the river, we began our ascent. There were times in ascending the trail when all below was out of sight and thought, and one was just lost in the wonder of the height of the Canyon, of continually going up and up, with always more above and beyond, until finally the very expanse of the heavens seemed to roof the Grand Canyon, beyond which one's sight could not go.

The ascent over, and again on the Canyon's rim, I could not leave till I had one last view with *the afterglow* of the sunset upon it. From darkness to dawn,—from full sunlight to twilight, this wonder work of God had poured out a wealth of inspiration.

Only this once have I seen the Grand Canyon, and that was twenty-eight years ago, but to-day, with eyes closed and memory active, its stands out before me as though it were seen only yesterday. In those two days the Grand Canyon became a part of me.

Ephesians is the Grand Canyon of Scripture. A well-known Bible teacher says of it, "In this epistle we enter the Holy of Holies in Paul's writings." Dr. A. C. Gaebelein writes, "This epistle is God's highest and best. Even God cannot say more than what He has said in this filling-full of His Word."

So will you spend a while in this Grand Canyon of Scripture with me? Let us first just skirt the rim of Ephesians to get some first-hand, vivid impressions and viewpoints of this masterpiece of God's supernatural creation, a sinner transformed into a saint, and the Body of Christ constituted from Jew and Gentile as fellow-members.

Do not stop for details, but just let your eye run to and fro over the entire epistle, and get God's own description of the high lights of its truth. "The saints"; "in Christ"; "his calling"; "his inheritance"; "the purchased possession"; "the Church, his body, the fulness of him"; "his workmanship"; "one new man"; "one body"; "the household of God"; "an habitation of God"; "a perfect man"; "members of his body"; "members one of another"; "a glorious church"; "the wiles of the devil"; "principalities, powers, world rulers of this darkness"; "the whole armour of God." What vast distances we have scanned, and what glories of our salvation in Christ have been silhouetted upon the horizon of our thought! Does it not give us food for many a day's study?

But now let us get a nearer view of the majesty and might and matchless grace of the sovereign God in His own workshop, as opened to our view in the first three chapters. Here man is scarcely seen save as the recipient of God's grace and the beneficiary of His mercy and love in salvation. Our first glimpse is into the eternity of the past, where God formed His eternal purpose which he purposed in Christ Jesus our Lord. All the rest is the execution of that purpose. Let us note a few outstanding impressions of His workmanship.

The Sovereign God is Working according to the Good Pleasure of His Will

1:5. "Having predestinated us *according to the good pleasure of his own will."*

1:11. "Being predestinated according to the purpose of him *who worketh all things after the counsel of his own will."*

The method by which man comes into the family of God as His child, and all other matters pertaining to his life in God's household, are predetermined by God. Man has nothing whatsoever to say about these things. In man's redemption God's will is the first cause and the determining factor. If man is not saved God's way, then he is not saved at all.

The Sovereign God is Working according to His Eternal Purpose

3:11. *"According to the eternal purpose* which he purposed in Christ Jesus our Lord."

The sin in the garden of Eden did not take God unawares, nor was man's salvation an afterthought of God. He had anticipated the fall, and was prepared for it. Before the Cross of Christ was ever set up in history on Calvary, or even in promise in Eden, it was existent in the heart of God in the dateless eternity of the past. The blueprints for the holy temple in the Lord which was to be God's habitation on earth were made by the triune God before the foundation of the world.

The Sovereign God is Working to Magnify His Grace and His Glory

1:6. *"To the praise of the glory of his grace."*

1:12. *"That we should be to the praise of his glory."*

Whether in creation or in redemption, God never acts save for His own glory. The salvation of sinners magnifies His wondrous grace in giving His only begotten Son to die that they might live.

The Grand Canyon of Arizona,—the workmanship of God in natural creation,—may one day give place to something even more wonderful in majesty and beauty in the new earth which He will make. But the Grand Canyon of Ephesians will abide in all the ages upon the ages to come, "that he might shew the exceeding riches of his grace in his kindness toward us through Christ Jesus."

The Sovereign God is Working according to His mighty Power

1:19. "The exceeding greatness of his power to usward who believe *according to the working of his mighty power."*

3:20. *"According to the power that worketh in us."*

6:10. "Be strong in the Lord and *in the power of his might."*

His mighty power is at work *for* us in Christ, our Saviour; *in* us in Christ, our Life; and *through* us in Christ, our Lord.

May we now move on to another point on the rim of this Grand Canyon of the Word to get another view. In Chapter two the impression is of the vast distances, the far-reaching and all-inclusive breadth of salvation. We see the richness of God's mercy and the greatness of His love in creating a saint out of a sinner. We see His masterpiece in workmanship in the constitution of the Church out of two races, irrevocably far apart by nature, but made one in Christ by grace. The gospel of conciliation with one another through reconciliation with God has made of the Jew and the Gentile one Body over which Christ is the Head.

Now at the end of our first day with the Grand Canyon of Scripture, let us go back to a time before time, and with a divine field-glass look on down through the centuries at the Church as God purposed it, even on to a time after time. For Ephesians is "the meeting-point of two eternities" in God's conception of the Church. As we trail the Church from glory through grace to glory, we shall comprehend a new measurement,—the length of the love of Christ for lost sinners.

14

1:4. "According as he hath chosen us in him *before the founda-tion of the world.*"

2:7. *"That in the ages to come* he might shew the exceeding riches of his grace."

Now let us rise before dawn that we may see sunrise in the Grand Canyon of Scripture. I promise you it will be a never-to-be-forgotten sight. We will travel along the road mapped out in Romans I-III, for it is this road that leads to Ephesians 2:1-3:11, 12; 4:17-19; 5:8. Here we stop at the rim of the Canyon before sunrise. What do we see? A gaping gorge where all is darkness, degradation, death. There is not one ray of light to relieve the terrible darkness; not one ray of hope in the midst of enveloping death. "Dead"; "trespasses"; "sins"; "ignorance"; "blindness"; "lasciviousness"; "uncleanness"; "greediness"; "darkness"; "children of disobedience and wrath.'·

There may be degrees in the degradation to which a sinner goes. He may go the full length of sin in the eyes of the laws of earth and be imprisoned as a thief, a gangster, a murderer; or he may be a highly respected citizen, even occupying a professor's chair, or a pulpit, in whose inmost heart God sees pride, unbelief, and enmity toward Him. But one is as "far-off" from God as the other, for both are "without Christ" and "without God," and so "without hope." Standing on the rim of 2:1-3, one trembles in anguish of heart at the thought of the present condition and the future destiny of the sinner left in his sins.

2:12. "That at that time *ye were without Christ . . . having no hope;* and *without God* in the world."

But look up and behold the glory light in the heavens! God has come to the sinner's rescue, and in His infinite mercy and love has made a way of escape out of the pit of sin and death.

2:4-5. *"But God,* who is rich in mercy, for his great love wherewith he loved us, even when we were dead in sins, *hath quickened us together with Christ* (by grace ye are saved)."

1:7. "In whom we have *redemption through his blood.*"

A Saviour provided for the sinner! A Redeemer gone down into the slave market of sin to buy the slave and to set him free.

Light now shines into the sinner's heart and brings life. A touch here and a touch there; "chosen"; "predestinated"; "accepted"; "redemption"; "forgiveness"; "obtained inheritance"; "sealed'; and the sinner is delivered from the power of darkness and is translated into the kingdom of his dear Son. The Sun of righteousness has arisen and shone into his heart, and has begun His transfiguring work.

Tarry a bit longer. The sinner is saved, but God would have him sanctified also, for he was "chosen to be holy." The believer in Christ is now a saint, for he is positionally separated unto God, by which the fountain of fulness in Christ has been opened to him. But as there are degrees of degradation in sinnerhood, so there are degrees of holiness in sainthood. As the trend of the sinner's life without Christ is always down, so the trend of the saint's life in Christ is always up. Christ came that we might have life, and might have it more abundantly. So for the Church and for the Christian there is fulness of life in Christ.

1:23. "The church, the fulness of him *that filleth all in all*."

3:19. *"Filled unto all the fulness of God."*

5:18. *"Be filled with the Spirit."*

Have we not now come to the end of the truth brought to our view in Ephesians? Surely we have seen enough to occupy us in contemplation and assimilation for the rest of our lives! No, we have not yet gone down to the deepest depth, nor reached the highest height of our scriptural Grand Canyon. Do not become a spiritual tourist, soon surfeited with the beauty and glory of this precious bit of Scripture, and rush superficially on into some other field of study. Take time to go down to the river bottom, though the trail is steep and narrow. As far as possible know the unknowable love of Christ for sinners; aye, fathom the depths of the Saviour's love for you before you leave Ephesians.

1:20. "Christ—*dead*."

He went to the deepest depths to which He could go to bring us from death unto life. Christ, the Saviour, became the sinner's substitute; taking the sinner's position; becoming sin in order to bear sin; dying to abolish death. "Christ dead" that the sinner might live.

1:20. "Christ—*raised from the dead* and *set at his own right hand in the heavenly places."*

Coming out of the grave, Christ ascended to the highest heights to which He as the God-man could go. He ascended to glory as victor over Satan and all the forces of evil, and upon His triumphal return was exalted to the place of Lordship over the universe, and was made Head over all things to the Church.

1:21. *"Far above all principality, and power, and might, and dominion."*

1:22. "And gave him to be head over all things to the church."

Christ, risen, ascended, exalted, shares not only His glorified life but even His exalted position with the new-born race of men who become one with Him through faith.

2:4-6. "God—*hath quickened us together with Christ—and hath raised us up together,* and *made us to sit together in heavenly places in Christ Jesus."*

Can we grasp the significance of these words? We, who are in Christ, are seated together with Him in that position of power and victory, "far above all." This is the highest height the saint can reach. Even in the eternity of the future we shall not obtain a higher position than we now occupy in Christ, for there is nothing higher. Christ, as the crucified Saviour, went with us to as deep depths as He could go that, as the exalted Lord, He might raise us up with Him to the highest heights to which we can go.

Now may we pause for one last look at Ephesians as a whole before we begin a study of its component parts? May it be to us a glimpse of our Grand Canyon of Scripture in the afterglow of the setting sun.

The Scope of Ephesians:
    The Church—Christ's Body—Its $\left\{\begin{array}{l}\text{Heavenly Calling}\\\text{Earthly Conduct}\\\text{Satanic Conflict}\end{array}\right.$

The Keynote of Ephesians:
    Christ—The Fulness of Church
    Church—The Fulness of Christ

The Key Thought of Ephesians:
    In Christ

The Content of Ephesians:
    Wealth—The Christian in Christ
    Walk—Christ in the Christian
    Warfare $\left\{\begin{array}{l}\text{Christ}\\\text{Christian}\end{array}\right.$ $\left\{\text{versus}\right\}$ $\left.\begin{array}{l}\text{Satan}\\\text{Satanic hosts}\end{array}\right.$

After quiet contemplation, will you answer these three questions to yourself:

What is *your* most vivid impression of this Grand Canyon of Scripture?

What is the greatest desire this study has aroused *in you?*

To what extent has this Grand Canyon of Scripture become *a part of you?*

Pause again for another moment of worship and adoration of God, our Father; of His Son, our Saviour; and of His Spirit, our Sanctifier.

Part I

THE WEALTH OF THE CHRISTIAN

———

PART I

THE WEALTH OF THE CHRISTIAN

THERE is one word that has been on the lips of mankind these past few years. The whole world has talked depression. I even heard of parents who gave their baby girl "Depression" as her middle name. Has it been the middle name of any reader of this book? Has the financial depression with its debilitating atmosphere caused within any of us a mental or a spiritual depression?

If so, it is time for us to move into the epistle to the Ephesians and take up our permanent residence there, where not the slightest trace of downheartedness is found, even though it was written in a Roman prison. On the contrary, one step over its threshold brings one into an atmosphere of unbounded spiritual affluence that creates within one's heart deepest peace and assurance. It is impossible to live habitually in Ephesians and be depressed.

A vast deposit of riches has been made for the Christian in the bank of heaven. It is the oldest bank in existence. It dates way back to B. W.—before the world was. It does not belong to time and earth, but to eternity and heaven. Unlike the banks of earth, it is as unshakable and steadfast as the triune God who founded it. Its doors are never closed day or night to a child of God, and as for a run on it nothing would please the heavenly Father more than to have a daily, hourly, moment-by-moment demand for its treasures.

He has placed a deposit for us in Christ of unsearchable riches that can be drawn upon according to our need and our desire. In the recent depression a bank in which I had a small sum of money deposited was hard pressed. A notice was received from it that only ten per cent a month could be drawn from my account. Now here in God's Word do we find a ten per cent limit imposed upon those who have any riches in the bank of heaven? On the contrary, God has put in our possession His own promises, given in the name of our adorable Saviour, which we may claim any time and to any limit by an act of appropriating faith.

The Resources of Heaven's Bank

These resources are ample for the saint to cover all past debts; to meet all present liabilities, and to provide for all future needs. They are three-fold.

$$\text{The Riches of} \begin{cases} \text{His grace} & 1:7 \\ \text{His glory} & 3:16 \\ \text{Christ} & 3:8 \end{cases}$$

The very words and phrases of Ephesians all speak of wealth. Let us examine some of them. They are indeed gilt-edged: "grace" used twelve times; "glory" eight; "inheritance" four; "riches" five; "fulness" three; "fill" or "filled" four; and the incomparable phrase "in Christ," or its equivalent, twenty-seven.

Ephesians also shows us some of the current coins which the Christian may use daily in claiming his wealth. They are such words as "blessed"; "abounded"; "obtained"; "worketh"; "give"; "know"; "saved"; "made nigh"; "access"; "strengthened"; "filled"; "loved"; "able to stand"; "able to withstand"; "able to quench"; "praying always."

The Reserves of Heaven's Bank

Recently I noted on the stationery of a National Bank these words: "Capital, Surplus and Reserves $2,250,000." During the recent depression one bank was forced to close its doors, not because of insufficient capital, but because of inadequate reserves. Can any spiritual depression ever lessen the power of God to meet the needs of His child, however great these may be? Will the reserves of heaven's bank be unequal to any demand made upon them? What, then, are these reserves? Ephesians tells us they are the fulness of the triune God.

The Fulness of God	3:19
The Fulness of Christ	4:13
The Fulness of the Spirit	5:18

May not our hearts rest quietly and confidently in the assurance of the all-sufficiency of our spiritual resources and reserves? Dear reader, if you are in Christ you are a child of a King who owns heaven and earth and all that is therein. If a child, then an heir and a joint-heir with Christ.

The Security of Heaven's Bank

There is great fear in these days of all financial institutions; in many countries even the finances of the government are in such a precarious condition as to cause alarm and a haunting sense of insecurity. An insidious fear often possesses even the Christian's heart and makes him doubt a bit the absolute safety of the bank of heaven. If anyone who reads Ephesians is the victim of spiritual jitters and needs to have his sense of security in his unlosable wealth restored, let his mind be riveted for a while upon an oft-repeated, three-lettered word which, connected with ten other words, furnishes a guarantee of absolute security:

HIS		
will	1:5, 9, 11	good pleasure 1:9
grace	1:6, 7	purpose 1:11; 3:11
glory	1:12, 14	calling 1:18
power	1:19	inheritance 1:18
love	2:4	workmanship 2:10

Is this not a sufficient guarantee to everyone who is a member of *His* Body of the security of His riches?

So we see that the wealth of the Christian is royal, munificent and unlosable; altogether sufficient to meet the requirements of his moral and spiritual delinquency and bankruptcy, and wholly adequate for even the greatest trial, financial, physical, mental or spiritual.

Only as we go deeper into Christ and He goes deeper into us will we know increasingly just how rich we are. But even eternity will not suffice for us to plumb the deepest depths or to measure the magnitude of our wealth in Christ (2:7).

Let us continue with receptive mind and eager heart a more detailed study of our unsearchable riches in Christ.

1. THE WEALTH GLIMPSED

1:3. "Blessed be the God and Father of our Lord Jesus Christ, who hath blessed us with all spiritual blessings in heavenly places in Christ."

In this cryptic sentence the apostle Paul opens the door into Ephesians, and gives us a glimpse of what awaits us. It is the key to this house of spiritual treasures. Paul could not wait to unfold gradually these riches, so he places, as it were, a nugget of gold in our hands at the threshold, an earnest of what we shall find within.

We shall see the Christian pilgrim's journey from grace to glory; the Christian's biography from the eternity of the past to the eternity of the future; the Christian wrestler's warfare with the Satanic hosts. It takes time for Paul to write all this, and it will take time for us to comprehend it. So in this one sentence he gives us the revelation in anticipation. The rest of the epistle is the unfolding of these words.

2. THE WEALTH BEQUEATHED

1:3. "Blessed be the God and Father of our Lord Jesus Christ, *who hath blessed us."*

The Blesser

For His beloved Son's sake the God and Father of our Lord Jesus Christ blessed us. We shall miss one of the deepest truths in Ephesians if we fail to see that everything the Father does for the Church and for the Christian, He does primarily for the glory of His own grace and for the sake of His dear Son who voluntarily laid down His human body on the Cross in a moment of time that He might possess His mystical Body in the heavenlies now and in all the ages to come.

Years ago a very dear friend of mine died, the only child of her parents. I had gone in and out of the home as another daughter. Among her papers was an envelope addressed to her parents, to be opened in case of her death. It contained just one request, that they would regard me as a daughter and do for me as they would have for her.

Is this not the request which the Son made of His Father for all the other sons who had believed on Him? Did He not express His desire to share with them all that was His, even to His oneness with the Father and their home in glory?

John 17:21 "That . . . as thou, Father, art in me, and I in thee, *that they also may be one in us."*

John 17:24. "Father, I will that *they also, whom thou hast given me, be with me where I am;* that they may behold my glory."

The Blessed

How can we know whether or not we qualify as recipients of the blessing? Two personal pronouns give us the answer.

"Our Lord Jesus Christ." Is He yours? To those who receive Christ as their Saviour and Lord, the Father opens His household and takes them into the family circle. Then the Father fulfils His Son's request and, as sons, shares with them the Son's blessings and, as heirs, grants them their part in the inheritance of the saints.

24

"Who hath blessed *us.*" The "us" very evidently refers to a distinct and restricted group of people. 1:1 tells who they are: *"The saints at Ephesus."* A saint is one who is set apart specially unto God as His own by union with Jesus Christ through the baptism with the Spirit. The saints to whom Paul wrote had their temporal abode in Ephesus while pilgrims on earth. *"The faithful in Christ Jesus,"* —are those who have made Christ Jesus the object of their faith and who live by faith in Him. They are in Christ as their other-worldly abode as citizens of heaven. From this salutation and from the content of the whole epistle we see that this oft-repeated "us" refers to all saints. Ephesians is really a family letter from the heavenly Father to all His children everywhere.

While on the very threshold of Ephesians your chief concern and mine is to know if we are indeed in this "us." We may know with unquestioning certainty. Have you received Jesus Christ as your personal Saviour from sin through faith in His atoning blood? If so, then you are one of the "us" and are eligible for the wealth bequeathed.

The Blessing

One question remains: When is the blessing ours, now or in the future? The tense of the verb gives the answer. *"Hath* blessed." It is all ours *now.* "All things *are* yours." All that God ever can give to His children is already given in Christ, who became poor that we through His poverty might become rich. To live as spiritual paupers when God has bequeathed us such unsearchable riches must grieve our Father deeply.

3. THE WEALTH DESIGNATED

1:3. "With all *spiritual* blessings."

The word "spiritual" designates the character of the blessings bestowed. A saint is one who has left the sphere of the natural and has come into the sphere of the spiritual. Henceforth his paramount needs are spiritual. He has become the possessor of a heaven-born nature, so he must have heaven-sent supplies to nourish and develop it. The saint has had implanted within him the eternal life of the Holy One, but he is travelling through an ungodly world, so moment by moment he needs life from above that he may live holily. Living in a non-spiritual world, he needs a spiritual atmosphere in which to breathe; spiritual food to eat; spiritual garments to wear; spiritual companions with whom to fellowship; spiritual exercise to keep fit and strong; spiritual strength to endure suffering and affliction; spiritual weapons with which to war.

The human personality consists of spirit, soul and body, as God has shown in I Thessalonians 5:23. In quoting man usually says "body, soul and spirit." God's order cannot be reversed. He always begins with the inner man, and works out to the outer man. To Him the spirit is paramount and is always put first. So God's concern is for a daily spiritual renewal which will cause the saint to grow up into Christ in all things, working ever toward the goal of a greater perfection. Life in Christ commences with a spiritual birth; continues through spiritual growth; and consummates at His coming in spiritual perfection.

3:16. "That he would grant you . . . *to be strengthened with might by his Spirit in the inner man.*"

4:15. "May *grow up into him in all things.*"

4:12. "For *the perfecting of the saints.*"

God's love is very Fatherly and His care of us is very practical. His concern reaches to the outermost rim of our every need and includes provision for the needs of soul and body. The blessing includes things physical, temporal and material, but always as related to and working toward the spiritual goal He has set for us—conformity to the image of His Son. Sometimes He allows times of trial and testing because He purposes our spiritual growth and perfecting through the process. "For whom the Lord loveth He chasteneth . . . that we might be partakers of his holiness" (Heb. 12:6, 10).

The word "spiritual" also designates the One through whom the blessing is procured. Ephesians teaches very clearly that the blessings purposed by the Father and provided in the Son are procured through the Spirit. Every spiritual blessing bestowed upon the saint is Spirit-communicated.

4. THE WEALTH MEASURED

1:3. "With *every* spiritual blessing" (R. V.)

"*Every.*" Study the word from the Godward side. What a revelation it gives of the elasticity of God's grace, stretched full length to the uttermost of our need; of the generosity of God's heart —nothing that love can give has been withheld from His children; of the amplitude of His treasury—not one thing that God wants to give is He unable to give. For there is not one of the thousands of promises that He has made that He has not the power to fulfil.

Study the word from the manward side. What a conception it gives of the saint's capacity for the infinite! If God has bequeathed to the Christian every spiritual blessing in Christ, then He must have given him the capacity to receive and to hold these blessings. What a call to an enlargement of his whole being so that he may abound in the blessings of the Lord and live an overflowing life! What a challenge to thirst for the living water and to come to that fountain of life to drink and to continue to drink that he may "be filled unto all the fulness of God!"

Friends, is not the trouble with most of us that we do not thirst? We are too self-satisfied and self-complacent. We have the attitude of the Laodicean who says, "I am rich, and increased with goods, and have need of nothing." There is spiritual stagnancy in our lives because we are content to live as beggars in the midst of plenty.

The life of the truly spiritual Christian is quite otherwise. He is a paradox in that he is always satisfied, yet ever seeking. He never thirsts, yet is always thirsting. He is perfectly content; yet ever wants more. He enjoys to the full what he possesses moment by moment, yet knows there is always more beyond, and eagerly longs for it.

"Every"—what a bountiful word! Every blessing needed for spirit, soul and body; for the past, present and future; for salvation, sanctification, sustenance, and service; for time and for eternity. There is every blessing for all saints, for any saint.

From memory recall every spiritual blessing mentioned in Ephesians which is yours in Christ; then all you remember from any part of Scripture. How many of these blessings are yours in practical possession? What ones do you honestly desire? Sit quietly before your Lord and name them, one by one, and then confidently appropriate each one by faith and thank Him for it.

Every spiritual blessing IS already *yours* in Christ!

5. THE WEALTH LOCATED

1:3. "In *heavenly places*"—(literally, in *the heavenlies*).

This phrase is used only in Ephesians, where it is found five times. It is seen to be Christ's seat of power (1:20); the Christians' sphere of life as identified with Christ in position, privilege and power (2:6); and the battlefield where Christ and His saints are in conflict with Satan and his hosts (6:12). "The principalities and powers" of both light (3:10) and darkness (6:12) have access to this sphere. In this phrase the Christian's wealth is definitely located.

As Scripture interprets Scripture, it is thus clear that the heaven-lies is not heaven, a future place reached after death, but it is the sphere where Christ is, which is heavenly in nature, privilege and blessing. Where Christ is the Christian also is in virtue of his union with Christ. To be in the heavenlies is to be living on a celestial level even while on the earth and to be in a heavenly state of mind and heart, even in the midst of earthly trials and sorrows. Dr. A. T. Pierson illustrates this most beautifully in telling of a visit he once made to an earnest Christian to condole her on the death of her saintly mother. "The woman said to me with a smile, 'For forty years, my dear mother's *mind* has been in Heaven.'"

A very dear friend of mine, now in her eighty-sixth year, suffered a stroke ten months ago and has been gradually failing physically, and at times even her mind has been clouded with hallucination. The one book she loves most to read, understands best, and talks of most readily and lucidly is the Book. This week the daughter who cares for her wrote: "From the first of her illness I have noticed that Mother is clearer *on all spiritual things* than on secular."

Paul was in prison in Rome; yet just as truly, yes, even more so, he was in the heavenlies in Christ. The tremendous reality to him of this other-worldly abode explains the paradoxes of such language as he used, as:

"Sorrowful,	yet always rejoicing."
"Poor,	yet making many rich."
"Having nothing,	yet possessing all things."
"Troubled on every side,	yet not distressed."
"Perplexed,	yet not in despair."
"Cast down,	yet not destroyed."

6. THE WEALTH DEPOSITED

1:3. *"In Christ."*

In these two words we have the whole of Ephesians in essence. They are the master key to heaven's treasury. The wealth of the Church and of the Christian is deposited wholly and only in Christ.

"In"—the biggest, little word in Ephesians, a preposition denoting position; the simplest of words, yet it introduces the mightiest of thoughts. When connected with the word "Christ" it forms the most significant expression in all Scripture. Of these two words Dr. A. T. Pierson wrote: "A very small key may open a very complex lock and a very large door, and that door may itself lead into a vast

building with priceless stores of wealth and beauty. This brief phrase—a preposition followed by a proper name—is the key to the whole New Testament. Those two short words, "in Christ," are, without doubt, the most important ever written, even by an inspired pen, to express the mutual relation of the believer and Christ. They occur, with their equivalents, "in him," or "in whom," over one hundred and thirty times. Such repetition must have intense meaning. When in the Word of God a phrase like this occurs so often and with such manifold applications, it cannot be a matter of accident; there is a deep design. God's Spirit is bringing a truth of the highest importance before us, repeating for the sake of emphasis, compelling even a careless reader to give heed as to its vital teaching."

Considering the number of times these two words or their equivalents are used in Ephesians,—fourteen times in Chapter I alone—it is not exageration to say that the whole message of the book is compressed within them. "Without Christ," a sinner, spiritually dead and a moral bankrupt: "In Christ," a saint, spiritually alive and a joint-heir with Christ. "Without Christ" one is, has, and can do, nothing. "In Christ" one is, has and can do, everything. Is this not what the Lord said: "Without me ye can do nothing."? Yet Paul said, "I can do all things through Christ that strengtheneth me." Some one has put it tersely thus, "If you take Christ out of Christ-i-a-n, what is left? I am nothing!"

What, then, does it mean to be in Christ? Primarily, it means a change of *position*. The whole human race was *in Adam in sin,* and therefore subject to death. The Church and the Christian are *in Christ* through salvation, and therefore are the recipients of eternal life. The saint has been wholly delivered from the old sphere of the devil, the world, and the flesh, and has been translated into the new sphere of Christ, the Church, and the Spirit.

Secondly, it means a difference in *possession.* In Adam the sinner possesses only a sinful nature, inherited from Adam, the federal head of the first creation. In Christ the saint possesses also a divine nature, imparted to him in Christ, the federal head of the new creation.

In Christ, the saint is both ensphered and enriched. Christ is to be the source, sustenance, and security of his life. In His Son the Father has stored up all the riches of His Grace and of His glory which He purposes to bequeath to His other sons. Outside of Christ the Father has nothing to give.

Outside of Christ there is nothing the true Christian wants. Everything his heart could desire is to be found in Him. Christ is his satisfaction and sufficiency. In Him we are separated from the trinity of evil unto the triune God; we are supplied with everything needed for a worthy walk; and we are secured from defeat by our Satanic foes.

IN CHRIST	denotes our position	—where He is, we are.
	defines our privileges	—what He is, we are.
	describes our possessions	—what He has, we share.
	determines our practice	—what He does, we do.

7. THE WEALTH DEFINED

In the Greek 1:4-14 is one sentence, said to be the longest in the Bible. There is no place where a stop can be made. Paul is carrying us in God's eternal purpose from the eternity of the past to the eternity of the future; through grace to glory.

May we now let 1:4-14 define for us more in detail the wealth of the Christian in Christ. That wealth is eightfold.

Chosen

1:4. "According as *he hath chosen us in him* before the foundation of the world, that we should be holy and without blame before him in love."

Perhaps we can best get at the deep and precious meaning of this glorious truth by answering six simple questions: Who? What? Whom? How? When? Why?

Who? *"He"*—the God and Father of our Lord Jesus Christ.

What? *"Hath chosen"*—picked out for Himself a people to be His own peculiar possession. God is love, and love cannot live alone. God has selected those who will be the habitation in which He dwells.

Whom? *"Us"*—the saints of 1:1, 3. Let us see very clearly that Ephesians has only the Church and the Christian in view. The unsaved are mentioned in only a few passages. So here there is no reference to them. There is no intimation that God has chosen some out of the vast number of *sinners* in this world to be saved, or that He has chosen *any sinners* to be saved. It is not a choice of one sinner versus another sinner, but it definitely states it is the choice of "us" who are saints.

God acts sovereignly in making the choice because of His inherent right to choose those who will live so intimately and eternally with Himself. The choice is both absolute and final, but it is not capricious or partial. God has not acted on the principle of favouritism, nor has He arbitrarily elected some and damned others. His election was made on an absolutely just and reasonable ground which gives to sinners a fair and equal chance. This leads directly to our next question:

How? *"In him."* The sinner is always and only the object of God's superabounding grace. In himself he merits nothing but God's wrath. In making the choice God is not looking at man in himself, but only as he is in Christ. So 1:4 teaches that those who are chosen are those who are in Christ. The rest of the epistle shows that those who are in Christ were sinners who put faith in the redeeming blood of the crucified Son by virtue of which they have been united with Him as members of His Body in an eternal oneness, and have become saints. So every saint has been chosen.

Is it not very plain, then, that those who are lost are lost because they refuse to accept Christ as their Saviour? They choose not to be among God's elect. D. L. Moody stated the truth of election in his own inimitable way: "The whosoever-wills are the elect, and the whosoever-won'ts are the non-elect."

When? *"Before the foundation of the world,"*—in the timeless eternity of the past, when there was neither a world nor men to inhabit it.

Why? *"That we should be holy and without blame before him in love."*

The best commentary to be found on this phrase is in I Peter 1:15, 16. Note the utter simplicity of the reasoning.

> "But *as he* is holy, *so be ye* holy . . .
> Be ye holy, *for* I am holy."

The Father must have children of like character, that there may be unity and harmony in the divine household. Because He is holy, those who are His habitation must be holy.

Oh! the pure, incomparable joy of being in the company of "chosen" ones! Are you there, my friend? How may you know? The answer is very simple: Are you "in Him"? If you are not, you may be this very moment if, by an act of faith, you open your heart to receive Christ as your personal Saviour.

Predestinated

1:5. *"Having predestinated us unto the adoption of children by Jesus Christ to himself,* according to the good pleasure of his will."

"Predestinated"—Are we fearful of the word? Does it sound cold, formidable, and theological? Not so, if we understand its meaning in relation to God's purpose for His chosen ones. The word means "to mark out the boundaries beforehand." It indicates God's next step in His gracious plan for those whom He has chosen.

"Unto the adoption of children by Jesus Christ to himself." Christ Jesus is God's Son in a unique way. He is the eternal Son, "the only begotten in the bosom of the Father." Yet it was the Father's purpose to have a family of sons and to set up a household of "brethren" from every nation and people over which He would be Father. How were these to become His sons and what would be their position in the family?

Through regeneration, which is not at all in view here, the believer in Christ is made a son. Through rebirth he has imparted to him a divine nature and implanted within him a supernatural life that fits him for membership in God's family and for companionship with God.

Now the question arises, What is his position and what are his privileges and responsibilities as a son in the divine family? Dr. L. S. Chafer, in *The Ephesian Letter,* answers this question so clearly that I quote his words:

"The believer is constituted a legitimate child of God by spiritual birth with all its attending relationships, but he is also, at the moment of that birth, advanced to maturity of *position,* being constituted an *adult* son by virtue of that legal placing which in the Scriptures is termed *adoption.* There is therefore no childhood period in the sphere of the Christian's responsibility. Whatever appeal as to a holy walk and service God addresses to one He addressed to all regardless of the length of time they may have been saved."

"By Jesus Christ." As with every other phase of our salvation, this work is wrought also solely through Jesus Christ. Every believer in Him has been marked out for the son-place, and in this son-position he has the present privilege of free and unlimited access to the Father (2:18), with all its attendant blessings and responsibilities and the pledge for the future inheritance as a joint-heir with Christ. In choosing us in Christ God marked us out as sons who would share all the possessions and privileges of the risen, ascended Son for all the ages to come.

Accepted

1:6. "To the praise of the glory of his grace, *wherein he hath made us accepted in the beloved."*

"Accepted"—what a gracious word! What a wealth of significance in it! Those that were by nature "children of disobedience and wrath" (2:2, 3); so "far-off" from God that they were called "strangers" (2:19); so deep down in the abyss of death and depravity that they were "without hope" (2:12); yet here said to be "accepted." How could such a change ever be wrought in the sinner? If so utterly disobedient, he would not want acceptance; if so utterly depraved, he could not make himself acceptable, even if he desired to. The sinner of 2:1-3 is rendered both hopeless and helpless by sin. Then by whom and on what ground was the change wrought by which he was taken into the very heart and home of God?

"Made accepted." God has left to the sinner not an inch of ground for boasting. Not an atom of anything either in his character or in his conduct can avail to bring him into God's favour. If he is ever accepted by God, God Himself must act on his behalf.

"In the beloved"—the Son of His love. How marvellously tender is the relationship between the Father and the Son! How dearly the Son is loved! So dearly that three times the Father opened heaven to tell men on earth, "This is *my beloved Son,* in whom I am well pleased." Christ was the perfect satisfaction of the Father's heart.

"In"—Can we ever grasp fully the meaning of this little word to us? *In Him* whom the Father loves supremely *we are.* In the Beloved whose righteousness and holiness satisfy every demand of the Father's justice and holiness we stand. The Beloved Son is our divine rainbow, God's pledge to us who are made accepted in Him that we will never again be cast out from His presence. In the Son of His love the Father receives us as He receives Him and loves us as He loves Him. It would be impossible to believe such an apparently incredible statement did not Christ Himself declare it. Then we must believe it and rejoice in it.

John 17:23. "That the world may know *that thou hast . . . loved them as thou hast loved me."*

"Near, so very near to God
    Nearer I could not be;
For in the person of His Son,
    I'm just as near as He.

Dear, so very dear to God,
    Dearer I could not be:
For in the person of His Son,
    I'm just as dear as He."

"To the praise of the glory of his grace." Surely every saint

should have a singing heart, and the theme of his song should ever be the matchless grace of God. The saints on earth and the redeemed in heaven unite in one grand, glorious symphony of "praise to the glory of his grace" wherein He took sinners like us and "made us accepted in the beloved."

Let us take one backward glance at our immeasurable wealth in the Father's grace before we look forward to that in the redemptive work of His Son:

Through His grace   —chosen   —loved

Through the riches of His grace   —predestinated—loved as adult
                                                      sons

Through the exceeding riches of
  His grace   —accepted   —loved as the Son
                                                   is loved.

Could our Father do more than this for us? Could He do less for His Son? Then should not our fearful, trembling hearts rest full-length upon the exceeding riches of His grace in His kindness toward us in Christ Jesus? And should not the dominating passion of our lives be to live to the praise of the glory of His grace?

Redeemed

1:7. *"In whom we have redemption through his blood,* the forgiveness of sins, according to the riches of his grace."

In the work of creation God showed forth His wisdom and His power, but only in the redemption of man could He manifest His grace.

In 2:1-3 we see the sinner in the pit of sin and the special character of deliverance needed. It pictures him as a slave, in bondage to Satan and Satanic forces. How, then, can he be freed?

"In whom we have redemption." While still in the slave-market of sin as a captive of Satan, the sinner is purchased by the Redeemer, brought out of the market and set free. He is brought out of all that he was that he may be brought into what he never had been but henceforth eternally would be. He ceased to be a slave that he might become a son.

"Have redemption"—the verb shows us that our redemption is a present-tense possession; something that is now ours as completely as it ever will be; made ours in such a way that it can never be taken from us.

"Through his blood." It was release through a ransom and the ransom was the life of the Son of man (Matt. 20:28), laid down in

death. "The life of the flesh is in the blood" (Lev. 17:11), and only as His life was poured out upon Calvary's Cross through the shedding of His blood was the sinner redeemed. Oh! what a price He paid for your redemption and mine!

"The forgiveness of sins." Out of the many blessings procured for the sinner through redemption only this one is mentioned. Surely no one could be the companion of a holy God who still had the guilt of sins upon him. Nor could he ever feel perfectly at home as a son in the divine family, fully assured of his Father's acceptance, unless he knew with certainty that all his sins were fully forgiven. On the ground of the shed blood of His Beloved Son the Father cancels all the sins of the believing sinner and gives him a clean bill of pardon. He assures His child that, when once He has thus remitted the punishment for his sins, He remembers them no more.

"According to the riches of his grace." Just here a question must thrust itself upon every sensitive mind. If Christ is the dearly Beloved of the Father, how could He ever let Him suffer, even unto the death of the Cross, for the sake of such sinner-slaves? How could His love for sinners who were alienated from Him both by nature and by choice seem to outweigh His love for the Son who was His own counterpart in oneness of life?

The only adequate answer is in that rarely precious phrase "according to the riches of his grace." Only when we look at the sinless Son upon the Cross can we begin to comprehend the meaning of the riches of His grace, there bestowed upon us far, far above measure. God's undeserved bounty toward the sinner was manifested by the planned-in-eternity redemption through the blood of the Lamb slain. Is it any wonder Paul says that it will take all the ages to come to show forth the exceeding riches of His grace?

Enlightened

1:8, 9. "Wherein he hath abounded toward us in all wisdom and prudence, *having made known unto us the mystery of his will.*"

God has an eternal purpose in Christ Jesus which He is steadily carrying out. Into the knowledge of what this purpose is and how it is being fulfilled God wishes every redeemed child of His to enter intelligently and sympathetically. So He has given to us a revelation of it in His Word, and in His abounding grace He enlightens us regarding these divine things. He gives His children the capacity to know and endows them with the spiritual qualifications for knowing and for acting upon their knowledge.

"All wisdom"—Through wisdom the spiritual senses of the saint

are quickened and he is made alert to God Himself. Insight into the deep things of God and into His far-reaching plan is also given him. He does not perceive superficially, but goes to the very heart of things and grasps spiritual truths with penetrating discernment.

"*All prudence*"—The apprehension of truth, especially the knowledge of God's wondrous plan of salvation, made effectual through practical application.

"*Having made known unto us the mystery of his will.*" God wants the Christian to know fully the counsels of His will as they relate to His Son and the outworking of His plan of redemption and reconciliation through Him. So He unfolds them to us in the unveiling of "the mystery of his will," truth once hidden but now clearly revealed.

God's purpose centres wholly in Christ. In Ephesians He gives in perspective both a near and a far view of His eternal purpose in Him. First in this age of grace He reveals the risen, ascended Christ as the One exalted to be Lord over the universe and Head over all things to the Church (1:20-23). As yet His authority is not fully acknowledged, even by those who belong to Him, nor is it openly manifested to the world. But in the age to come all things both in heaven and upon earth are to be gathered together into one in Christ (1:10), and His authoritative Headship over them will be both manifested and acknowledged. Christ as the centre and the circumference of all things in God's wonderful plan will fulfil His stewardship to the glory of God. Regarding this gracious and glorious plan God would have every Christian fully enlightened.

Obtained an Inheritance

1:11. "*In whom also we have obtained an inheritance,* being predestinated according to the purpose of him who worketh all things after the counsel of his own will."

"*In whom we have obtained an inheritance.*" In Christ the Christian has everything he needs for his entire pilgrim journey on earth. Of this we are assured in Ephesians and in other passages of Scripture.

I Cor. 3:21, 23. "For *all things are yours* . . . whether things present, or things to come; *all are yours;* and ye are Christ's, and Christ is God's."

Romans 8:32. "He that spared not his own Son, but delivered him up for us all, *how shall he not with him also freely give us all things?*"

But our present blessings are as nothing compared to the inheritance that awaits us in the future. Our rights as children of God extend far beyond our earthly life. The moment we are born into the family of God we become heirs to an inheritance beyond our power to estimate.

Romans 8:17. "If children, then heirs; *heirs of God, and joint-heirs with Christ.*"

The Son's prayer that we might share His life in glory will assuredly be answered. We who now are possessors of "the riches of his grace" will also be partakers of "the riches of his glory." All that He now is in His glorified life we shall be. We shall even reign with Him and share with Him His governmental authority on the earth.

II Tim. 2:12. "If we suffer, *we shall also reign with him.*"

Rev. 5:10. "And hast made us unto our God kings and priests; and *we shall reign on the earth.*"

Such a thought seems incredible. Perhaps at this moment we are feeling like spiritual weaklings and cowards, not able to face courageously even the burdens and tasks of the day that lies before us. The thought of such a position and such power is preposterous! Dare we believe that any such inheritance is really ours? Let God answer the question and silence our doubt.

"*Being predestinated according to the purpose of him who worketh all things after the counsel of his own will.*" In the eternity of the past God marked us out for that son-place in his family which relationship puts us in line for heirship. Our redemption in Christ was the first step in the outworking of the counsel of His own will. Can God's eternal purpose be thwarted half-way? Can His sovereign will be stalemated? What God has sovereignly purposed will He not sovereignly perform? In God's eternal purpose and His sovereign will we have an all-sufficient ground for assurance that we shall obtain our inheritance in full.

Then stop just here for one moment of silent praise for such an inheritance as you have in Christ. That act of praise will double your assurance of obtaining it and increase your appreciation of its value. If you are not in the royal line of inheritors because you are not a child, will you not this moment become a child and heir by opening your heart to receive the Lord Jesus Christ as your personal Saviour?

Sealed

1:13. "In whom ye also trusted, after that ye heard the word of truth, the gospel of your salvation; *in whom also after that ye believed, ye were sealed with that holy Spirit of promise.*"

"Ye *heard—ye believed*—ye were *sealed*." These are the biographical steps in every soul's salvation.

"*Ye heard*"—The Word of truth which is God's instrument in the sinner's regeneration. This Word presented to you the good news of a perfected salvation, and showed the way of deliverance from the bondage of Satan and of entrance into the liberty of Christ.

"*Ye believed*" in Christ as your Saviour and received Him into your heart, and that moment you were born into God's family as His child. But how many earnest Christians there are who have truly believed, yet have no joy in salvation because they lack assurance of their acceptance by God. Thus they become the prey of the enemy who delights in torturing them with doubt. How strategically God has guarded against every such attack, and how graciously He has provided for victory over it! He wants us to have the unwavering assurance that we are His.

"Ye were *sealed with that holy Spirit* of promise." God marks us as His very own by sending the Holy Spirit, to indwell us according to the promise He Himself had given. God seals every redeemed person as His purchased possession, and the Spirit Himself is the seal. But perhaps the doubt of someone is not fully dispelled because of his fear of grieving the Holy Spirit through sin so that He will depart. Ephesians teaches us with equal clearness these two truths, that we can and do grieve the Holy Spirit through sinning, but that we can never grieve Him away.

4:30. "And grieve not the holy Spirit of God, *whereby ye are sealed unto the day of redemption*."

Upon the authority of the Lord Jesus Christ Himself we can rest assured that when the Holy Spirit once takes up His abode within us, He will abide with us forever (John 14:16). The work He was divinely appointed to do will not be finished until He presents us faultless before the presence of His glory.

The Seal is a Mark of Genuineness

II Cor. 3:3. "For as much as ye are manifestly declared to be the epistle of Christ ministered by us, written not with ink, but *with the Spirit of the living Lord*."

There are professors of Christianity, and there are possessors of Christ. God makes a clear distinction between the two. The professors are those who refuse to enter in by the door, but have tried to climb up some other way. They have trusted in their morality, good works, or religious ordinances for acceptance with God. Christ calls such "thieves and robbers" (John 10:1). Christ disclaims them as His. "Ye believed not, because *ye are not of my sheep.*"

The possessors have heard the voice of the Good Shepherd who said He was the door of the sheep, and have come through Him into the fold (John 10:9). To such He says, "My sheep hear my voice, and I know them, and they follow me." His distinguishing mark between the false and the true is the indwelling of the Holy Spirit.

John 14:17. "Even the Spirit of truth; *whom the world cannot receive,* because it seeth him not, neither knoweth him; but *ye know him;* for he dwelleth with you, and *shall be in you.*"

The Seal is a Mark of Ownership

John 10:14. "I am the good Shepherd, and *know my sheep, and am known of mine.*"

Christ speaks of His own sheep. How does He establish His ownership? By His own special brand. Vast herds of cattle roam over the plains belonging to different masters, yet ownership is easily established because each of a herd has the owner's mark branded upon its body. Christ has no unmarked sheep. He knows His own, and they know their Master because of the Holy Spirit who indwells each Christian.

Rom. 8:9. "But ye are not in the flesh, but in the Spirit, if so be that the Spirit of God dwell in you. *Now if any man have not the Spirit of Christ, he is none of his.*"

Do you know that the Holy Spirit dwells within you? Then you may have the assurance that you possess Christ and that He possesses you.

Secured

1:14. "Which is *the earnest of our inheritance,* until the redemption of the purchased possession unto the praise of his glory."

Another question haunts many true believers, which is, "Once saved by grace, are we eternally saved?" Even though here and now we have the assurance that we are His own, and though we enjoy the privileges of salvation and sanctification provided for us in Christ, is it not possible for us to fall short of future perfected redemption through some failure on our part? Has God given any guarantee of eternal security in Christ and of obtaining our inheritance in full? Yes, a thousand times yes! God's *promise* for the present is also His *pledge* for the future.

"*The earnest of our inheritance.*" When God purchased us as His very own, He gave the Holy Spirit as a *down-payment,* which was His pledge of perpetuity of His right in us and our right in Him. The Holy Spirit in us is God's earnest of the full consummation of our redemption.

"Until the redemption of the purchased possession." Ephesians more than any other epistle reveals the eternalness of our redemption. It begins in the dateless eternity of the past with God's choice of a Body and Bride for His Son who were to be holy and without blame; it continues through time with the work of the triune God in the salvation and sanctification of the purchased possession; it ends in the dawn of the eternity of the future, when the Son presents unto Himself the Church glorified, sinless and spotless, even as He Himself. God views His whole redemptive plan from one eternity to another. Can we then conceive of His stopping in its fulfilment at some period of *time?* Extract from that word "until" every bit of the sweetness of assurance God placed in it for you.

"To the praise of his glory." Here is the simple but sufficient reason for God's steadfastness in the perfecting of the redemption of His own. If a single redeemed one, if even one sinner saved by grace, missed the final glorification of that coming day, God's own glory would be diminished to that degree, and Christ's prayer would be to that extent unanswered. "To the praise of his glory" every saint must one day be glorified and be forever with His Saviour in glory.

8. THE WEALTH REVEALED

Paul in one breath, as it were, has proclaimed the wonderful message of redemption according to the riches of His grace. He has told it out; now he must pray it in. So without laying down his pen,—for Paul has only begun to tell of the unsearchable riches of Christ,—he prays. His prayer is for those who already belong to the company of saints through faith in the Lord Jesus (1:15). He asks that through divine revelation they may know what Christ possesses in them and what they possess in Christ.

As he prays with his mind steadfastly fixed upon the Saviour in whom he personally had found such immeasurable wealth, his thought goes up, up, up, until it is quite out of the realm of earth and reaches the highest heavenly heights of revealed truth about Christ and His Church.

Christ { seated in the heavenlies.   Head of the Church.
        { exalted far above all.   Lord of the Universe.
Christ—The fulness of the Church. Church—the Fulness of Christ.

This, then, is a prayer that we, too, should pray for ourselves and for all saints (6:18). So let us enter with reverent hearts into a study of this inspired prayer.

1:15 *"Wherefore."*

This word links 1:4-14 with 1:15-23. The prayer is not a parenthesis, but is closely connected with what has gone before. Paul seems to be thinking aloud: I have written what the triune God, Father, Son and Spirit, have done to redeem you. But oh! do you grasp the full scope of it? Do you truly appreciate how precious and priceless is your inheritance in Christ? I know of your faith in the Lord Jesus and your love unto all the saints, which proves that you not only have life in Him, but even a measure of abundant life; yet I long for you to have a full knowledge of Christ that you may know all that you possess in Him: and that your potential riches may be made personal and actual. "Wherefore I pray."

1:17. "That the God of our Lord Jesus Christ, the Father of glory, *may give unto you the spirit of wisdom and revelation in the knowledge of him;* the eyes of your understanding being enlightened."

We have the *revelation of the Spirit* in the Word, but we must also have the *Spirit of revelation* in our hearts. The same Spirit who indited the Scriptures must illumine them if we are to have spiritual apprehension, for no human intellect can apprehend spiritual things unaided. So Paul prays.

"That God may give unto you the spirit of wisdom and revelation." This was not a prayer for the bestowal of the initial gift of the Spirit, for He was already theirs. Now, as the indwelling Spirit, He was to function as their Teacher and Revealer.

There is amazing ignorance among us Christians of our unsearchable riches in Christ, and tremendous need of supernatural light to be shed upon the Word as we study it, that the nuggets of gold contained in every part may be found. We all need this Spirit of revelation made ours by prayer. But it is not enough merely to find the gold; it must be mined if it is to be of practical use. The heavenly principles revealed must be inwrought into experience. To transmute this heavenly truth into our earthly life, we need the divine operation of the Spirit of wisdom. What the Spirit of revelation makes objective, the Spirit of wisdom makes subjective.

"In the full knowledge of him." The prayer is restricted in its range. Paul is not praying that the saints may be made intelligent students of truth in general, or even of particular segments of truth. There are Christians who have made a special study of the Lord's

Second Coming who have never yet clearly grasped the essential truths nor richly appropriated the blessings of His first coming. A minister of the Gospel for seventeen years, who ardently preached on the millennium, declared before a Conference assembly that he had known almost nothing of the truth about the Holy Spirit, and had at that Conference received the fulness of the Spirit for the first time. It is one thing to be conversant with Bible themes; yet quite another to have full knowledge of the theme of the Bible— the Lord Jesus Christ Himself. It is for just this that Paul prays.

They already knew Christ, but it was for a deeper, growing knowledge that Paul prayed; for a thorough versus a superficial understanding; for a heart versus a head knowledge. Paul could never be content to have his converts know only the elementary principles of salvation. Now that they were *in* Christ he longed to see them grow up *into* Christ in all things (4:15). Having received Christ into their hearts as Saviour by faith (1:13), he prayed that Christ might dwell there in full possession and become the very Life of their life (3:17).

"The eyes of your understanding being enlightened." Paul prays that their innermost being might be flooded with light. So far the petitions have been preparatory. The real subject and scope of the prayer is for spiritual apprehension of the three "whats" of the following petition:

1:18, 19. "That ye may know *what is the hope of his calling,* and *what the riches of the glory of his inheritance in the saints,* and *what is the exceeding greatness of his power to usward who believe."*

"What—the hope of his calling"

God has called the Church to be Christ's Body, the fulness of Christ, the visible part of the invisible Christ to an ungodly world. God has called the Christian, as a member of Christ's Body, to be as holy and as heavenly as Christ is.

What, then, is the *hope* of His calling? Hope is a word that looks to the future. It always leads our thought onward in expectation; belonging as truly to the to-morrow of time as to the eternity beyond time; having both a near and a far horizon.

For the Church it means the expectation now of steady growth unto an ever-increasing spiritual maturity reaching toward the measure of the stature of the fulness of Christ (4:13). What of the hope when the last chapter of the Church's life on earth is written and, God's cycle for this age having run out, the eternal morrow dawns?

Oh! what a hope! The Church now sanctified becomes the Church glorified.

5:27. *"That he might present it to himself, a glorious church, not having spot, or wrinkle, or any such thing; but that it should be holy and without blemish."*

For the Christian the hope means that he will be more like Christ to-morrow than he has been to-day; filled more and more unto all the fulness of God; transformed into Christ's image from moment to moment.

II Cor. 3:18 (R.V.). "But we all, with unveiled face beholding as in a mirror the glory of the Lord, *are transformed into the same image from glory to glory,* even as from the Lord the Spirit."

One day Christ will come again to take every Christian into His immediate presence. In that eternal to-morrow there will be perfect likeness of every Christian to his Lord, for he will be glorified both in spirit and in body.

I John 3:2. "Beloved, now are we the sons of God; and it doth not yet appear what we shall be; *but we know that, when he shall appear, we shall be like him;* for we shall see him as he is."

Oh! is it any wonder that Scripture describes such a calling as high (Phil. 3:14); holy (II Tim. 1:9); and heavenly (Heb. 3:1)? What does the hope of such a calling inspire in you? Is it glorious enough to inspire hatred of all that is of the world, the flesh and the devil? Is it attractive enough to wean you from the world with all its soul-destroying pleasures and pursuits? Is it real enough to make you loathe self that would dethrone Christ as your Lord? Is it precious enough to make you seek those things which are above, where Christ sitteth on the right hand of God? Is it strong enough to create within you the passionate desire to have Christ all and in all to you?

"What—the riches of the glory of his inheritance in the saints"

Could any words express more perfectly the preciousness to God of His purchased possession? Ponder the words prayerfully:

"His *inheritance* in the saints."

The *glory* of his inheritance in the saints."

The *riches* of the glory of his inheritance in the saints."

How seldom we think of what we are to God! We so selfishly begin in our thinking with ourselves. What we can get from God rather than what we can be to God is our continued concern. But Ephesians emphasizes God's inheritance in the saints.

Someone has so well said, "God was not satisfied in possessing suns and stars; He wanted sons and saints." We are dearer to Him than all the worlds He has ever made; more precious than all His other creation. When this heaven and earth shall have passed away and a new heaven and earth shall have come, God's child, the redeemed sinner made a saint in Christ, shall abide forever.

The Church as Christ's Body and the Christian as a member of that Body are the manifestation of God's glory on earth to-day, feeble and inadequate as it is. But a day is coming—oh! that it might be soon!—when His heart shall, be fully satisfied in His inheritance, for His glory shall be prefectly manifested in the saints. Let this incomparable truth stir within your heart a passionate desire that He may be glorified in you more fully each day until that great day dawns for which both He and we look with such fervent expectation.

Dear fellow-Christian, are you ready to give up in complete discouragement because you think of how miserably you have failed in walking worthily of so high a calling and in glorifying your Lord? Are you saying that the standard set is too high and the life required impossible? So would Paul himself have given up, and every saint since his time, if the power to live such a life were required of them.

"What—the exceeding riches of his power to usward who believe"

Let us consider the meaning, the manifestation, and the measure of His power.

The Meaning

"His power"—From the Greek word for power come the words dynamo and dynamite. The power of which God speaks here is that which is inherently His as God; a power of surpassing, incalculable greatness which reveals the full strength of His might.

"To usward"—God would then tell us that in this wonder-working power is all that is needed for the commencement, continuance and consummation of our salvation: that it is all-sufficient for every demand made upon the saint in appropriating his wealth, in walking worthily of his high calling, and in wrestling victoriously against Satanic powers.

"Who believe." This mighty power is at the Christian's disposal upon one condition only—that of faith. The surpassing-all-limit power of God can be limited in its working only by the believer's failure to believe. The only check that can ever be imposed upon

the continuous current of His mighty power to usward is the self-imposed check of unbelief.

The Manifestation

No true believer should ever doubt His power. All His marvelous work in creation proves His mighty power; again, it is revealed so clearly in His deliverance of the children of Israel out of the bondage of Pharaoh and out of Egypt. But what guarantee is given to the present-day Christian that in its working it is able to overcome all the counter-working of sin and death in us, and to overthrow all the powers of evil working against us? God gives an absolutely assuring answer.

"According to the working of his mighty power." The only hindrance to the continuous, active working of His mighty power in us is found within us. Back of every purpose of God is the power for its fulfilment.

"Which he wrought in Christ." It is a power tested and proven; able to work in us as it wrought in Christ.

The Measure

How much power dare we depend upon to be manifested in our case? Dare we believe it will be sufficient to conquer all our foes; to break the hold of all our old sinful habits; to give deliverance from all temptations? To live above all our handicaps in environment and circumstances?

God gives the exact measurement of His power as He tells us what He wrought in Christ. The measure is foursquare and is summed up in four words: resurrection, exaltation, lordship, and headship.

Resurrection

1:20. "When he *raised him from the dead.*"

Christ *dead*—Christ *raised.* What a mighty chasm is bridged by the mighty working of God's power! Christ not dormant, as some say, but *dead.* Christ under the power of death and held by "the pains of death" (Acts 2:24); Christ buried in a tomb sealed with a stone "to make it as sure as ye can" (Matt. 27:65), and guarded by a watch lest "that deceiver should rise again, as he said he would." But God's mighty power in-worked in Christ to break the bonds of death. Christ arose.

This same power that wrought in Christ is to work in us who believe and in the same way. Having already in-worked to bring us out of death into life, its working will continue to make us walk in newness of life. Christ was raised as the representative Man who became the Head of a new race of men, each one of whom was to become like Himself.

Exaltation

1:20. "And *set him at his own right hand in the heavenly places.*"

The Father welcomes His Beloved home to glory and exalts Him to the place of greatest honour and power in relation to the throne.

Lordship

1:21, 22. *"Far above all* principality, and power, and might, and dominion, and every name that is named, not only in this world, but also in that which is to come, and *hath put all things under his feet.*"

"Far above all." Christ was crowned Lord of all, having become victor over all human, angelic and Satanic power. He has been placed in a position of supreme authority over all created beings, which includes every rank and order of celestial hierarchy, whether good or bad.

Still further is His unique Lordship shown in the pre-eminence of His Name over the name of every created object in this age or in the age to come. How terrifying to-day are the names of even some men who seem to have an almost uncanny power which is being wielded to the hurt and death of many! How even more, the very names "Satan"; "the devil"; "the great dragon," fill us often with stultifying fear. But oh! how precious to know and to rest upon that Name that is above every name!

"Hath put all things under his feet." Christ,—"far above all" and "all things" far beneath Him! *"Hath* put"—a past tense, an accomplished fact. *"All things."* Let us not tone it down by our wretched unbelief to mean some things. *"Under his feet,"*—the place of accomplished defeat and complete subjection. Christ has become both Victor and Ruler. While the full realization of the subjection of all things to the absolute Lordship of Christ awaits His triumphal return to rule on the earth, yet in God's purpose His Son is already King of kings and Lord of lords.

BEHOLD THE MAN ⎰ Commander of hosts of loyal angels.
⎱ Conqueror of hosts of rebel angels.
⎱ Controller of all things.

Headship

1:22, 23. "And gave him to be head over all things to the church, which is his body, the fulness of him that filleth all in all."

46

"Gave him to be head over all things to the church." Headship gave Christ full dominion in the affairs of the Church to direct all things pertaining both to its inner life and outer activity.

"To the church"—that company of saints chosen in Him; called out and separated from the world, the flesh and the devil; identified with Christ in His death, resurrection and ascension by which He becomes their Saviour, Lord and Life.

"His body,"—that company of saints gathered from both Jews and Gentiles; united to the Lord and to one another through reconciliation by the Cross and made one Body.

"The head—His body"—The Head and the Body become organically one so that each is vitally necessary to the other. All that the Head is and has in the heavenlies is the possession of the Body. And all that the Body is and has on earth is the possession of the Head.

"The fulness of him that filleth all in all." In Himself as God Christ is absolutely complete. He needs nothing added to Himself to make for perfection. "In him dwelleth all the fulness of the Godhead bodily" (Col. 2:9); and out of this fulness He meets the need of the Church and of every Christian. "Ye are made full in him" (Col. 2:10).

"The fulness of him"—But as the God-man He is not complete without the Church. As His Body, the Church is the complement of Christ. "He would be no more complete in His resurrection glory without the Church than Adam would have been without Eve."

Christ the Head ⎧ Source of Wealth
⎨ Sufficiency for Walk ⎬ Fulness of Church
⎩ Strength in Warfare ⎭

Church the Body ⎧ Filled with the Spirit
⎨ Filled unto all fulness with God ⎬ Fulness of Christ
⎩ Filled with Christ ⎭

Thus Christ is seen to be the invisible Head of the Church in the heavenlies, while the Church is the visible Body of Christ on earth and each is the fulness of the other.

Oh! just here will you pause for a moment to bow in silence before Him as you think of the sacred privilege and the solemn responsibility of the position and possession you have in Christ! To just what extent have you claimed Him as your fulness, and in what measure are you the complement of Him? Do you cower and collapse before human and Satanic powers, or do you conquer as

47

one "far above all"? Do you yield in repeated defeat to discouragement and depression, or are you the victor through your unshakable confidence in the victory of your Lord and Head? Are you above or beneath your circumstances? Is the measure of your faith according to the measurement of His power?

9. THE WEALTH UNFOLDED

A wondrous spiritual panorama now unfolds before us; God's grace and power in operation in the creation of a Christian and in the constitution of the Church; the Master-Workman at work forming "the new man."

It is sometimes helpful in understanding a portion of Scripture to let it fall loosely into fragments, and then to gather up these parts and put them together. By using this method in this study we discover four sharply-drawn contrasts.

Two Persons

2:2. *"The prince* of the power of the air, the spirit that now worketh in the children of disobedience."

"The prince"—The word shows the Holy Spirit is speaking of a person. Surely 2:2 teaches that he is a person of mighty, supernatural power; the ruler in the realm of evil, which has two spheres of activity: the air, the abode of evil spirits; and the earth, the abode of unregenerate men. This prince is the No. 1 public enemy of the whole universe.

2:6. *"Christ Jesus."*

The Son; the Father's Beloved; the sinner's Saviour; the saint's Lord and Life; Satan's Conqueror.

Satan is the source of all in the life of the sinner. Christ is the source of all in the life of the saint. Out of these two sources flow two streams; one the putrid stream of sin and death, and the other the pure stream of salvation and life. These two streams are the exact opposite, both in direction and in destiny.

Two Parties

Open your Bible to Ephesians II and let your eye run down the page. *"Ye—We"*—Here we find a marked *personal* contrast between two parties. It would be a great help at this point to turn to the epistle to the Romans and read the first three chapters where God says that all humanity, whether Gentiles or Jews, are sinners. In the whole world of mankind "there was not one righteous, no, not one"; "all have sinned and come short of the glory of God," so that all the world is guilty before God.

This may seem to some like a too sweeping and almost unwarranted indictment of mankind, and we need to go further into Romans V if we would understand God's basis for it. Here we see two men in sharp contrast,—Adam and Christ. Adam is the federal head of a race of sinners by natural generation; Christ is the federal head of a company of saints by supernatural regeneration. By disobedience Adam himself became a sinner, and all men who remain in him are "the children of disobedience." By obedience Christ became the sinner's Saviour, and in Him believers are made righteous.

So here in 2:1-3 the Gentiles, "ye," and the Jews, "we," as individuals, are in the same position and condition of sin and death. They are on an equality as sinners. The individual Jew is as great a sinner as the individual Gentile. As sinners they are equally "far off" from God, and need to be "made nigh" through reconciliation. "By nature" both Gentile and Jew are "the children of wrath," both facing the same awful destiny.

Let your eye run a second time over Chapter two, and we see a marked *racial* contrast between Gentile and Jew.

Uncircumcision	Aliens	Strangers
Circumcision	Commonwealth of Israel	Covenants of promise

Still a third time glance down the page and make a wonderful discovery: a wholly different and a very pleasing contrast.

Twain	Both	Foreigners	Far off
One new man	One body	Fellow-citizens	Made nigh

We both—
$\left\{\begin{array}{l}\text{household of God}\\ \text{holy temple in the Lord—One new man}\\ \text{habitation of God}\end{array}\right.$

Is it not fascinating to trace these very sharp, exclusive contrasts followed by such clear, all-inclusive unity? What is the meaning of it all? Scripture throws light on the meaning.* In another of Paul's epistles noonday light is shed on this entire section. Let us quote it:

I Cor. 10:32. "Give none offence, neither to *the Jews*, nor to *the Gentiles*, nor to *the church of God*."

Here the whole of mankind is divided into three races of people

---
* It would be helpful also to read Romans IX-XI and the Acts, especially chapters 2, 10, 11, and 15.

as distinct from each other as black from white. The Jew and the Gentile are the two divisions of mankind on earth. They are separated from each other nationally, racially, socially and religiously. The Church of God is neither Jew nor Gentile, yet is composed of both. It is a super-race, above all nationalities, classes, and religions; heavenly in origin and nature, though composed of men of earth.

How and why in God's economy did the human race, which had its origin in Adam, become divided into two such mutually hostile parties? This necessarily takes us back to God's explanation in Genesis. The entire human race had its origin in God's first man, Adam, who for two thousand years of human history was the only recognized head of mankind. Sin, which entered into mankind through Adam, brought God's judgment first upon Satan and his tool, the serpent. An age-long conflict was declared between two persons and between their seed.

Gen. 3:15. "And I will put *enmity between thee and the woman,* and *between thy seed and her seed;* it shall bruise thy head, and thou shalt bruise his heel."

How helpful it would be to trace "the seed" of the serpent and that of the woman on down through the Bible. It would throw much light on our previous study of the two persons. But we can go only as far as Genesis XII, where we find the beginning of the two parties.

The Jews—Called the Circumcision

"What advantage then had the Jew over the Gentile? Or what profit is there in circumcision? Much every way" (Rom. 3:1, 2). In Genesis XII we see God doing a new thing. He chooses one man out of whom He promises to make a great nation. From this nation "the seed of the woman" will come. Thus God sovereignly chose one nation from among the nations for His own glory and use.

Deut. 7:6. "For thou are an holy people unto the Lord thy God; *the Lord thy God hath chosen thee to be a special people unto himself,* above all the people that are upon the face of the earth."

From Genesis XII on the river of human life is divided into two distinct and distinguishable streams, flowing ever further and further apart. Israel, the chosen nation, and the Gentile nations are now distinct entities, nationally, socially and religiously.

As God's chosen people, the Jews became a *privileged* people above all other nations. To them was given a threefold trust; the conception of the coming Messiah, the custody of the oracles of God, and the covenants of promise. Through His chosen people the seed of the woman, Christ, the world's Saviour, will come forth. Through them the revelation of Christ and of God's redemptive purpose in Him will be given in the Scriptures. Through them also the unconditional promise of blessing to the peoples of the whole earth will be fulfilled.

As God's chosen people, the Jews became not only a people of privilege, but of responsibility to keep the life-stream pure, and to be a true witness of the one Lord among all the other nations. To accomplish this God commanded a clean-cut division between this chosen nation and all other nations, and the rite of circumcision was to be its covenant sign.

Gen. 17:9-11. "God said unto Abraham, . . . *Every man child among you shall* be circumcised . . . and it shall be a token of the covenant betwixt me and you."

Thus we see the Jewish nation drawn nigh unto God, formed nationally into the "commonwealth of Israel," "called the circumcision," and made the possessor of God's special "covenants of promise."

The Gentiles—Called Uncircumcision

The Gentile bore no sign in his flesh of his relationship to God, so he was "called uncircumcision." Regarded by the Jew as "an alien" and "a stranger," he became an outcast. He was "far off" from God, for he had no share in nor claim upon the promises of God made in His covenants with Israel.

The Church of God

The Church of God according to Ephesians is constituted of Jew and Gentile, each individually reconciled unto God and so unto one another. "We both" made one in Christ. God again does a new thing. He creates a new race which is super-racial, super-national, super-social, and super-religious.

2:15. "For to make in himself *of twain one new man.*"

Two Positions

The biggest little word and the most ubiquitous in Ephesians is the word "in." It is a preposition denoting *position*. God's Word gives our position precedence over our condition, because *where* we are determines *what* we are. Much of spiritual defeat and failure lies in our ignorance of and indifference to this fact. We are so concerned over what we are that we give no thought to where we are. Ephesians primarily emphasizes our position, and shows our condition to be the outgrowth of it. There are but two positions in which men may be: The sinner is in sin, and the saint is in Christ.

In Sin

The sinner is ensphered by and encased in sin. He is at home in sin. He lives and walks in sin.

2:1. "And *you,* who were dead *in sins.*"

2:3. "Also *we* all had our conversation in times past *in the lusts of our flesh.*"

As sinners, both Gentiles, "you," and Jews, "we," share the same position. All were dead in sins. However unequal the status of the Jew and the Gentile may be racially, as individual sinners they are on an absolutely equal footing. There is no privileged class in sin. High or low; educated or illiterate; Aryan or non-Aryan; occidental or oriental; professional or industrial; capitalistic or proletarian; all are brothers born in sin. The only place where all men meet on a common level and share the same position is in their natural birth in sin.

In Christ

The saint is ensphered by and encased in Christ. He is at home in Christ. He lives and walks in Christ.

2:5, 6. "God hath quickened *us* together with Christ and raised *us* up . . . and made *us* sit together in heavenly places *in Christ.*"

Before his rebirth Paul was one of the most bigoted of Jews, thinking himself doing God's service to imprison and slaughter the Christians. Yet here he uses that word "us," which includes the Gentile Christians. All barriers are down now; all racial enmity is gone, and Paul is the arch-champion of the equality of all saints in Christ.

As there is no privileged class in sin, so there is none in Christ. Every sinner is a bankrupt and an outcast, and only by God's unmerited favour, shown to him in Christ, is he ever anything else. One's nth degree human pedigree; one's Ph.D. education; one's multimillionaire estate; one's highly refined culture; one's publicized philanthropies; one's name in *Who's Who* avail for nothing in grace. Clergy and laity; the aged believer and the newborn convert; the most noted citizen and the most notorious criminal, saved by grace, all have the same position in Christ. God has no favourites in Christ. Grace exalts all saints to the same high and heavenly position in Christ.

In sin is where all sinners are by nature. In Christ is where all saints are by grace. God is no respecter of persons, either in sin or in Christ.

Two Periods

Another glance down the page of Ephesians II gives us a marked contrast in periods of time:

> In time past⎫
> At that time ⎬ But now.
> Sometimes.⎭

Also we see *"Ye were"* silhouetted against yesterday's horizon, while *"Ye are"* marks the dawn of a new day for the believer in the Lord Jesus. In these two periods of time a great and transforming miracle has taken place which separates the believer eternally from his past sins and sanctifies him forever unto his Saviour. Let us now consider what this glorious miracle is:

The Creation of a Christian (2:1-10)

As we come out of Chapter one into Chapter two, it is a startling drop from the pinnacle of redemption to the abyss of ruin. It is a sudden change from the purest air of the heavenlies to the putrified atmosphere of the pit.

Praise God! We may go on into 2:4-10, where we see the sinner becoming a saint through the mighty operation of God's mercy, love and grace. The process in the creation of a Christian is given here with a clarity and beauty found nowhere else in the Word. The passage falls naturally into a three-fold division:

> The sinner in his sins (2:1-3);
> The saint in Christ   (2:5-7);
> The way of salvation (2:4, 8-10).

Let us study the process of transition from the old position to the new.

The Sinner in Sin

2:1. "And *you* . . . who were *dead in trespasses and sins.*"

"And *you*"—This "you" refers to Gentiles; the "we" of 2:2 to Jews; so in this category of sinners is included every human being without a single exception. It means you, your family, your country, your race, and every man of every race. All are now, or once were, sinners.

This "you" refers also to Gentile *Christians.* Paul is writing of what they were "in time past." He is allowing one backward look, that their hearts may be quickened into deeper gratitude, greater love and fuller appreciation of the exceeding riches of God's grace toward them in Christ. Oh! that your heart and mine might be thus quickened as we read this book is my most earnest prayer!

"Were dead in trespasses and sins."—"Trespasses" indicate the element in which the sinner lives; one of rebellion and refusal of obedience to divine authority and law. The noun being in the plural gives the impression that the breaking of God's law is the habit of the sinner. *"In sins"*—which are the fruit of sin; the outward manifestation of the inward nature. There are many kinds and degrees of sins, and the sinner is capable of committing any or all of them, for the seed of sin is in him, and no one can forecast what fruit it will bear. The sinner may be held in restraint by personal pride; public opinion; selfish interest; or fear of consequences; but by nature he is still a child of disobedience, and is at heart opposed to God's will and purpose. Every sinner has preferred to follow the devil rather than God. He is therefore a spiritual outcast.

"Dead."—Let the word stand by itself. I beg of you, do not trifle with this word; do not ignore it, evade it, or whittle it down to anything less than its Scriptural significance. It describes as no other one word can the sinner's broken relationship to God. Sin severed the cord that bound the human spirit to God, and so entirely "alienated him from the life of God" (4:18) that he is henceforth in a state of spiritual death. The sinner is not merely morally degraded or diseased; *he is spiritually dead.* Unless he is saved by grace through faith, his present spiritual death will end in "the second death" (Rev. 20:14), which is eternal separation from the presence of God.

The sinner is a helpless, hopeless derelict; a powerless bankrupt, with no resources within himself for spiritual recovery. As a dead man his first need is life, but he has no way to generate it and no access to the One who can. Left to himself, he can do nothing, and faces his destiny as a child of wrath, having no hope. What a direful, pitiable position is his!

His position determines his condition. The sinner belongs to the underworld of sin, where there is but one walk possible.

2:2, 3. *"Ye walked* according to the course of *this world,* according to the prince of *the power of the air,* in the lusts of *the flesh."*

"Ye walked" according to the *direction* of the world, the *dictation* of the Devil, and the *domination* of the flesh.

"By nature—the children of disobedience and wrath." Every sinner is born with a nature inherently hostile to God and opposed to doing His will. If he refuses the Saviour he thereby hardens himself in his enmity toward God, and so by his own deliberate choice continues to be a child of disobedience. He is therefore under divine displeasure, and is a child of wrath. If the love of God manifested in Christ is rejected, then the wrath of God must be revealed.

So we see that the sinner is wholly out of adjustment with God. If he is set right, it must be with God first. But in 2:1-3 there is not one ray of light or one gleam of hope. Unless God intervenes and takes the initiative, the sinner will forever remain in his sins.

The Way of Salvation

2:4, 5. *"But God, who is rich in mercy, for his great love wherewith he loved us, even when we were dead in sins."*

"But God." Oh! if you have not encircled and underlined these words in your Bible, do it now. Here is a floodlight on the sinner's path; a signpost which marks a movement of God toward the sinner. Though our sin is inconceivably repulsive to His holiness, yet our soul is inconceivably precious to Him. So He will open a way of reconciliation for every sinner that he may be delivered from that awful pit.

"Who is rich"—God did not lack in resources for such a task, nor did He have to go outside of Himself to perform the miracle of regeneration. Out of His own inherent riches He met our abject poverty and transformed us from spiritual bankrupts into spiritual multimillionaires. God draws upon the riches of His mercy. He looks in pity upon the sinner utterly undone, and His great heart of love is moved to take the initiative in providing a way of salvation.

But we have learned that all sinners are children of wrath. They have incurred the displeasure of the infinitely righteous and holy One, and are deserving of the full penalty for their sin. Then how will God's mercy and love operate to satisfy the righteous demand of His holiness and at the same time meet the need of rebellious sinners?

2:5. *"By grace ye are saved."*

The first movement in salvation is not from men to God, but from God to men. This wondrous redemption was planned and executed *in the heart of God* in the eternity of the past, before even the world was. There and then a way to save to the uttermost was wrought out in the counsels of the triune God.

In what way and through whom would God's grace work to provide for sinful men a Mediator between God and them? For this is the sinner's greatest need if he is to be brought to the place of reconciliation. Who could act both as God's representative and the sinner's?

Just here let us look to the Holy Spirit for His own divine light and love to be poured into our inmost being, that we may not only apprehend more fully, but may also appreciate more deeply the worth and work of our adorable Saviour.

The Saint in Christ

2:1. *"You dead."*   1:20. *"Christ dead."*

"You dead."—How can a dead man be made alive? "Christ dead." What an amazing answer! Christ, the source of all life, even life itself, *dead!* This is the almost unthinkable thing that grace has done. It has put Christ, the sinless One, in the sinner's place. "The wages of sin is death"; "the soul that sinneth, it shall die." The penalty must be paid, and there was no other way to do it. He bore the sinner's sins by taking the sinner's place.

2:5. "Even when we were dead in sins, *hath quickened us together with Christ."*

Believing upon Christ as his Saviour and receiving Him into his heart, the sinner becomes the possessor of eternal life and is made one with Christ. Shall a live man remain in a grave?

1:20. *"Christ raised from the dead."*

2:6. "And hath *raised us up together with him."*

The grave could not hold Him that was alive. Neither can it hold the quickened sinner. The grave of sin is no place for a saint. An evangelist said in a meeting, "We shall never be anything but sinners saved by grace, with one foot in sin and one foot in grace." Never, oh! never, according to Ephesians. If 2:1-10 teaches anything, it is the exact opposite of such a statement. True, the sinner is saved by grace, and by grace alone, and this fact should ever be kept fresh in his memory, that he may forever praise God for His wondrous goodness. But it is equally true that through God's grace the believer in Christ has left forever the old position in sin, and has come into a totally new position in Christ. Indeed the *sinner* has become a *saint*. God lifted him altogether out of that awful pit of sin and placed *both feet* on the solid rock "in Christ" wherein he is to walk in the future, as in times past he walked "in sin." How could a saint walk worthily (4:1) with one foot in sin and one foot in grace? It is just such teaching and such practice that excuses the unworthy and inconsistent walk of many a Christian. Being raised together with Christ, the saint is now to walk in newness of life. To do this Christ must become the Life of his life.

But God's grace is not yet exhausted, nor His redemptive plan yet completed. Wherever Christ is the Christian must be, for he is now bound together with Christ for all time and eternity. Christ and the Christian are eternally one. The earth could not hold the risen Christ any more than the grave could retain the dead Christ, for His redemptive work demands something more.

1:20. *"He set him at his own right hand in the heavenly places."*

2:6. *"He made us to sit together in heavenly places in Christ Jesus."*

Dare we believe this glorious truth that He who went down to the very deepest depths of sin for us now carries us up to the very highest heights of glory with Him? That is hardly the way to put the question. Dare we *not* believe it? God has written both of these truths in His Word and, if we do not believe the latter, we do not really believe the former. God has said it, and to disbelieve is to make God a liar.

"Made us *sit together."*—Seated; how restful and relaxed it sounds! Yet how many of us are most of the time anything but that, but rather buzzing around in a fretful, feverish fashion which is far more earthly than heavenly in the impression it makes upon the world about us.

"In the heavenlies in Christ."—Yes, at home in the heavenlies, where our citizenship really is (Phil. 3:20). Not visiting this glorious place from time to time as trial, sorrow and conflict drive us to a higher plane, but settling down in the heavenlies in possessive and permanent occupancy as our abiding-place.

Paul was in a Roman prison when he wrote this epistle, but one would never know it. There is no smell of a prison in Ephesians. As you open the book it is just like going into some vast, open expanse and breathing the fresh air of heaven. There is no clank of prison chains to be heard, for Paul is not bound in spirit. He is there as the prisoner of Rome, but this he will not admit, and claims to be "the prisoner of Jesus Christ." What is the secret of such victorious otherworldliness? Paul's spirit is with Christ in the heavenlies though his body languishes in that foul Roman prison.

To whom did Paul write this epistle and to whom is it addressed? He wrote it to the saints *at Ephesus*, but addressed it to the faithful *in Christ*. Their temporary residence was at Ephesus, which was the centre of idolatry, superstition, luxury and vice. The shrine of

Diana was there, the place of the midnight darkness of paganism. Yet their real abode was in Christ, which was to them the centre of worship, light, life and holiness. It was at the right hand of the throne of God, the place of the midday light of Christianity.

Oh! my friend, where do you live? "At" or "In"? Do you just live down on earth as a Christian all wrought up into a frenzy of anxiety over life's perplexities and problems; its trials and tribulations; its sufferings and sorrows? You will surely have them, for they are permitted, even intended by God for your discipline, growth and training. Or do you daily take afresh by faith your position in Christ in the heavenlies and there find His peace, joy and rest; yes, and the courage and strength to bear and to endure victoriously?

Still one further thought out of "together with Christ:" Where is He? *"Far above all."* Ponder these words until they sink into your innermost consciousness and become a very part of you. Where are we? In Christ. Then we, too, are "far above all" in God's purpose, sharing fully in all the conquest, victory and power of that exalted position. In Christ we are as far above the power of Satan as Christ is; therefore we may be more than conquerors, always triumphing in Christ (Rom. 8:37; II Cor. 2:14). Is it any wonder that through all the ages to come we shall be praising God for the exceeding riches of His grace in His kindness toward us through Christ Jesus?

The saint in Christ is God's workmanship; a creation of God's own. Man's works have no part in this wondrous miracle. Good works will be the fruitage of his life as a Christian, but they had no part in making him one. God was the sole Creator of the Christian, who was created through union with Christ.

2:10. *"For we are his workmanship,* created in Christ Jesus unto good works."

What part does man have in the translation from sinnerhood to sainthood? God tells us quite plainly:

2:8. "By grace ye are saved *through faith."*

But the helplessness of the sinner is so complete that in himself he has not even the faith necessary for salvation. This, too, is God's gracious gift to him.

2:8, 9. "And that not of yourselves; it is the gift of God: Not of works, lest any man should boast."

Our salvation is not the result of anything we are or know or do. This leaves no place for pride. Our new life and new position in Christ, even the faith by which on the manward side these unsearchable riches become our possession, are all the outright gift of God.

We have studied together the blessed truth of the creation of the Christian. Let us stop for a moment to get it clearly in our mind's eye before we pass on to our next theme.

PONDER
$\begin{cases} \text{Dead in sins.} & \text{— By nature.} \\ \text{BUT GOD—} & \text{— CREATED IN CHRIST JESUS} \\ \text{Alive in Christ.} & \text{— By grace.} \end{cases}$

PRAISE

Together with Christ
$\begin{cases} \text{quickened} \\ \text{raised} \\ \text{seated} \end{cases}$

In Christ
$\begin{cases} \text{in the heavenlies} \\ \\ \text{far above all} \end{cases}$

The Constitution of the Church (2:11-3; 12)

Our approach to the study of this great theme will be from a somewhat new angle. Let us see not only how God constituted the Church in the beginning, but how His method of doing it with its glorious results is the only effective way of meeting the desperate need of human society to-day, which is in such a serious state of maladjustment.

There are two distinct and divergent lines of teaching in the Church to-day. There are those, who, interpreting the Word of God literally, say that God has commissioned the Church primarily to save the individual sinner, and, therefore, its first obligation is to preach the gospel of redemption through regeneration. There is another group who, interpreting the Bible liberally, say that the primary work of the Church is to salvage human society, which is in such a deplorable state. So they advocate preaching a social gospel which aims at the reconstruction of society with the expectation of the reformation of the individual. Let the Word show us what God says and does. He clearly teaches that sin's primary work was to separate man from God (4:18). Adam and Eve, when once conscious of sin, "hid themselves from the presence of the Lord" (Gen. 3:8). So the first work of salvation is to bring the sinner out of hiding into real and joyous fellowship with the Lord. This necessitates preaching the Gospel of redemption to the sinner, that he may get right with God. For, if he is out of adjustment with God, he will most certainly be out of alignment with men.

Therefore the personal aspect of salvation is presented first in 2:1-10, where God creates a saint out of a sinner, thus making him fit for both divine and human society, rather than reconstructing human society to make it fit for men still in their sins. God created the saint before He constituted the Church out of the aggregate of saints. He has used His Church as a powerful and effectual factor in the remaking of society, as the unprejudiced study of any mission field will prove. Ephesians has place for a social gospel, but it follows the individual gospel as a fruit rather than taking precedence over it as the root.

The aim of the social gospel is to bring a right adjustment in all the manifold relationships of men with men, and nations with nations, so that wrongs and enmities may be abolished; that righteousness and love may prevail, and that men may live in peace one with another. That the Church has a responsibility in social as well as individual salvation no student of the Word will deny. But the Church itself is divided over the method to be used for its achievement. One section, stressing primarily the brotherhood of man, works to strengthen the human ties which bind men together through political, economic, social and religious alignments, so they give themselves to the advocacy of the World Court, the League of Nations, disarmament, labor legislation, and World Conferences on Unity of Churches. Another section of the Church, stressing primarily the necessity of men's reconciliation with God, works to bring about the conciliation of man with man by the mediation of Jesus Christ, who is able to do away not only with the fruit of enmity, but with the enmity itself, and thus open the way for a true brotherhood based on mutual fellowship in Christ. Again let us see from the Word God's way of conciliation:

Sin's secondary work was to separate man from man. When Adam was brought face to face with his own sin of disobedience to God's command, he immediately placed the blame for his transgression upon Eve his wife. And when the Lord asked Eve, "What is this that thou hast done?" she promptly laid the blame upon the serpent. Men and women have been shifting the responsibility for their own sin upon someone else ever since that day.

Sin caused friction between that first husband and wife. Sons were born into the family. Cain, the elder, was the follower of Satan and his works were evil; while Abel chose to follow God and his works were righteous (I John 3:12). This caused jealousy between them which ended in the murder of Abel by Cain. The sin in that first family on earth, like a pebble thrown into the ocean of humanity, has caused an ever-widening circle of friction, jealousy and enmity, until to-day the world is one colossal war camp. One of the greatest of world problems is how to keep men and nations from each others' throats.

Sin has separated human society into hostile peoples and parties. Sin has caused a mighty schism in humanity, dividing men *racially* into Semite and anti-Semitic, Aryan and non-Aryan; *nationally* into the totalitarianism of Bolshevism, Nazism, and Fascism, and into democracies; *socially* into caste and outcast, titled and common, white, black and yellow; *economically* into capitalistic and proletarian; and *religiously* into Christendom and paganism; while Christendom is subdivided into wheat and tares, truth and error, an organism and an organization. Sin has also created in individuals and nations a superiority complex that has led to aggression and invasion and made the weak a prey to the strong.

Surely human society is in desperate need of reconstruction. There must be a conciliator between man and man if hatreds and enmities are to be put away and any real brotherhood established. But who is sufficient for such a task? Can any nation produce such a conciliator? Woodrow Wilson was a man of high international ideals, and hoped against hope that he could step into the breach between the nations and be used to bring peace to the world through his Utopian dream of a League of Nations. He died, some believe, of a broken heart, and his dream has become more like a nightmare for others.

Men have resorted to pacts and treaties of all kinds and descriptions to cement international friendship and to court peace. Internationally-minded statesmen, passionately devoted to the cause of peace, have laboured long over the preparation of these treaties. Representatives of many nations have travelled long distances and spent many millions to meet in conferences to discuss them. Nations have signed these documents, publicly pledging thereby to do their part to keep the world's peace, and have speedily gone to incredible lengths as international kidnappers of neighbour nations.

No treaty ever made or to be made can weld antipodal nations into peace. It may temporarily disarm a nation, but it can never destroy its will to war. The heart of peace is not an "it," but an "He." "*He is our peace,*" and there is peace in no other way. God works to unite men, not by the reconstruction of human society, but by the construction of a divine society on an altogether new basis, as Paul shows in 2:11-3:13, where he passes from the personal to the corporate aspect of salvation.

So let us turn now to a study of the constitution of the Church, which is Christ's Body. 2:11-22 falls naturally into three parts:

| We | Israel | Circumcision | Commonwealth of Israel | Made Nigh |
| Ye | Gentiles | Uncircumcision | Aliens | Foreigners | Far off |

Twain—separated by
$$\begin{cases} \text{the middle wall of partition.} \\ \text{the law of commandment contained in} \\ \quad \text{ordinances.} \\ \text{enmity.} \end{cases}$$

We have already considered the great gulf between Jews and Gentiles, dividing them into two camps which bear toward each other mutual hatred and contempt. The privileged Jew looked upon the unprivileged Gentile as outcast even from the love of God.

Let us consider the spiritual condition of the Gentile pagans:

2:12. "Ye were *without Christ.*"

The Messianic idea of a coming Deliverer for Israel welded the Jews together as citizens in a commonwealth. As a nation they looked for the Promised One who would be prophet, priest and king. The nation, as a whole, might depart from God and serve other gods; yet there was always a remnant of the true Israel that kept its faith fixed on that Coming One. While the Gentiles were just a race of individual pagans having no essential oneness except in sin. They had no part in the promised Messiah and no claim upon Him.

2:12. "Having *no hope.*"

They were "strangers to the covenants of promise," so they had no anchor. They were as sailors in a captainless boat on an uncharted sea. They had no divine revelation and so no divine plan for their course of life. "Their future was like a night without a star." They had only the horizon of earth, with nothing to satisfy them here or hereafter.

2:12. "Ye were *without God.*"

The Jews had one God in whom their national life centred. The Gentiles had innumerable gods; so their racial life disintegrated into many nations with no common meeting-point. The Old Testament reveals the nations as utterly opposed to God, and under the domination of Satan. Such was the condition of the Gentiles; outcasts from both human and divine fellowship.

At that time—Without
$$\begin{cases} \text{Christ} \\ \text{Hope} \\ \text{God} \end{cases} \text{——BUT NOW.}$$

God intervenes for the hopeless Gentiles and provides a way of salvation through a world Saviour. These Gentile Christians at

Ephesus had heard the Word of truth and had believed on the Lord Jesus Christ. They had been brought home to God by the redeeming blood.

2:13. "But now in Christ Jesus ye who sometimes were far off are *made nigh by the blood of Christ.*"

The Conciliation of Jew with Gentile

A way must be opened for the conciliation of Jew and Gentile. and 2:14-18 shows us what it is. A threefold cord of peace binds them in indissoluble union in Christ.

1) *Christ Himself is their Peace.*

2:14. "For *he is our peace.*"

Christ is not merely a peace-maker; He Himself is "our peace." So to receive Him is to have peace and is the preliminary for making peace, as this passage so clearly shows. How different is the way of man, who both tries to make and to preach peace with Christ altogether left out of the transaction!

2) *Christ made peace.*

2:14. "He hath *broken down the middle wall of partition* between us."

2:15. "Having *abolished in his flesh the enmity,* even the law of commandments contained in the ordinances."

2:15. "For *to make in himself of twain one new man.*"

2:16. "That he might *reconcile both unto God in one body by the cross.*"

There are four distinct steps mentioned here in Christ's work of making peace. First, by breaking down the middle wall of partition between them. We have seen that God had made a choice of Israel as a special people for Himself, and had separated Israel from the Gentile nations. This separation was typified by the wall in the olden temple by which the court of the Gentiles was separated from that of the Jews; to go beyond which would have meant death to the Gentile.

Many Jews were just as evil in the sight of God as the Gentiles. They were Jews outwardly, but not inwardly (Rom. 2:28, 29). Their nearness to God was a *privileged* nearness because of God's choice of them as His peculiar people rather than a *personal* nearness because of their choice of God as their satisfying portion.

But this wall of separation tended to make the Jews bigots in their attitude to the Gentiles. The further away from God they went personally, the more bigoted they became racially. Their distinction as God's chosen people created within them a superiority complex. In order to make "both one" this wall of separation must be done away with entirely. This is what Christ first did in making peace.

Secondly, He made peace by abolishing the enmity between them. The separation between Jew and Gentile was emphasized by certain institutions designed to isolate Israel from other nations. Such, Paul says, was the law of commandments contained in the ordinances, which was given to Israel only. Just here read Romans 2:11-29, and note that the Gentiles were without law, while the Jews rested in the law, considered themselves teachers of the law, and made their boast of the law, while the majority of them were dishonouring God through breaking the law, and thus they blasphemed His name among the Gentiles. So, though they were more privileged than the Gentiles in being the custodians of the law, yet they were under its curse for having broken it. Therefore they were as guilty before God as the Gentiles.

This enmity must be abolished if peace were to be made. This could not be done by either race, for a Jew as a Jew, and a Gentile as a Gentile would never find a way of conciliation. There is no meeting-place in the natural where Jew and Gentile can be made one, but God provided one in Christ.

The Gentile had sinned "without law," and the Jew had sinned "in the law"; so both were under the penalty of death and of judgment. Someone must pay that penalty and bear that judgment for both. This Christ did in His own flesh. The law was good and holy. As the incarnate Son He obeyed its every command. Could the Father accept the perfect life of His Son for the imperfect life of sinners, and so cancel their debt? Oh! no, "the wages of sin is death." Christ must die. "Cursed is every one that continueth not in all things which are written in the book of the law to do them" (Gal. 3:10). Christ must be made a curse. In His own body on the tree He bore the full penalty of the law and cancelled the guilt of both Jew and Gentile. The Cross of Christ is the only place where the enmity between the Jew and the Gentile could be, or ever has been, abolished, and where they could meet on an equal footing. There they met on an equality of sin and of salvation.

Thirdly, He made peace by making in himself of twain one new man. So far all that has been done has dealt with the past and has centred in the removal of barriers to peace. But as yet there is not an established basis for real unity and continued peace. Now the Lord does a marvellous and a totally new thing.

"Of twain—one new man." The two old parties, Jew and Gen-

tile, are superseded by a new race and given a new name. God did not convert Jews into Gentiles, nor Gentiles into Jews, nor did God raise the Gentile to the earthly position of the Jew or lower the Jew to the earthly position of the Gentile. But through redemption by the blood of Christ the old racial and religious divisions were thrown into the discard, and in Christ both Jew and Gentile were raised to a heavenly position far transcending anything ever promised to or possessed by either.

"One new man"—super-racial and super-national. God welded Jew and Gentile into a new race of men in which all the old distinctions and differences, bonds and barriers, are obliterated. No longer does either Jew or Gentile count his citizenship as of the earth, for he has become a citizen of heaven (Phil. 3:20). True, he is still a pilgrim on earth, but he is here as a stranger passing through to his heavenly home. But "the new man" is more than just redeemed Jew and Gentile.

"One body"—It is redeemed Jew and Gentile united on earth as the Body of Christ with the risen, ascended Lord in heaven as Head of the Body. Over this new society Christ is to be the Lord, and in it He is to be the Life. The Jew forgets that he is a Jew, and the Gentile that he is a Gentile. Each now thinks only of what he is in Christ. Christ is to be all and in all to both. In such a glorious oneness every racial, religious, social and class distinction is utterly wiped out.

Col. 3:11. "Where there is neither Greek nor Jew, circumcision nor uncircumcision, barbarian, Scythian, bond or free; but Christ is all and in all."

Here is a oneness that is inward and vital. A new start has been made from a new center. Here is no camouflage of a patched-up, man-made peace, but a divine reality in a positive brotherhood of goodwill and love, born out of a true family relationship established by life in Christ.

Fourthly, He made peace by reconciling both unto God in one Body by the Cross. Before Jew and Gentile were conciliated and both made one, there had to be a reconciliation of "both unto God." The Cross was the place where a twofold enmity was slain; that between the Jew and the Gentile toward God, and that between the Jew and the Gentile toward each other. Each had to be at peace with God before they could be at peace with each other. But when once God had become their Father, then they gladly called each other brethren.

"By the Cross"—There is, however, but one place for such con-

ciliation. At the Cross both are alike condemned as sinners and redeemed by the Saviour. At the Cross both met as equals on the ground of grace, for both are lowered to the same depth in sin, and both are exalted to the same height in Christ. So the moment they were united to God through faith in the blood of Christ, they were united to one another as members of His Body. Such is the mighty, severing and unifying power of the Cross of Christ.

Oh! why is the crucified One not invoked to remove enmities and to secure peace in our war-torn, hate-infested world to-day? At heart the whole world is at war. Many countries are deliberately preparing for war, while others are actually engaged in wholesale murder through undeclared wars. In Spain it is brother against brother; in the Orient it is neighbour against neighbour. Every attempt yet made to bring peace has utterly failed. The reason is evident.

Because man's way of making peace is by seeking to secure conciliation of man with man before men are reconciled unto God. Nations seek to heal the breaches made by sin by man-made negotiations, alliances and treaties that are worthless scraps of paper almost as soon as the signatures are dry, and by world conferences on every conceivable point of friction. But over every one of them, written in capital letters, is the word FAILURE. So they meet only to compromise for the present and to postpone to the future. They persuade themselves that peace is just around the corner, but they never get to the turn of the road that leads to the goal. And they never will, for the reason that they are not even going in the direction of peace. The Prince of Peace is not invited to sit at their council table, hence they do not even know the right road to take. Conciliation between man and man must have a divine basis, which is the blood of Christ shed on the Cross. This is God's way to peace. If God now allowed men to make peace their way, He would confess that His way was a failure. God would never so betray His Son.

And God's way works wherever men have been willing to co-operate with God in bringing peace. When we see God removing the enmity between two such absolutely opposite peoples as the Jews and the Gentiles and welding them together into a new race, as He did in that first century Church; then we know that He can do the same thing in this twentieth century between opposing nationalities. He is doing it in our day. In a conference on revival in Europe I witnessed a very touching scene: Two women, one French and the other German, neither of whom in the natural had any love for the nation of the other, stood with eyes moist, with hands clasped in true Christian love and fellowship, and each fervently pledging prayer for the other. *"He is our peace."*

Let this quotation from a letter received very recently prove how wonderfully God's way of peace works: "Last Wednesday at our prayer-meeting we listened to a story from one of our missionaries, who has been working in Manchuria, of the behaviour of the Japanese towards the Chinese Christian leaders. The story she told seemed almost incredible. We were told of one pastor who had been tortured to make him confess that he was a Communist, but although he almost died owing to the tortures, he refused to tell this lie. After considerable pressure the Japanese authorities agreed to bring him up for trial. There was a bright side to this dark picture in that a Japanese Christian barrister went over from Japan to defend this Chinese brother. He said he knew he was doing this at the risk of his life, but he felt constrained to go." *"In himself of twain one new man, so making peace."*

In 1907 it was my privilege to attend a conference of the World Student Christian Federation, where there were representatives from more than forty nations. As a hymn was sung, one caught the strains of music in six languages. Only one word could I understand, but in each language it was clearly distinguishable;—that one word was the name of Him who made us all one family in the Lord: the precious name of "Jesu." *"That he might reconcile both unto God in one body by the cross."*

Let us, then, sum up finally God's way of conciliation as set forth in 2:14-16:

"In Himself"
$\left\{ \begin{array}{l} \text{Christ is the Mediator between Jew and Gentile.} \\ \text{Christ is the Eradicator of all barriers between Jew and Gentile.} \\ \text{Christ is the Reconciler of Jew and Gentile unto God.} \\ \text{Christ is the Conciliator of Jew and Gentile with each other.} \\ \text{Christ is the Centre of the new man composed of Jew and Gentile.} \end{array} \right.$

"Of twain"—Jew and Gentile—*"Both one"*—Out of every kindred, tongue, people, and nation (Rev. 5:9). Though they differed in tradition, temperament, or training, Christ has been able to unite men in Himself. He has eliminated race prejudice, nationalistic superiority, class distinction, religious bigotry, and personal dislike, and welded men together in one Body.

"One new man"—Note very carefully that God is not making a new world, but a new man. God makes no attempt to improve world conditions by repairing the old systems, but He replaces the old, earthly nationalisms by a new order whose citizenship is of heaven.

3) *Christ Preached Peace*

2:17. "And came and *preached peace to you* which were afar off, and to them that were nigh."

Having become peace and having made it, Christ now preaches peace. It was His personal message after His resurrection (Luke 24:36; John 20: 19, 21, 26). He preached it later through His apostles, and continues to preach peace through His Word faithfully given by His ministers.

It is God's clearly declared purpose to heal the schism made by sin in humanity; otherwise His plan of salvation would be incomplete. In this present age He would do it *through grace.* Peace has not been established on earth because men will not follow God's way. But in the age to come, *through government* the Lord Jesus Christ shall rule over the earth as King of kings and Lord of lords. Then righteousness shall prevail and peace shall be its fruit.

The Construction of the Church (2:19-22)

2:19. "Now therefore ye are no more strangers and foreigners, but fellow-citizens with the saints, and of *the household of God."*

"Now therefore." Paul now summarizes the results of God's workmanship, and shows the benefit of His work to God as well as to the saints. Connecting 2:19 with 2:18, these words also show that now the Gentile and Jew have equal access to the Father through the Son by the Spirit.

1) *The Church Becomes the Household of God*

Here is a picture of the felicity and harmony of the divine family, gathered about the Father's hearthstone. Oh! what joy there is in the Father's heart. For the prodigal son has at last come home!

"Ye are no more strangers and foreigners." The "ye" undoubtedly refers to the Gentiles, who once knowing God had not glorified Him as God, but in the blindness of their minds and foolishness of their hearts had given themselves up to idolatry (Rom. 1:21-23). Having departed from God they went out into the far country of utter moral degradation.

But note the marvellous change in the heart of that elder brother, the erstwhile bigot, Saul of Tarsus! Listen to that Hebrew of the Hebrews, as he welcomes the prodigal son home:

"But fellow-citizens with the saints, and of the household of God." By the Cross of Christ all racial prejudice and enmity have been abolished. Now in Christ the Jew can say to the repentant, believing Gentile, Ye are no longer strangers, but home-born ones; not now foreigners, but fellow-citizens and fellow-members of the Body of Christ. "We both," as members of the household of God, have the same access to the Father's heart and home.

2) *The Church Becomes an Holy Temple in the Lord*

2:21. "In whom all the building fitly framed together groweth unto *an holy temple in the Lord."*

Paganism had its temple there in Ephesus, the magnificent temple of the Asian goddess Diana. Its fame was world-wide, and worshippers came there from far distant places. Judaism had its temple in Jerusalem, which was the stronghold of the Jewish faith. So Christianity has its temple, a building not made with hands, but builded by God, Jesus Christ Himself being the chief corner-stone.

Upon this divine foundation God lays one living stone upon another, the saints born into the family of God since the day of Pentecost. Each is put in his own place by God, and in such a way that they exactly fit together. The building is not yet completed, but grows day by day, as a soul here or in a far corner of the earth is won to the Lord and made a living stone.

3) *The Church Becomes an Habitation of God*

2:22. "In whom ye also are builded together for *an habitation of God* through the Spirit."

God must have a dwelling-place on earth as well as in heaven. Where His family is there He must be. Also where needy, sinful men are, there He must have some way of revealing Himself to them and of reaching them with the Gospel message. So during this age of grace God takes up His residence in the Church and in the Christian. We are the habitation of God, the visible part of God on earth. Oh! what a challenging truth! Is God seen in us?

The Constitution of the Church (3:1-12)

God states in this passage that He is doing an altogether new thing. A "mystery," or secret, hid in Himself from the beginning of the world, was now made known by special revelation to Paul, and through him to the apostles and prophets of the new dispensation.

3:3, 5. *"By revelation he made known unto me the mystery* . . . which in other ages was not made known unto the sons of men, as it is now revealed unto his holy apostles and prophets by the Spirit."

What this new thing was cannot be stated more clearly than in God's own words:

3:6. "That the Gentiles should be *fellow-heirs,* and *of the same body, and partakers of his promise* in Christ by the gospel."

That the Gentiles were to be saved and that they were to be blessed through the promise given to Abraham was revealed in the Old Testament. But that God purposed to create this new man out of Jew and Gentile, and constitute them one Body over which Christ would be the Head, and in which the Gentile would be a co-equal with the Jew in every respect, was indeed a new thing. Jews and Gentiles are to be fellow-partakers in everything in Christ.

Were Paul here to-day witnessing the anti-Semitism which is sweeping like a tidal wave over the world, and, sad to say, has caught some Gentile Christians in its devastating onrush, would he have to reverse Romans 3:29 to read, "Is he the God of *the Gentiles only? Is he not also of Jews?* Yes, of the Jews also."

What would this "prisoner for *the Gentiles"* (3:1) think if he read the following paragraph?

Just recently a decree was issued by a Christian church that hereafter no Jew could worship there because of governmental threats. A very consecrated Hebrew Christian missionary in that country who had membership in that church and often preached there, was among those ejected. He and other Christian Jews were compelled to form a *Hebrew Christian church.* Christian Jews not allowed to worship with Christian Gentiles as *fellow-heirs, fellow-members, fellow-partakers!* Not "both *one,"* but both *two.* Not *"both* one body," but *each* one body. Oh! the awful shame and sin of such an act!

In the light of such a murderous wound inflicted not only upon the Body of Christ, but upon Christ Himself, let "the prisoner of Jesus Christ for you Gentiles" make his last appeal to us present-day Gentile Christians.

2:11-12. *"Wherefore remember* . . . that at that time ye were without Christ, being aliens from the commonwealth of Israel, and strangers from the covenants of promise, having no hope, and without God in the world."

Did not God put that word "remember" in 2:11 for such a day as this? *"Remember"* that "in time past" you were an helpless, hopeless outcast in the deepest depths of sin. *"Remember"* you would still be there, as "far off" from God as any Jew you know to-day, had you not been "saved by grace." *"Remember"* that you were then the "alien" and the "foreigner" belonging to a pagan, unprivileged race, while the Jew belonged, and still does, to God's chosen people, a nation privileged in God's sight beyond all nations of the earth. *"Remember"* that apart from the blood of Christ you could never have been "made nigh" unto God. *"Remember"* that, as a Gentile, you have nothing in yourself or in your race of which to boast; and that your position as a "wild olive tree grafted into the good olive tree as a branch" is held only through faith, and not because of any personal, national or racial merit or superiority (Rom. 11:11-34). *"Remember"* that God has no favourites in His family, and that both Jew and Gentile have the same access unto the Father, through the Son, by the Spirit. *"Remember"* that, when once either Jew or Gentile has been incorporated into Christ through faith in His blood, he is a fellow-member of Christ's Body and a "fellow-citizen" with all saints. *"Remember"* that "we twain" are made "one new man" in Christ, and that henceforth we belong to a heavenly race that is super-racial and super-national, sharing alike both the privileges and the responsibilities of the Christian Church. O yes, ye Gentiles *"remember"* that your two most precious possessions, your Saviour and your Bible, came to you through *the Jew;* that the door to the Church was opened to you by Peter, *the Jew;* and that the revelation given of your equal possession of all its blessed privileges came to you through Paul, *the Jew.* And to any Gentile Christian who gives over all the curses to the Jew pronounced upon him in God's Word, while he glories in all the blessings as promised to himself, even those plainly and exclusively given to the Jewish nation, *"remember"* the Word of God spoken centuries ago to the father of the Jews:

Gen. 12:3. *"I will bless them that bless thee* and *curse him that curseth thee;* and in thee shall all families of the earth be blessed."

And the Word of God through the Psalmist:

Ps. 122:6. "Pray for the peace of Jerusalem; *they shall prosper that love thee."*

And our Lord's own touching word regarding "my brethren":

Matt. 25:40, 45. "Inasmuch as ye have done it unto one of the least of these my brethren, *ye have done it unto me. . . .* Inasmuch as ye did it not to one of the least of these, *ye did it not unto me."*

10. THE WEALTH REALIZED

There is a marvellous interdependence between the two prayers in Ephesians. In Chapter one there is a prayer for *revelation:*— *"that ye may know";* a petition for spiritual apprehension of the riches of His grace. Now Paul stops again to pray. This prayer is for *realization:*— *"that ye might be";* a prayer for spiritual appropriation of the riches of His grace.

Let us get this interdependence between the two prayers in our mind's eye. Note the contrasts and the complements.

First Prayer (1:15-23).	Second Prayer (3:14-21)
Revelation	Realization
Enlightenment	Enablement
Light	Life
Know what you are	Be what you know
Know the power of God	Experience the fulness of God
Power working for us	Power working in us
Ye in Christ	Christ in you
Christ fulness Church	Church fulness Christ

Process of Realization

As we know from experience, the realization of Christ's abundant life in us is a process. While we become the potential possessors of the fulness of Christ the moment we are reborn, yet the personal possession of that fulness is a continuous process after the initial appropriation of it by faith. No matter how much of that fulness one has enjoyed to-day, there is more beyond, and every to-morrow should be for us unto still greater fulness.

So in this prayer for realization there is a process. There are a series of petitions; each one is an advance upon the one that precedes, and a preparation for that which follows. As the petitions in the first prayer were introduced by three "whats," so these in the second prayer begin with four "thats."

"That he would grant you to be strengthened."

"That Christ may dwell in your hearts by faith."

"That ye may be able { to comprehend"— and to know the love of Christ."

"That ye may be filled unto all the fulness of God."

Possibility of Realization

The possibility of an answer to this prayer seems so remote that there may be hesitancy in voicing the petitions. The scope of the prayer staggers us. We know the wealth which God has purposed and provided for us in Christ, but can it be procured? Let us have our hearts set at rest on that question.

The prayer is buttressed at each end by two reassuring phrases. They should convince us that the realization of our riches in Christ is based on something very stable and sure; objectively upon "the riches of his glory," and subjectively upon "the power that worketh in us."

3:16. "That he would grant you *according to the riches of his glory.*"

"*According to.*" God is not promising something which He is unable to perform. He estimated His own resources before He promised to bequeath such wealth to His children. God's budget has always been balanced, and there need be no fear of His prodigal program of spending for the salvation and sanctification of believers in His Son. Nothing is unstable in the plan of redemption, for God is not experimenting with men's souls, nor has He left anything to chance. He counted the whole cost of building this wondrous habitation of God long ages before He laid a single living stone upon the foundation, and knew that He was fully able to carry it to completion.

In his book *In the Heavenlies* Dr. H. A. Ironside unfolds the deep meaning of the words "according to" in a simple illustration:

"It does not say 'out of' His riches, but 'according to' His riches. Here is a millionaire to whom you go on behalf of some worthy cause. He listens to you and says, 'Well, I think that I will do a little for you,' and he takes out his pocketbook and selects a ten-dollar bill. Perhaps you had hoped to receive a thousand from him. He has given you 'out of' his riches, but not '*according to*' his riches. If he gave you a book of signed blank checks all numbered, and said, 'Take this, fill in what you need,' that would be 'according to' his riches."

This is precisely what the King of glory has done for us, as we saw in 1:3. He has given according to the sublime measurement of His own immeasurable riches.

"*The riches of his glory*"—the wealth of His own glorious perfections. The riches of His grace are provided in Christ crucified, risen, ascended, and exalted. The riches of His glory are in Christ, the glorified, regnant Lord. All that He is and has is ours. He is our fulness.

Subjectively the realization comes through the in-working of a resident power.

3:20. *"According to the power that worketh in us."*

Perhaps we are quite convinced by now that through our position in Christ we are heirs of God and joint-heirs with Christ. Objectively, we apprehend this fact, and doctrinally we believe it. But our great problem is how to live like heirs. We *know* what we are; our difficulty is to *be* what we know. How may we subjectively appropriate this wealth, so that experimentally it is manifested in a consistent walk and a conquering warfare?

God assures us that He has made provision for this experimental realization through the in-working of a resident power. It is the power of a Person who is none other than God's own Spirit. All that Christ was and did as the incarnate Son was through the power of the Holy Spirit. He promised to send the Holy Spirit to be to the disciples all that He had been to Him. From the day of Pentecost this same Spirit has been in every member of Christ's Body as a mighty power working to make these riches of glory his personal possession. This we shall see more fully as we now begin our study of the prayer petitions. We feel like saying in the words of Dr. Scroggie, "All that we can hope to do is to mark the order in this tumult of holy words."

Provision for Realization

The trinity of the Godhead work together to make this wealth ours. The riches which the Father provides in the Son are possessed through the Spirit.

3:16. "That he would grant you, according to the riches of his glory, *to be strengthened with might by his Spirit in the inner man."*

"To be strengthened with might," or as Way translates, "to be made strong with power." Is there any greater need in the Christian's life than to be made strong and with a power outside of himself? How often he feels that he is going backward rather than forward. He is conscious of weakness, failures, defeats, and backslidings that are well-nigh overpowering. More than once he cries out in anguish of spirit, "Is it worth while to try to keep on? I just have not the strength for this conflict." Nor has he, and God rejoices whenever a child of His comes to the end of himself and acknowledges his own utter impotency, for then God can begin to work. The Pentecost promise was for power. We are to be made strong with power through a Person.

"By his Spirit." The Holy Spirit who worked for us to implant life now works in us to impart power. He lives within us to strengthen and energize with divine might and by a definite and continuous

process. The life bestowed by the Spirit through rebirth is to be realized in fulness through renewal.

"*In the inner man.*" Into the most secret springs of our spiritual life this Spirit-strengthening power is infused. God always begins at the innermost part of our being and works outward.

Purpose of Realization

It is threefold: to establish Christ's presence in possession of us; to enhance Christ's preciousness to us through the deepening knowledge of His love for us; and to ensure the plenitude of Christ's life in us.

To Establish Christ's Presence in Possession of Us

3:17. "*That Christ may dwell in your hearts* by faith."

"*That*"—a very definite advance upon the first "that." The Spirit working in power in the inner man discovers and discloses that which hinders Christ's fullest indwelling; demands the emptying of the life of self and the enthronement of Christ as Lord; and establishes Him more effectually in the possession of every part of the Christian's life.

"*Christ may dwell.*" This has no reference to Christ's initial entrance into the Christian's life. He is already there as Saviour. He has crossed the threshold and been given *a* place in the life. Yet in some lives He seems to be far more like a house-guest than the sole and rightful owner. This does not satisfy Christ's heart, nor fulfil God's purpose. When God exalted His Son to be Head over the Church, He gave Him the right to become the Lord over every Christian. The word "dwell" connotes the fixed, permanent abode of the One who owns; it is illuminated and interpreted by Paul's other word, "To me to live is Christ." This word "dwell" makes the human personality of the Christian the home of Christ into which He may settle down and be absolutely at home, possessing, controlling and using it as He wills. His is to be the presiding Presence, permeating and possessing all.

"*In your hearts.*" In the innermost sanctuary Christ is to be given *the* place of pre-eminence, enshrined and enthroned as Lord over all.

"*By faith.*" On the Godward side Christ's indwelling is due to the supernatural power of the divine Spirit, while on the manward side it rests upon the willing yielding of the Christian to Christ's possession and upon the appropriation of Christ Himself by faith.

Thus the presence of Christ is made a living, luminous reality, and the first purpose in the realization of our wealth is fulfilled.

To Enhance Christ's Preciousness through His Love for Us

We love Him because He first loved us, but who loves Christ as he ought? His gifts are often more appreciated than the Giver. Many a Christian who rejoices in salvation would have to confess to coldness of heart toward the Saviour. The one outstanding sin of this very Ephesian church mentioned in Revelation 2:4 was "Thou hast left thy first love." Their warm, intense love for Christ Himself had waned. Against many of us would not God have to record this same sin? If the next petition is prayed with true understanding it must make the Lord Jesus Himself more precious to us.

3:18. "That ye may be able *to comprehend with all saints what is the breadth, and length, and depth, and height.*"

3:19. "And *to know the love of Christ,* which passeth knowledge."

"That." As we read what lies beyond this third "that," it is as though a tidal wave swept over us. The onward rush of the wave picks us up and carries us to the shores of our redemption in Christ, where we comprehend through the Spirit's inward illumination its fourfold measurements. But the outward rush of that same wave sweeps us out into the shoreless ocean of His unknowable love.

"Ye may be able to comprehend,"—to stretch your mind over so as to grasp with a divine insight and a human response which makes it your own, and this to the limit of an ever-growing mental and spiritual capacity. But only as we are strengthened by the Spirit in the inner man, and as Christ indwells us deeply, can we so comprehend.

"With all the saints." No one saint or group of saints of any one generation has the spiritual capacity to grasp the whole counsel of God, or the reach of His eternal purpose. Each saint may comprehend in part, but it takes all the saints "in the unity of the faith and in the knowledge of the Son of God to come unto a perfect man" (4:13). And it is equally true that it takes every saint to enable all the saints to become full-grown. What a divine rebuke this is to insulated denominationalism and to prejudiced nationalism! Recently someone told me of a devout Christian who openly declares to those who are not of her denomination that they are not saved. How each of us needs all the saints to help us comprehend our wealth in Christ! Who can excel a regenerated, spiritually-minded Jew in an explanation of the Old Testament Scriptures? And how often some

passage of Scripture has taken on new meaning and beauty for the missionary when seen through the eye of an oriental Christian.

"What is the breadth, and length, and depth, and height." Paul prays that we may be able to comprehend the dimensions of something that is both comprehensible and measurable, yet the petition stops abruptly without telling what it is. May it not be the work of the triune God in our redemption so clearly taught in Ephesians I-III? Salvation through grace to glory lies within the boundaries clearly marked and measured as we have seen it purposed and proclaimed in this epistle. What could possibly enhance Christ's preciousness to us more than a daily richer comprehension of the measurements of this glorious salvation? For that very purpose may they pass in review before our minds and hearts once more.

The Breadth—the $\begin{cases} \text{Jew} \\ \text{Gentile} \end{cases}$ made into $\begin{cases} \text{one new man} \\ \text{Body of Christ} \end{cases}$ (2:11-22). redeemed

The Length—God's eternal purpose from eternity to eternity $\hspace{2cm}$ (1:4; 2:7).

The Depth—depravity from which the sinner was delivered $\hspace{0.5cm}$ (2:1-3). death in which the sinner was found

The Height—position to which saint was raised $\begin{cases} \text{in Christ} \\ \text{in heavenlies} \\ \text{far above all} \end{cases}$ (2:4-6; 1:21).

"To know the love of Christ." We can know that Christ loved us and gave Himself for us. We can know the faithfulness of His love as manifested in countless ways every day of our lives; its tenderness as it comforts us in suffering and sorrow; its fellowship as it shares with us everything it possesses; its patience as it forgives us the seventy times seven. We can also daily add to our knowledge of the love of Christ as we company with Him in prayer and in the study of His Word; as we fellowship with other saints who know and experience deeply the love of Christ; and as we enter more fully into the fellowship of his sufferings, "filling up on our part that which is lacking of the afflictions of Christ for his body's sake" (Col. 1:24).

"Which passeth knowledge." But there is a love of Christ that is knowledge-surpassing. The expression of Christ's love is knowable, but the essence of it is unknowable. We can never know the love that paid the cost of leaving His eternal home in the Father's bosom in the heavenly glory and of coming to a world that rejected and crucified Him. We can never know the knowledge-surpassing

77

love that voluntarily emptied itself of its inherent glory and was made in the likeness of men and became obedient unto death, even the death of the cross. We can never know the love that on Calvary's Cross suffered the anguish of heart compressed in that cry, "My God, my God, why hast thou forsaken me?" We can only confess our utter inability to comprehend such love and tell Him that it makes Him unspeakably precious to us, more precious than anyone or anything in heaven or upon earth. We can respond with a love for Him that sweeps our life clean of all counter-loves and that leads us to go to the uttermost limit of our capacity in adoration of and devotion to Him.

> "It passeth knowledge, that dear love of thine,
>   My Jesus, Saviour; yet this soul of mine
>   Would of thy love in all its breadth and length,
>   Its height and depth and everlasting strength,
>   Know more and more."

To Ensure the Plenitude of Christ's Life in Us

3:19 (R.V.). *"That ye may be filled unto all the fulness of God."*

"That." This fourth petition is the final fruitage and the climax of the strengthening by the Spirit in the inner man, as it introduces the ultimate purpose of God in the realization of our wealth and the goal towards which He has been steadily working.

"Ye may be filled." Is not this word "filled" (5:18), with the kindred words "fill" (4:10), "filleth" (1:23), and "fulness" (3:19; 4:12), the keynote of Ephesians? Is this not the objective in the realization of God's deepest desire both for the Church in its corporate capacity and for the individual Christian? Does God not clearly state the ultimate goal for the Church, that it shall come "unto the measure of the stature of the fulness of Christ"?

The Holy Spirit strengthens us in the inner man that Christ may dwell in every corner and cranny of our lives, thus emptying us of self and enthroning Christ in us as a living reality. He strengthens us that we may comprehend ever more fully the measurable love of Christ expressed in salvation, and that we may know the unknowable love that made Him our Saviour, thus making Christ so precious to us that we are satisfied in Him. But Satan is always at work to destroy the work of the Spirit and to win us back to allegiance to himself. There is but one safeguard to his cunning wiles; to be filled with Christ that all such temptation be resisted, and that we may in all things and at all times be more than conquerors.

"All the fulness of God"—the grand, glorious sum total of all

that God is. There is nothing conceivable beyond the fulness of God. It is all the divine perfections of the Godhead as expressed in Christ.

Col. 2:9. *"For in him dwelleth all the fulness of the Godhead bodily."*

This is the doctrinal meaning of the fulness of God, but what does it mean tangibly and practically in relationship to the Church and to the Christian? Is it not just all that vast wealth stored in Christ out of which God draws for the achievement of His purpose (3:11); the fulfilment of His good pleasure (1:9); the carrying out of the counsels of His own will (1:11); the manifestation of the riches of His grace and glory (1:7; 3:16); the working of His mighty power (1:19); the expression of the richness of His mercy and the greatness of His love (2:4)? Is it not also those unsearchable riches in Christ which the saint appropriates for the satisfaction of every Spirit-inspired desire; for the supply of every need of the spirit, soul and body; for the sustenance of life on that highest plane in Christ in the heavenlies, far above all; and for the strength to stand and to withstand in the warfare with Satan?

How can we ever hope to become the recipients of the fulness of God? The very thought is overwhelming. Let Scripture answer and let us not sin against God through unbelief.

Col. 2:10 (R.V.). *"Ye are made full in him."*

John 1:16. *"Of his fulness have all we received."*

Are we not beginning to see more clearly why Paul writes of the *unsearchable* riches of Christ? At the same time are we discouraged because we have appropriated so meagerly of our wealth, and seem to have so little evidence of this plenitude in our lives? Perhaps there has been the reception of a measure of that fulness, but this petition is that we "may be filled unto *all* the fulness of God." Who could ever measure up to such a standard as this? Why, then, should we offer this petition?

"Filled unto." What comfort that word *unto* gives and what hope it inspires within us! Yet what a challenge to possess our possessions in Christ and to realize our wealth to the full! There is no limit placed upon the plenitude that may be ours except that which we ourselves make. For we shall be filled according to the measure of our emptiness, our thirst, our appropriation, our capacity, and our communion with the fountainhead.

Daily we may be "filled *unto*"—a process continuous but never completed while we are here on earth. But one day the process will be perfected, and we shall be filled full when we together with all

79

other saints "come unto the measure of the stature of the fulness of Christ."

Power for Realization

God has revealed our immeasurable wealth in Christ, and has led us to offer petition after petition for its realization. While the words have fallen from our lips have we been saying secretly in our hearts, "It cannot be done; anyhow, it cannot be done *in me*"? Whoever looks within at himself for this power, or around at others, however spiritual they may be, may rightly say that it is impossible. But there is another way to look—up to Him who has promised that His own mighty power will work in us for the realization of our riches in Christ.

3:20

"Unto him

"That is able to do

All that we ask or think

Above all that we ask or think

Abundantly above all that we ask or think

Exceeding abundantly above all that we ask or think

According to the power that worketh in us"

"*Unto him*"—The Purposer is the Promiser, who is also the Performer. Look unto Him, our

R ich
R esourceful Father.
R eliable

"*That is able to do.*" Our petition, however great, can never exceed God's ability to grant. Through God's power every saint has been lifted from the deepest depths in sin to the highest heights in Christ; he has been incorporated into Christ as a member of His Body and made the habitation of God. Surely the God who has had power to thus save and sanctify him can now strengthen him with power, that His purpose for the saint may be fully realized. What God has commenced He will surely consummate.

"*All that we ask or think.*" What petitions have we asked? What desires have flooded our hearts that we dared not voice? Is it possible He has power to do "*all*" for us? Yes, "*above* all"; still God's power has scarcely been tapped: "*abundantly* above all"; surely the limit of even God's power has been reached. No, not yet; "*exceeding* abundantly above all." And yet God's power is not exhausted, for He continues to give even after we stop asking and only harbour the unuttered thought; yet still there remains a vast residue of power

80

unused after unbelief has stopped our asking and stifled our thinking,—*"above all that we ask or think."*

"According to the power that worketh in us." The Promiser provides the power. The power is a Person—none other than God's own Spirit, who abides in us to make Christ real and regnant, and thereby ensure to us the realization of our wealth in Christ. The indwelling Spirit is God's pledge of His limitless power to do.

"That worketh in us." If God is able to work with such superabundant, limitless power, why does He not do it? Why do we see so few Christians who seem to have drunk of the fountain of the fulness of God? There is but one possible answer. The limitless power of God is limited by the unwillingness to have it work, or by the unbelief that it can. But in the light of this prayer could there be a greater sin in the life of a saint than to live on the lower level of the carnal when God's provision and power make possible life on the highest plane of the spiritual? Someone has tersely said: "You have your Bible and your knees; use them." Let us use them so that these treasures in Christ may become in fullest measure current coin in our lives.

The presence of God—abiding; the plenitude of God—abounding; the power of God—achieving; this realized through prayer in the Christian's life is the sum total of his vast wealth in Christ.

Praise for Realization

3:21. *"Unto him be glory,* in the church by Christ Jesus throughout all ages, world without end. Amen."

How fitting that the petitions of this prayer should glide into praise, and that not only this prayer but these chapters should close with a doxology! *"Unto him"*—the Master Workman who has wrought in the Church through the presence of His beloved Son in the power of His mighty Spirit to make it the manifestation of His glory, both now and throughout all the ages—be praise!

PART II

THE WALK OF THE CHRISTIAN

———

1. A WALK IN UNITY

2. A WALK IN HOLINESS

3. A WALK IN LOVE

4. A WALK IN LIGHT

5. A WALK IN WISDOM

6. A WALK IN PRAISE

7. A WALK IN HARMONY

THE WALK OF THE CHRISTIAN

EPHESIANS I-III has given us a revelation of our wealth in Christ. Wealth is never to be hoarded, but rather kept in circulation, that it may minister to the needs of all. The wealth of the Christian should be manifest in his walk. This revelation of divine truth becomes fruitful only as it is transmuted into life. Revelation must eventuate into realization; illumination into application.

One of the brightest converts of a Gospel Mission had become a backslider. In an interview with him, he thought he would gladden my heart by telling me that he believed everything in the Bible from Genesis through Revelation. The only reply that seemed applicable was, "If you believe it, then why do you not live it?" When a friend was speaking to the prisoners in Sing Sing prison, one prisoner said to her very boastfully, "I would have you know that I did not come in here as these other fellows did. I came in here a Christian." My friend quietly replied, "I am very sorry that being a Christian did not keep you out of here." The more we know the truth and believe it, the greater is our responsibility to live it. Head knowledge must become heart experience. Consistency in his daily walk should be the vital concern of the Christian.

Ephesians I-III tells us how God sees us in Christ in the heavenlies; IV-VI, how men should see Christ in us on earth. They unfold with crystal clearness the sevenfold walk of the Christian which is the divine standard for every Christian's life.

4:1. "I, therefore, the prisoner of the Lord, beseech you that *ye walk worthy of the vocation* wherewith ye are called."

Paul's Approach

"*Therefore*" does not indicate the commencement of something altogether new, but rather the consequence of what has preceded. Here it does not present a change of thought, but a call to prove the reality of our wealth through the rightness of our walk. "To turn from the doctrinal to the practical is not a break or a breach. There is no divorcement between Christian doctrine and Christian doing." The condition of the Christian must harmonize with his position. Being *in* Christ he should grow up *into* Christ.

Paul's Appeal

"*I beseech you*"—Oh! the intensity of desire and the deep sense of responsibility which the aged apostle writes into that word "*beseech!*" He has already given them a marvellous revelation of their heavenly calling. Now with equal clarity he would show their responsibility for a corresponding conduct. It would well repay you to make a study of such words and phrases as "therefore," "wherefore," "for," "that," "as," "so," "let," "be ye," "be not ye," "see then," in Ephesians to see how Paul's appeals are always made on the ground of one's condition corresponding with one's position. "*Ye are*"—"*therefore be ye*"—is invariably the basis of Paul's appeal.

"*That ye walk worthy of the vocation wherewith ye are called.*" Before making this appeal Paul has shown them what is their high calling. How could they be expected to walk worthily without knowing what their calling was? Yet this is the mistake which many Christians make. They know that they are not living as they ought, and they try to mend their ways and improve their manner of living without having knowledge of the divine standard and its requirements. They try to "*be*" (4:32; 5:1), before they "*know what*" (1:18). There is tremendous danger in some present-day movements that ignore or even discard doctrine and place emphasis primarily, or even solely, upon experience. Such experiences are as untrustworthy and unacceptable to the Lord as the premises upon which they are built.

"Therefore—*walk.*" To walk indicates motion. There are many words that indicate motion, such as leap, run, float, drift, creep, but you cannot substitute one of them for the word walk. To walk implies purpose, starting for a goal; progress, steadily advancing step by step; perseverance, keeping on until the goal is reached. Walking stands for steady, sustained motion, and involves the action of the mind in the decision to start; of the heart in the desire to continue, and of the will in the determination to arrive.

Then what does to "walk" mean in relation to the Christian's life? The whole course of his daily living; his habitual conduct before men; his life lived out in the open.

"Therefore—walk *worthy.*" The characteristics of a worthy walk are given in 4:1-6:9, which we shall study in detail. But here let us consider briefly the Godward and the manward aspects of such a walk. God has already determined both its starting point and its goal, and the road over which the walk is to be made. His starting-point is 1:4, His goal is 5:27, and His path of travel is 5:18. God has determined that we shall "walk even as he walked" (I John 2:6). God's goal for every Christian is complete conformity to the image of His Son, and He would have every step in our walk bring us that much nearer to the goal.

Such a walk requires on the manward side fullest co-operation with God. It demands a set purpose, a steady progress, and a strong perseverance. The Christian must resolutely purpose to "put off the old man," and to "put on the new man"; he must not be content without a step-by-step growth "up into him in all things"; and he must keep steadily on his course without faltering or fainting in spite of all opposition by not "giving place to the devil," or "grieving the Spirit," but rather by being filled with the Spirit and empowered by Him.

But how exceedingly difficult is such a walk! The old habits of life are so binding; the worldly currents about us are so strong; the temptations of the world, the flesh, and the devil are so subtle; the fear of being considered peculiar is so gripping; the opportunity of fellowship with spiritually-minded Christians is so limited. To maintain a steady, sustained consistency in daily conduct is not an easy task. It is far easier to float downstream with the tide of nominal Christianity; to drift in the listlessness and lukewarmness of a worldly church; to creep along as a spiritual babe, fed on the milk of elementary doctrines of salvation; easier even to mount up with eagle's wing and soar to spiritual heights of sudden inspiration on some spiritual Mount of Transfiguration only to relapse into a back-slidden condition when facing the stern realities of Christian living in an unsympathetic atmosphere; very much easier, even, to run, rising to some particular task such as teaching a Bible class, or leading a meeting, or preaching a sermon, than to practice consistently in the home, office, or social circle the truth preached. A daily, consistent Christlike walk; no stagnancy, slump or sloth—how hard!

So the aged apostle devotes the very heart of this epistle to telling us what a worthy walk is. Eight times he uses the word "walk." What shall we do with this divine standard set for the Christian's walk? We may reject it as impossible and impracticable, or we may receive it as possible and livable and rejoice in it, as daily our faithful Father enables us "to walk even as he walked" by the power of the divine Spirit. Let us now consider the sevenfold walk of the Christian.

1. A WALK IN UNITY

If someone asked what is the first essential of the Christian's walk, it would seem most fitting to say it was holiness. Did God not choose us in Christ that we should be holy? Then is not holiness the fundamental essential in the Body of Christ? The divine order in Ephesians is otherwise, and God's order can never be reversed.

4:2-16 shows that the first characteristic of a worthy walk is unity. What is the primary necessity for wholeness and health in a human body? It is the harmonious functioning of all the organs of the body; the perfect co-ordination in action of every part with every other part. A displacement of even an insignificant organ or the maladjustment of any parts of the body can cause disease and disability. A missionary in China began to have convulsions. She had the best of medical attention. She was told she had an incurable disease and advised to go home. On the way back to her station she consulted an osteopath. Two little bones were found to be out of adjustment, which caused pressure on the nerves. Quickly they were brought into unity through adjustment, and the incurable disease was cured.

So in the Church, the mystical Body of Christ, spiritual health is dependent upon the harmonious functioning of all the members and upon their perfect co-ordination in action. But what awful maladjustments we see in Christ's Body to-day! What sinful failure in co-ordination between its members! What shameful divisions over secondary matters which dishonour the Lord in the sight of the world! How desperately we need to come back to the divine standard set in Ephesians, and how humbly we need to acknowledge our failure and sin in not living according to it!

The Divine Standard

The unity to which God is calling His Church is distinctly defined and definitely declared. It is not a union of denominations or a federation of the churches of Christendom. Neither is it the unity of the Body. God nowhere asks us to make or to maintain the unity of the Body, for that is God's task. Through baptism with the Spirit the believer is united to Christ, the Head, and to every other member of the Body in an indissoluble bond, which unity is maintained by the indwelling Spirit. So with the making and keeping of the unity of the Body we have nothing to do.

But with the outworking of God's eternal purpose for the completion of the Body; for its edification and sanctification; and for its manifestation of Christ in glory and power to the world, we have much to do, which requires the harmonious, effectual working of every member. Hence God's call to keep the unity which He now defines.

The Unity of the Spirit

4:3. "Endeavouring to keep *the unity of the Spirit* in the bond of peace."

"Endeavouring to keep." God is not asking us to make unity, but to keep a unity that already exists. Just what unity we are to keep we are also told:

"The unity of the Spirit"—created and indwelt by the Holy Spirit, the Church, the Body of Christ, is a spiritual organism in which there is oneness of mind, heart and will; a spiritual fellowship of those who share the same life, purpose and power.

This Spirit-made unity every Christian should set himself to keep with purposeful, determined, watchful endeavour. He should do his utmost to keep a zealous, jealous custody over this Spirit-fashioned oneness with which the Church began on the day of Pentecost. Such unity is not an intangible, uncertain thing but, on the contrary, is dependent upon definitely-stated principles. The basis is in truth, and the bond is in love. Unity is rooted in God's truth, and it fructifies through God's love.

The Basis of Unity

Having charged us with the sacred responsibility of keeping the unity of the Spirit, the Lord now tells how to do it.

The Sevenfold Unity to be Kept

4:4-6. "There is *one body,* and *one Spirit, . . . one hope* of your calling; *One Lord, one faith, one baptism; One God and Father* of all who is above all, and through all, and in you all."

The Lord Jesus prayed for visible oneness in the Church before the world. Ephesians 4:4-6 interprets for us the meaning of His prayer. Our Lord never asked for a man-made union of organized churches into a grand federation, but He prayed for a Spirit-made, Christ-centred, God-controlled unity in the living organism, the Body of Christ.

It was to be oneness of fellowship through oneness of faith; an inward unity expressing itself in outward harmony.

One Body

Note that it does not say "one Church." Were that so then each of the three great divisions into which Christendom is divided would claim that distinction. It is even conceivable that some denomination or sect, of which there are hundreds, would make this unique claim. Neither does it say there is one federation of all organized churches forming, as it were, a "Christianized world trust."

"There is one body," which Ephesians teaches is eternal in calling, heavenly in conception, divine in creation, and supernatural in constitution. The living members of this Body have been called out of every kindred, tongue, people and nation. They differ in nationality, colour, language, education, training, ability, temperament, and outlook. Through the human blood running in their veins they have inherited dislikes, prejudices and animosities that separate them as far as the east is from the west. But through the blood of the Saviour and the baptism of the Spirit they are united to Christ as living members of His Body.

5:30. *"For we are members of his body,* of his flesh and of his bones."

Being organically united with Christ, the Head, each member is then made one with every other member of the Body. The oneness is so complete that we are literally a part of the life of each other. United to the Head there is one mind, one heart, one spirit.

One Spirit

On the day of Pentecost the Holy Spirit descended to form the Body of Christ. The hundred and twenty individual persons in the upper room were fitly joined together into one Body through the Spirit's baptism. This same Spirit took up His abode in the Church and in each Christian, and by His indwelling and inworking He maintains a visible, vital unity in the Body of Christ. "Every impulse of the Spirit is toward unity. He cannot suicidally lead against Himself."

One Hope

The hope of the saint is to be with and to be like his Lord. While he praises God for the progressive sanctification which goes on day by day on earth, every truly earnest Christian longs for that day when the partial will give way to the perfect and redemption will be consummated in glorification. The one hope that in these days unifies the Lord's own as perhaps no other is the blessed hope of His soon return to take them unto Himself.

One Lord

Note that "one Lord" is the centre of this sevenfold unity. It must be so. Everything centres in and around the Lord Jesus Christ. The eternal purpose of the Father and the mighty power of the Spirit are directed toward making the Lord a living reality within the Church and the Christian.

Note also that the central figure of Ephesians is not "the Jesus of history," but the Lord Jesus Christ. In the opening verses of the epistle we are shown how we are redeemed through His blood, but having crossed the threshold of salvation we are quickly led right into the throne room where the whole stage of the epistle is set. We are brought into the presence of the risen, ascended, exalted Lord upon whom throughout Ephesians our eyes are fixed and held.

It is *one* Lord" and a *solitary One* who is in a class and on a plane all by Himself, as far above all other men and even angels as the heavens are above the earth. He is "Lord of lords, the Lord God Almighty." Note also that this "One Lord" is Head of the Church, which automatically excludes any other temporal head of the visible Body of Christ. To no man has the Lord ever delegated the headship over the Church. His headship, on the contrary, is mediated directly by the Holy Spirit whom the ascended Lord appointed.

One Faith

The apostle Paul writes both of "the faith" and of "faith" (Gal. 1:23; 3:26). "The faith" is the divine standard of truth as revealed in the New Testament which embodies the Christian doctrine once for all delivered unto the saints (Jude 3) as essential to salvation, and which is the very foundation of unity in the Body of Christ. The faith is, no doubt, what Paul means here. "Faith" is the way of access unto God through an act of believing in the Lord Jesus Christ, who is the heart of "the faith." The faith gives us a Person in whom to believe. Faith accepts the gift and receives the Person.

One Baptism

Accepting the whole standard of divine truth in "the faith" which centres in the "one Lord," one is united to Christ and to all other Christians through the sovereign work of the Holy Spirit, which Scripture designates as the baptism with the Spirit. Of all the manifold ministries of the divine Spirit for the believer, this baptism, which joins him to the Lord and opens the fountain of His fullness to him, is the most fundamental and essential. Surely then the "one baptism" is that with the Holy Spirit. It is an inward process wrought by God alone. But this inward union should be manifested by an outward symbol, for this community life in the Body of Christ should be acknowledged publicly. Hence the baptism by the Spirit is followed by water baptism.

One God and Father

"*One body—one God.*" The apostle begins with the visible circumference, the Body, scattered throughout the world, and ends with the invisible centre, God, the generating source of everything.

"*One God*"—who is absolute Sovereign, working after the good pleasure and counsel of His own will (1:5, 11) to carry out His eternal purpose in Christ for the Church.

"*One Father*"—of us whom He has "chosen" and "predestinated unto the adoption of children by Jesus Christ" to be His habitation on earth.

One God and Father
$\begin{cases} \text{"above all"—} & \text{Sovereign Purpose.} \\ \text{"through all"—} & \text{Pervasive Power.} \\ \text{"in you all"—} & \text{Indwelling Presence.} \end{cases}$

Such, then, is the sevenfold basis for unity in the Spirit which is God's standard for the Church.

The Professing Church—An Organization

But as we look at Christendom to-day, what measure of unity do we find? How far has the divine standard been followed? We see the professing Church divided into three major parts, Protestant, Roman Catholic, and Greek Orthodox. In Protestantism we find two clearly-defined sections, called Liberals and Conservatives, between whom there is a cleavage that is inevitable, caused by a totally different interpretation of each of these divinely appointed unities. Both sections are becoming more audible and aggressive in their opposition to each other, so that the gulf between them is not only fixed but is growing wider every day.

For such a division in the present-day Church there is a Scriptural parallel in the relationship of Jesus Christ to the outstanding religionists of His day, the Pharisees and the Sadducees. From both of these groups He had to depart because they had first departed from Him and from the clearly revealed truth of the Old Testament Scripture concerning Him.

The germ of such division was also in the early Church. The apostle Paul saw it and openly rebuked it. He also went straight to the cause and showed it to be twofold: a departure from the headship of Christ to accept the leadership of men and a departure from the truth of the Word to accept the traditions of men. In his farewell message to the elders of the church at Ephesus he warned against this very thing:

Acts 20:29-30. "For I know this, that after my departing *shall grievous wolves enter in among you,* not sparing the flock. Also *of your own selves shall men arise, speaking perverse things, to draw away disciples after them.*"

Col. 2:8. "Beware lest any man spoil you through philosophy and vain deceit, *after the traditions of men,* after the rudiments of the world, *and not after Christ.*"

The True Church—An Organism

The Holy Spirit was appointed to dwell within the Church as the sole and sovereign executor of the Father's eternal purpose in Christ for and through the Church. The early Church recognized and submitted to His sovereign control. So in the book of the Acts we read "The Holy Ghost said," and "It seemed good to the Holy Ghost and to us." What He said was accepted and accomplished. The affairs of the Church were managed in counsel and co-operation with Him. Hence the unity in the faith and fellowship, in the prayers and program of that first century Church.

Acts 2:42. "And they continued stedfastly in the apostles' *doctrine* and *fellowship,* and in *breaking of bread,* and in *prayers.*"

Acts 4:32. "And the multitude of them that believed were of *one heart* and of *one soul.*"

Signifying their union with Christ, the Head of the Body, they were designated by the name "believers"; and indicating their union with each other as fellow-members of the Body, they were called "brethren"—not capital B. And when some carnal Christians of the Corinthian church attempted to start rival sects and become Paulites, Apollosites, Cephasites, or even to misuse the blessed name of Christ for such selfish ends, they were severely rebuked by Paul.

I Cor. 1:11-13. "It hath been declared unto me that *there are contentions among you.* Now this I say, that everyone of you saith, *I am of Paul;* and *I of Apollos;* and *I of Cephas;* and *I of Christ.*

Is Christ divided? Was Paul crucified for you? Or were ye baptized into the name of Paul?"

The results of such unity in the Spirit were very marvellous. "The Lord added to the church *daily* such as should be saved." "And believers were the more added to the Lord, *multitudes both of men and of women.*" "Then the *churches were edified;* and walking in the fear of the Lord, and in the comfort of the Holy Ghost, *were multiplied.*"

As we look at the true Church, the Body of Christ, in this twentieth century, what do we see? The Church is split up into many churches, each called by its own name, separating it from all the others. Between these churches there is often even jealousy and rivalry. Such appalling division in the professing church is a sad enough spectacle to present to a godless world. But to behold such division in the true Church is nothing short of shameful. May we not go further, and ask if it is not the greatest sin of the members of the Body against the Head?

The tendency within the Church to-day is to divide over doctrines and to form little spiritual aristocracies composed of "the elect," who claim not only special revelation of truth, but often a special realization of that truth in experience beyond others. From such exclusive groups there are constant departures to form other select circles. I heard of one such group that had become so advanced that admission to its gatherings was only by ticket.

This shameful division is often caused by over-emphasis upon some phase of truth which is lifted quite out of its setting in Scripture and is made the central doctrine upon which a new sect is formed. The "One Lord" is displaced as the centre of the Spirit-made unity, and this particular doctrine takes His place.

Division is also caused by dogmatic insistence upon the interpretation of the truth regarding some divinely-appointed rite or ordinance of the Church. One missionary was refused the privilege of taking the Lord's Supper with the saints of one denomination in the United States *because she had not been immersed.* While in a European country a deeply spiritual pastor who, *because he had been re-baptized by immersion* from real conviction, was denied the privilege of fellowship in prayer with members of the denomination to which he belonged. Can one conceive of cubicles in heaven set apart for those belonging to each of these groups, so that they will be spared the pain of fellowship and worship together around the "One Lord"?

Disunity is caused also by one-sidedness of viewpoint due to

94

some particular experience or the manner of entering into it and the insistence upon putting every other Christian into the same mould. Once in China an invitation was withheld to have meetings in a certain mission with whose missionaries there was perfect agreement as to the truths of the sevenfold unities of 4:4-6. We differed only on one point—the method of entering into the life of sanctification provided for us in Christ.

Division is due also to the attitude which makes one hopelessly intolerant of another who differs with him on any point of either major or minor importance; even on points of doctrine about which equally spiritual and scholarly teachers do not see alike, as for instance the meaning of the baptism with the Holy Spirit, or some phases of Advent truth.

Those who are guilty of thus breaking the unity of the Spirit invariably justify themselves by claiming to be "contenders for the faith," when they may be contending only for their own private interpretation, or for some tradition of their denomination, or even for their own opinion.

All such need to be saturated with the truth of Ephesians. They need to pray that divinely-inspired prayer that they "may be able to *comprehend with all saints* what is the breadth, and length, and height; and to know the love of Christ, which passeth knowledge." They need also to be reminded of the divinely-given process for the growth of the Church into the full stature of the perfect man, "Till *we all come in the unity of the faith and of the knowledge* of the Son of God." Not, till a few select ones, like a little church within the Church, reach that goal; not, till we come through our segregations into little groups magnifying some specially deep truths within the Word of truth; not, till we came through the same knowledge of all doctrines to exactly the same experience in life of those glorious truths. Oh no; Ephesians does not teach that. But, "till we all," every single born-again child of God, "come in the unity of the faith," already declared to us in 4:4-6, and "in the knowledge of the Son of God," who is in Himself the middle unity, not only of doctrine, but of life. We are fellow-members of one Body, and each member needs every other member if we are all to reach spiritual maturity in Christ, and every saint has something to contribute to the edifying and the increase of the Body (4:12, 16).

What is the solution of this problem of disunity within the Church? Many in Christendom are greatly disturbed over it, and we see on the part of some leaders in Protestantism hectic attempts to solve the problem by ecclesiastical federation of existing churches;

by a union of separate units based on uniformity of order and organization. The approach to union is made by the alley-way of the social, ethical and ecclesiastical,—the mere externalities of religion. There are plans on now for such a world amalgamation of churches. Dr. I. E. Holt, of The Federal Council of Churches in the United States, has said, "The Protestant churches must first unite. Then a Catholic Protestant church could meet the Greek Catholic church and the Roman Catholic church, and work out a plan for a World Christian Church. That ought to come some day; and we have conferences and groups at work on plans which are influential."

This is as far from the catholicity for which Christ prayed, and which the Holy Spirit through Paul preached, as the sun is from the earth. Such a "World Christian Church" is not the "One Body" centering in the "One Lord" through the unifying presence and power of the "One Spirit." The unity for which Christ prayed and of which Paul wrote is "the unity of the Spirit" based on "the unity of the faith." It was oneness of life through oneness of faith. The approach to such unity is by the highway of the spiritual, divine, and heavenly—the true inwardness of Christianity. It is not the outworking of man-made *"plans,"* but of the divine *purpose.*

What is our part, then, in keeping the unity of the Spirit on this divinely-appointed basis? It is first of all to obey the Scriptural command, "Examine yourselves, *whether ye be in the faith;* prove your own selves" (II Cor. 13:5). If you are in the faith, then unite with every other saint who also is in the faith, of whatever section of the Church or of whatever denomination, in the unity of the Spirit. The Holy Spirit, who unites the Head with the Body and the members of the Body with each other, will then be able to maintain that unity in the bond of peace.

The Bond of Unity

Three times in this section on unity is love shown to be the bond:

4:2. "With all lowliness and meekness, with long-suffering, forbearing one another *in love.*"

4:15. "But speaking the truth *in love,* may grow up into him in all things, which is the head, even Christ."

4:16. "Maketh increase of the body unto the edifying of itself *in love.*"

We have considered the divisions within the Church over the basis of unity through doctrinal differences due often to sincere though misguided zeal. But Paul recognizes divisions due to a far more needless and sinful reason,—the breaking of the bond of unity through lack of love. Let us face the facts frankly and seek the cause of the disgraceful discords between true believers.

From years of observation and study through personal contacts in many lands, one is led to believe these discords are largely due to national and personal prejudices and to dislikes due to temperamental differences which are not overcome by divine love. For several years my work has taken me into several countries in Europe. Much has been heard about the "mentality" that characterizes each nation, and it has been intimated that one could not understand this people or that because of inability to understand their mentality. That there is a great difference in the national characteristics of peoples which leads to different ways of viewing things and to different standards of life one would grant immediately. But this does not mean that one mentality is wrong and another right, or even that in all points one is better than another. It simply means there is a difference, and for a purpose. God who created each race and each individual intended it to be so. That this strange, forbidding thing needs to raise walls as high as the heavens between fellow-members of the Body of Christ, one who has lived long in Ephesians refuses to grant. One wonders if a more clarifying word for this troublesome thing is not racial prejudice and national pride. A medical missionary, devoted to her work in China, said that after several years in the land she still found it difficult to sit by a Chinese at a table or in a train. While travelling on a boat with a deeply spiritual Chinese Christian, she implored me to sit next to her at meals so that an equally consecrated Indian Christian would not occupy that seat, "for," she said, "I could not eat anything if I had to sit beside an Indian."

What a bomb our Lord threw at the heart of such sinful racial and national prejudice in those who through rebirth share equally the life and privileges of the heavenly citizenship in Christ!

Col. 3:11. "Where there is neither Greek nor Jew, circumcision nor uncircumcision, Barbarian, Scythian, bond nor free; but Christ is all, and in all."

God grant that it may blow every shred of prejudice and pride of race out of everyone of us who are fellow-members of the one Body. Perhaps some of us will not know how deeply rooted we are in prejudice until we seek deliverance from it.

Another secret of discord lies in personal temperamental differences. Through observation and through confidences given in personal interviews with numberless Christian workers, one is convinced that the very greatest strain in Christian work, both at home and on the mission field, is due to these maladjustments in temperaments with their resultant friction and tension.

Under one roof, living and working together seven days in the week, are people of radically different temperaments, tastes, and training. One is quick and nervous; the other slow and calm. The former can do a half-day's work while the other is getting dressed in the morning. One is socially-minded and enjoys a bit of company sometimes; the other is solitary-minded and feels no need of anything outside of herself and her work. One is generous and open-handed; while the other is thrifty, sometimes perhaps tight. A fellow-missionary who was housekeeper for our little company once handed me my monthly bill for—dollars—cents, and 7/18ths of a cent. Never having been good at figures, I let her keep the change. One is spontaneous and outgoing, readily sharing her heart experiences; the other reticent and unapproachable, never revealing what she really thinks or feels. One gives herself to prayer and is accused of laziness; the other becomes a slave to work and is suspected of ungodliness. One is a replica of the mystical Mary, and the other of the practical Martha.

God intended these temperamental differences that we might be complements one of another. Had God meant us all to be alike, He would have put us into the same mould. Had He done so what a drab, monotonous world this would have been! The question we need to ask is, "Can there be unity in such diversity? How can members of His Body really be made members one of another?" The Lord answers our question.

Unity in Diversity through the Graces of the Spirit

Unity is not something intangible and indefinite. It is a spiritual fabric woven out of designated materials which are interwoven into spiritual relationships. Those materials are the graces of the Spirit, all of which are included in the spiritual blessings bequeathed to us in Christ. Therefore all these graces may be possessed by all saints alike. Paul mentions several which are essential in keeping the unity of the Spirit.

4:2. "With all *lowliness* and *meekness*, with *longsuffering, forbearing one another* in love."

"*Lowliness.*" Someone has defined lowliness as a "holy humbleness," which would mean negatively a lack of self-assertiveness and any tendency to pride and boastfulness. Positively may we not say that it is such a Scriptural estimate of one's self as Paul had? He was writing this highest and deepest truth, a revelation given by

God to him and to no other, yet he said, "Unto me, *who am less than the least of all saints,* is this grace given." Paul never forgot what his past life in sin had been, and delighted to say, "I am what I am by the grace of God." In Christ by grace he was chief of apostles, but always in himself by nature he was "the chief of sinners." His holy humbleness came from remembering always the depths to which he had gone and the heights to which he had come, and that it was all due to the grace of God. So there was no room for highmindedness or boastfulness even in Paul. Much less will there be in any one of us.

In the epistle to the Philippians Paul shows us that the source and secret of unity is first in having the mind of our Lord, and then in having a right mind regarding ourselves in relationship to others.

Christmindedness—willingness to $\left\{ \begin{array}{l} \text{empty} \\ \text{humble} \end{array} \right.$ Himself Phil. 2:5-8.

Lowlymindedness—
    willingness to esteem others better than ourselves. Phil. 2:3.

Like-mindedness $\left. \begin{array}{l} \\ \\ \end{array} \right\}$ —having the same love. Phil. 2:2.
One-mindedness

"Meekness"—our estimate of ourselves in relationship to God; a fitting complement to lowliness. Again we have our perfect example in the meek and lowly Jesus, who in relationship to His Father was "obedient unto death, even the death of the cross." There was in Him a whole-hearted acceptance of His Father's will in all circumstances. Even "when he was reviled, he reviled not again; when he suffered, he threatened not." He was called by the most humiliating names: "Thou art a Samaritan," and was even charged with "casting out devils through Beelzebub, the chief of devils"; yet He patiently endured all such reviling. This is true meekness, which is the very opposite of revenge, resentment and retaliation. It is a spirit that never takes offence even under the severest provocation.

"Longsuffering"—without irritation or annoyance, but with patience and endurance, meeting every harassing trial that comes in fellowship with others. Longsuffering is an unweariable spirit that is so strengthened by Christ that it outlasts the blasts of pain and provocation. Nevertheless, it does not mean long-facedness, for in Scripture it is almost invariably accompanied with joy.

"Forbearing one another"—which Dr. H. A. Ironside translates "lovingly putting up with all that is disagreeable in other people."

To forbear does not mean that we are blind to the sins and short-comings of others, nor to the difficulties which they produce. But it does mean that we have the love and patience of Christ in our attitude toward them. When one feels impatience, which tempts to criticism, it is a check upon one to put his own life alongside that of the spotless Son of man and thus see his own immeasurable shortcomings. How quickly it silences condemnation of others as we think of the patience the Lord has shown toward us. It is also a very wholesome antidote to uncharitableness to remember that, if we find it difficult to live with certain people who have disagreeable traits, they probably find it just as difficult to live with us.

In order that the whole Body of Christ may be edified and made to increase through the united faith and work of all members in the unity of the Spirit, Paul makes this great appeal: Be lowly-minded, be meek, be longsuffering, and forbear in love. Is there one of us who has measured up to this fourfold divine standard? Must each of us not confess that we have often failed in each of these divine characteristics? Are we prepared to-day to take an advance step in this matter of unity in our relationship to others?

"In love." We hesitate to answer that question. All of us believe in theory in such practical unity. We admit Christ prayed for it, and that the Bible teaches it. But——? We think of some person with whom it has been utterly impossible thus far to live or work without discord; and we ask, "Is it possible?" Yes, but only in one way—*"in love,"* and that the love of Christ which supersedes all human points of friction. It demands the loving Christ living out His love-life in us.

The unity that is rooted in truth ripens in love. The root is God's eternal, unchangeable truth which fructifies into life through a Spirit-produced humility and a Spirit-provided love.

Diversity in Unity through the Gifts of Christ

4:7. "But unto every one of us is given grace according to the measure of the gift of Christ."

"But"—is always an arresting word. Here it denotes an abrupt change in thought; in fact, introduces for consideration the exactly opposite truth of diversity in unity. Spiritual graces, which are included in the spiritual blessings of 1:3, are bequeathed equally to all God's children, but, when it comes to spiritual gifts, we find a divinely-determined diversity in the divinely-purposed unity in the Body of Christ.

The Individual Endowment of All Members

The Head of the Body is righteous and fair. Each person chosen in Him was also created in Christ Jesus unto good works, so for his particular share in the extension and edifying of the Body he has been given a suitable and a sufficient gift.

"Unto every one of us is given." As God has before ordained just what task each Christian is to have (2:10), He has set every member in the Body in just the place He wishes him to occupy (I Cor. 12:18), and has then bestowed upon him whatever gift is needed to accomplish his work effectually. There are no omissions and no exemptions. Every Christian has some gift, though it may differ both in kind and in degree from that of another, which is to be used for the mutual benefit and blessing of all saints.

4:16. "From whom the whole body fitly joined together and compacted *by that which every joint supplieth, according to the effectual working in the measure of every part,* making increase of the body unto the edifying of itself in love."

No matter how insignificant, weak or obscure a member of the Body may feel himself to be, yet he has a part to perform that is very essential to the spiritual health and functioning of the Body as a whole.

"The gift of Christ." Christ, the Head of the Body, in His infinite wisdom and impartial love bestows the gift upon every member for the glory of God and for the increase and the building up of the whole Body.

Then should not each of us know what his gift is? Should he not value it as a precious gift from the Lord Himself? Should he not be satisfied with his gift because chosen expressly for him as the one by which he can best glorify the Lord and fulfil His purpose? Should he not use it unstintedly for the benefit of the whole Body?

The Special Endowment of Some Members

In the bestowal of gifts, the supreme objective is the carrying out of the sovereign, eternal purpose of God in Christ Jesus. This is clearly shown in the verses we now study,—in the force of these three prepositions: "till"; "unto"; and "for."

4:12 (R.V.). *"For* the perfecting of the saints, *unto* the work of ministering, *unto* the building up of the body of Christ:

4:13. *"Till* we all come in the unity of the faith, and of the knowledge of the Son of God, *unto* a perfect man, *unto* the measure of the stature of the fulness of Christ."

4:14, 15. "That we henceforth be no more children, . . . But

. . . may grow up into him in all things, which is the head, even Christ."

"*Till*" suggests the working out of the predestined purpose.

"*Unto*" points toward the finished product.

"*For*" indicates the present process.

God is not working in a haphazard fashion. He is steadily progressing along planned lines with the ultimate goal ever in view. God has purposed that the Body shall be the fulness of Christ. To that end there must be steady growth out of spiritual infancy unto spiritual maturity. "No more children," but constant growth "up into Christ in all things." The goal is "the perfect man"; humanity in Christ perfected according to the standard of the Perfect Man, the Lord Jesus Christ.

Thus the standard for the Church is set, and it is the business of every Christian to ascertain what it is; to accept it; and to adjust his whole life to the achievement of it. How prone we are to say that God's standard is impossible and impracticable in such a world as this! How we try to persuade God to lower His standard to the level of our experience! But we cannot so deflect God. He resolutely insists upon our decision to accept His standard and to determine to bring our experience up to the level of His standard. God works steadily on to bring the Church "*unto* the measure of the stature of the fulness of Christ."

For the accomplishment of His purpose God has made ample provision through the bestowal of special gifts upon some members of the Body in order that they may be used to prepare every member for his particular task.

4:11. "And *he gave some, apostles;* and *some, prophets;* and *some, evangelists;* and *some, pastors,* and *teachers.*"

The foundation of the Church must be securely laid in the Lord Jesus Christ and made known in an authoritative body of teaching. This divinely attested truth must be thoroughly taught to the Church. So Christ gave to the Church in its infancy some to be apostles and prophets. Upon this foundation, laid once for all, a building was to be constructed for a habitation of God made up of living stones, to be added one by one. A mystical Body was to be created for Christ, the Head, out of sinners saved by grace and quickened by His Spirit. This required evangelists who would go far and wide to proclaim the gospel and extend the boundaries of the Church through winning souls one by one and "adding to the Church such as should be saved." But the sheep must be shepherded, so there was the need of pastors; the members of the Body must be built up in their knowledge of Christ through the Word, so there was need of teachers. As the evangelist labours to extend the Church, so the pastor and the teacher work to edify it.

"For the perfecting of the saints." The special gifts are bestowed with a definite, divine design. No gift is bestowed for the sake of the man himself. It is given to one for the sake of the whole. Neither does it place the monopoly of service in the hands of a gifted few. The evangelist, pastor and teacher are not commissioned by the Lord to do all the work of the Church, but rather to so feed, teach and train the saints individually that each of them be brought to spiritual maturity and thoroughly equipped to fill his place and do his work in building up the whole Body. Every Christian has been made a king and a priest unto God (Rev. 1:6). As the whole Body is bound together in faith and in life, so is it also united in service.

But what discord we see in the Church to-day caused by these very gifts! What unholy ambition! What sinful pride! What corroding jealousy! What spiteful envy. What ill-concealed resentment! What deep-rooted bitterness! What hateful backbiting! What colossal conceit! What domineering leadership! What arrogant presumption! And because of such sins, factions and divisions within the church. Just this week I heard of a tragic breach of fellowship within one church caused largely by the jealousy of a pastor over the fruitful work of one of his parishioners who taught a large Bible class. It is comparatively easy for one Christian to weep with another Christian in sorrow, but how pitifully few are able to rejoice with those that rejoice in success!

In Ephesians God has shown us what is our responsibility in this matter of keeping this God-ordained and God-designed unity of the Spirit in the Body of Christ. We should have a fixed determination that we shall not allow anything for which we are to blame to separate us even a hairs-breadth from any other member of the Body. We should study diligently how to keep this unity; and make it our personal business to advocate and advance it whenever possible. We should determine to stand together on the basis of truth and in the bond of love as an act of allegiance and devotion to Him who is our one Lord, and thus glorify Him by walking in unity.

2. A WALK IN HOLINESS

The second characteristic of a walk worthy of our high calling in

Christ is a walk in holiness as revealed in 4:17-30. Paul's call to such a walk is based on divine authority.

4:17. *"This I say therefore,* and *testify in the Lord,* that ye henceforth walk not as other Gentiles walk."

"This I say." In 4:1 Paul was persuasive in his appeal. He wrote beseechingly. Here he is pressing home truth with firmness, even with a tone of insistency. *"And testify in the Lord."* Way translates this, "I solemnly adjure you as in God's presence." One feels here the tremendous burden upon Paul's heart to impress deeply upon those to whom he writes the imperative necessity of a revolutionary change in their whole manner of living. So his language must be in accord with the truth he would frankly and faithfully give. Also Paul would have them know that he is not stating his personal conviction regarding the standard for their Christian life, but that it is the living Lord speaking through him.

Cleavage Between The Old and The New

"Therefore." We cannot escape this word in Ephesians. Like a sign-post on the road it arrests and compels attention. It is the verbal causeway between the heavenly calling of Chapters one to three and the earthly conduct of Chapters four to six. The word has a special significance here. These Ephesian saints had passed out of the old position in sin, and were now in Christ. *"Therefore"* this new position demanded a clean-cut cleavage from all that pertaining to the old. The new position in Christ was the pivot of Paul's argument for a new walk. Consistently a new practice results from a new position. So with invincible logic Paul proceeds to call them to an altogether different walk from that of the unsaved Gentiles among whom they still lived.

"Henceforth." There is also a clean-cut time element in Ephesians. In the spiritual history of those Christians there was a "sometimes" and a "now" (2:13). There was a moment of time when they crossed the boundary line from death into life. In that moment of rebirth something so tremendously revolutionary had taken place that the sinner had been made into a saint. *"Henceforth"* life could never be as it was before. Christ's presence is the most potent argument for a walk in newness of life.

Contrast Between The Old and The New

"Ye—walk not—as other Gentiles walk." How did these other Gentiles walk? In an appallingly vivid pen picture Paul tells us.

4:17-19. "In the vanity of their mind, *having the understanding darkened, being alienated from the life of God* through the ignorance that is in them, because of the blindness of their heart; who *being past feeling have given themselves over unto lasciviousness,* to work all uncleanness with greediness."

This is a full-length portrait of those "other Gentiles," sunk in the lowest depths of the mire and filth of sin. It is a revelation of the life to which every unsaved person is eligible and with nothing within himself to prevent him from going to the uttermost length. Not every saint in the Ephesian church had been such an advanced and abandoned pagan as here described, but every one of them had walked as sinners in just such a company.

In 2:1-3 we were told that all sinners walk according to the world, the flesh, and the devil. In 4:17-19 we see some of these sinners so walking, and the sight is terrifying and heartbreaking. It is a picture of:

Spiritual death—"being alienated from the life of God."

Mental darkness—"having the understanding darkened."

Moral degeneracy—"who being past feeling have given themselves over."

Physical depravity—"Unto lasciviousness to work all uncleanness with greediness."

The ignorance that was in them through wilful blindness of heart had produced an impotence which finally generated insensibility toward everything spiritual, ethical and moral. With deliberation and premeditation they had abandoned themselves to utter sensuality without any protest from conscience, reason or heart. They had sunk so low that they wantonly made it their business to sin in its vilest forms.

Let us turn from this depressingly dark picture and see the marvellous contrast wrought in some Gentiles by God's grace and power.

4:20, 21. "But *ye have not so learned Christ;* if so be that *ye have heard him,* and have been *taught by him,* as the truth is in Jesus."

"*But ye.*" These Ephesian Christians had had the great advantage of Paul's presence with them for more than two years. In his farewell message to the elders of that church he had said, "I have kept nothing back that was profitable unto you, but have *taught you publicly* and *from house to house.*" We may be very sure that Paul's teaching went beyond the elementary truths of salvation and included the deep, essential truth of sanctification through oneness of life with Christ. The mature, spiritual life of the church at Ephesus was, no doubt, the product of such painstaking, systematic indoctrination of full salvation in Christ. Oh, that every pastor, Bible teacher and missionary did the same thing to-day! The need for such indoctrination in the twentieth century Church is as great as it was in the first century Church.

"Learned Christ; heard him; taught by him." The central theme of Paul's teaching is perfectly clear. It had been such as to bring them Christ Himself in all the loveliness of His righteous, holy life. They had learned that to be a Christian is to have Christ in them living out His life again on earth in His mystical Body as He had lived it as Jesus in His earthly body.

"Walk not." There is a walk that befits each sphere. When in either one of the two positions full conformity to its life is the natural expectation. The walk in Christ should be as holy and heavenly as the walk in sin was defiling and degrading. So when one leaves the old sphere to enter the new, it involves the decision to renounce the old life in its entirety, and to abandon one's self whole-heartedly to the life of the new. This is the logic of Paul's appeal.

"In times past ye walked" (2:2); "Henceforth walk not" (4:17). To be *in* Christ and not grow up *into* Christ makes the Christian life an anachronism, a monstrosity, a lie. The revelation of Christ in truth must result in the realization of Christ in life. Paul writes, Ye have heard and accepted "the truth as it is in Jesus"; now you must live, act and speak according to this new standard. There can be no compromising alliances, no stultifying reserves, no divided interests.

"Ye were" ——— "Ye are" ——— "Be ye."

Here is Paul's forceful challenge to become what you are. It leads very naturally into his next practical exhortation:

Call to Put Off The Old and to Put On The New

4:22. "That *ye put off concerning the former conversation the old man,* which is corrupt according to the deceitful lusts."

4:24. "And that *ye put on the new man,* which after God is created in righteousness and true holiness."

This twofold clear, crisp exhortation marks the meeting-point between God's part and ours in our sanctification. It is the crossroads between God's sovereign work through grace and man's co-operative action through faith. It is an exhortation to practical holiness in every phase of one's daily life.

Paul takes us immediately to the very source of life in each sphere and shows us two things. The character of life is due to its source and the character determines the conduct. Life in the old sphere is tracked to its source, "the old man," and the conduct is corrupt because the character is such. Life in the new sphere is traced to its source, "the new man," and the conduct is righteous and holy because the character is so. The fountain determines the flow. Let us then consider these two fountain-heads and our responsibility in relation to them.

"The old man"—primarily the old, corrupt, sinful nature inherited from Adam; the inborn tendency to evil. But here it includes the whole manner of life in the old sphere. This term is used only three times in Scripture,—in Romans 6:6; Colossians 3:9; and Ephesians 4:22. There are three equivalents. It is all that a man is by nature, so is called "the natural man" (I Cor. 2:14). It is the "I" which is thrown into such sharp contrast with "Christ" in Galatians 2:20. It is "the flesh" of 2:3 which dominates the sinner, compelling him to fulfil its lust and desires.

"Concerning the former conversation," or better, "former manner of life," as in the R. V., which is a life in sin lived according to the debased standard of the trinity of evil. Their former manner of life was the unregenerate, unclean, unholy life of the sinner under the domination of "the old man."

"Which is corrupt."—"The old man" is utterly defiled and defiling in character, and waxes more and more degenerate in conduct even unto the point of depravity, as in the case of "the other Gentiles." "The old man" can do nothing but sin, for all his desires (4:22), as well as his deeds (Col. 3:9), are sinful. He is unchangeable and incurable because he doesn't want to be changed. He is also irretrievably incorrigible, for his attitude to God is one of habitual disobedience (2:2), hardened into fixed enmity (Rom. 8:7). "The old man," therefore, is the whole old creation in Adam. It is the sinner with only a sinful nature which contaminates everything from the centre to the circumference of his life.

"Put off the old man." God always takes the initiative in salvation. Before He asks or expects man to act, He has acted. The work of Christ in salvation is a completely finished work. So in regard to "the old man" God has already done His part, which is plainly recorded in Scripture as an accomplished historical fact.

Rom. 6:6 (A.R.V.). "Knowing this, *that our old man was crucified with him,* that the body of sin might be done away, that so we should no longer be in bondage to sin."

By the sovereign act of God that "old man" was crucified with Christ. In God's reckoning he died on the Cross as truly as Christ died. In that death God put an end to the old creation in Adam that He might replace it by the new creation in Christ. He put "the old man" out of employment, as it were, by depriving him of his dominion over the believer in Christ. In God's reckoning the crucifixion of "the old man" was a final, once-for-all act. From that moment God sees him only on the Cross. In God's purpose all the old, filthy, sin-infected garments in which "the old man" was clad went into the discard also as utterly unbefitting the life of the new sphere into which the believer was translated. Can you conceive of Mr. Bosshardt, when delivered out of 560 days of captivity by bandits in China, refusing to lay aside the filthy, vermin-infested garments he had been compelled to wear? Would not his deepest desire be to be rid of everything that in the slightest degree pertained to that experience, now past through God's grace and goodness?

What God has made true for us positionally, He longs to make real in us experimentally. This requires our intelligent, wholehearted co-operation in willing consent and in active choice as the imperative "that ye put off" clearly shows. There is a part for us to play if the crucifixion as historical fact is made an experimental reality. Therefore we should know what our responsibility is, and then fulfil it. May we consider three practical ways in which we may "put off the old man"?

Reckon the Crucifixion of the Old Man to be a Fact

Such reckoning means simply believing what God says in Romans 6:6, and knowing it as a fact in one's own personal salvation. This demands a definite act of faith, which results in a fixed attitude toward "the old man." We will see him where God sees him—on the Cross crucified with Christ. Faith will operate continuously to keep him where grace placed him. This involves us very deeply, for it means that our hearty consent has been given to God's condemnation of and judgment upon that old "I" as altogether unworthy to live and as wholly stripped of any further claim upon us. The first step in a walk of practical holiness is this reckoning upon the crucifixion of "the old man."

Recognition of the Manifestation of the Self Life

While God makes it perfectly clear that identification with Christ in His death and resurrection takes us in toto out of the old position in sin and in the flesh, He nowhere says that sin is taken out of us in our earthly life. All the verses of Romans 6 teach us God's perfect provision for deliverance from sin's *power*, but not one verse teaches us that we are here and now delivered from sin's *presence*.

Even in the new sphere in Christ the old, sinful nature remains in us. Were this not so there would be no point whatever in Paul's exhortation to "put off the old man" and to walk worthily of our calling. If the old nature were eradicated, and we possessed only the new nature we could do naught but walk righteously and holily, for that is the only way "the new man" can walk.

As a sinner each of us was the possessor of but one nature, a sinful one, which poisoned the spiritual blood-stream, and thus caused vitiating toxins to be carried into our spiritual, moral, and ethical tissues. Through rebirth we became the possessor of a divine nature which purifies the spiritual blood-stream, and causes vitalizing life to flow into our spirit, soul and body. So within every saint are two natures; one that always yields to the instigations of the devil, the enticements of the world, and the claims of the flesh; the other that chooses to live under the Lordship of Christ, according to the divine calling for the Church, and under the control of the Spirit. Paul's whole argument in "put off the old man" and "put on the new man" is based on the presence of these two natures within the Christian and the necessity of a choice being made as to which is to have the mastery of the life.

"To put off the old man" experimentally will mean, then, the recognition of his presence and the possibility of his further manifestation. It will demand a daily self-examination (II Cor. 11:28) to discover wherein we have given place to the devil or have walked in the ways of the world in our pleasures, pursuits and plans; or have been dominated by the flesh in our attitudes and acts, our desires and deeds, our conversation and conduct. Such wholesome self-examination may degenerate into morbid self-introspection that will be paralyzing and futile unless it ends in honest self-judgment (II Cor. 11:31) and confession (I John 1:7), as Scriptually prescribed. If one has walked in the old grooves and put on the old garments, then it must be frankly acknowledged and confessed. The definite sins must be named before the Lord and His forgiveness so freely given must be taken and praise be given for the cleansing of the precious blood.

Renunciation of the Old Creation in its Entirety

"Henceforth walk not." These words have an authoritative tone of finality about them. "Put off" demands unconditional renunciation. The Christian has begun a walk on a new road in a new sphere leading to a new goal. Then he must be prepared at the very beginning with deliberate determination to make a full and final abandonment of the old life in its entirety. But a walk is taken step by step. So as one goes along the new road and recognizes soft spots in character, backslidings in conduct, danger points in companionships, discrepancies in ethics, departures in morals, and compromises in standard, there must be an immediate putting off of that old remnant of the abandoned life. Paul makes this quite clear in Chapters four and five, as he mentions definite sins still to be found in the lives of these Ephesian Christians.

God has decreed that in the new creation old things have passed away (II Cor. 5:17), and here in Ephesians He places squarely upon us our responsibility for obedience to this decree. He calls upon us to make a complete renunciation, once-for-all, of all that pertains to our former manner of living, and to follow this decisive act with a definite attitude toward the master of the old life that will ensure instant refusal of his claims as soon as recognized.

"To put off the old man" is but the negative side of a holy walk, the casting off of the filthy sin-spoiled garments. The saint must be clothed upon with spotlessly white robes.

"The new man"—the new creation in Christ; the saint possessing a new spiritual divine nature, from which a pure river of life flows into every part of his being; the human personality with Christ at its centre, crowned as its Lord, and indwelt as its Life; the "I in you" of John 15:4; the "Christ in you" of Colossians 1:27.

"Which after God hath been created." If created, then something not already existent. It is not a spark of divine life just waiting to be fanned into a flame. No man is born the possessor of this divine nature. "The new man" is not the product of physical but of spiritual birth. Again, what is created is not evolved. "The new man" is not the product of self-culture, but is an outright creation of God.

"In righteousness and true holiness." As the old nature still in us can do nothing but sin, so the new nature cannot sin. As the old nature was irretrievably unrighteous and unholy, so the new is inherently righteous and holy. The Christian is patterned after Christ in the perfection of His character in its twofold expression of righteousness in relation to man and in holiness in relation to God. Christ has been made unto us righteousness and sanctification (I Cor. 1:30). We are, therefore, righteous in the righteousness of Christ and holy in the holiness of Christ. Paul's appeal, then, is for us to become what we are: to put on the garments with which we have already been clothed.

"Put on the new man." By the sovereign act of God "the new

man" was created. By God's grace the believing sinner was quickened and raised together with Christ. In the co-resurrection God created "the new man" and opened the way for him to walk in newness of life.

Rom. 6:4, 5. "Therefore were all buried with him by baptism into death; that like as Christ was raised from the dead by the glory of the Father, *even so we also should walk in newness of life.* For if we have been planted together in the likeness of his death, *we shall be also in the likeness of his resurrection.*"

From the moment of co-resurrection with Christ, God sees the Christian only in Christ and Christ in him. In God's purpose all the holy, heavenly robes in which the Lord Jesus is clothed have been bestowed upon the saint as the only ones befitting his new life in the new sphere.

But again we must do our part in putting on "the new man." May we consider three suggestions of how we may do this:

Claim Your Position in Christ

In 2:4-6 God is stating a fact of salvation which is true of every saint, whether he ever knows the fact or not. It is true that every believer was united with Christ in His death and resurrection the moment he believed, and is in Christ who is seated in the heavenlies at the Father's right hand. This new position in Christ is the very foundation of our sanctification and of a walk in newness of life. This every Christian should know; otherwise he will always be floundering in defeat and discouragement without knowing the God-appointed way of victory and peace.

This new position *is* ours. We *are* in Christ in the heavenlies, far above all principality, power, might and dominion. To take our position in Christ daily by a definite act of faith, and to see ourselves "far above all" before we are subjected to Satan's attacks is to begin the day in victory. Is this not the practical meaning of taking the shield of faith? (6:16). It is spiritual preparedness for a holy walk as well as for warfare.

In speaking once on this glorious truth in a home for deaconesses in Germany the suggestion was made that upon waking in the morning each one there should claim her position in Christ by a definite act of faith, and start the day from that vantage-point of victory. The next morning one of the older deaconesses whose work was a daily routine of monotonous and sometimes provocative tasks testified to the radical change wrought in her day by having it transformed into one of continuous victory with its resultant radiant joyousness and peace. If you have never done so, try it to-morrow, and see if it will not work to turn defeat into victory for you.

Covet Your Possessions in Christ

Every Christian *is* the potential possessor of *every* spiritual blessing by virtue of being in Christ. But how spiritually poverty-stricken the average Christian seems. How few of us give any adequate impression to the worldlings among whom we live of our incalculable wealth in Christ! Why is it so?

Perhaps our desire for spiritual treasures is at a low ebb. To claim effectually we must covet eagerly. There are even among reborn Christians those who would quickly reach out for a bit of earth's filthy lucre, who would not raise a finger to get the golden coins of heavenly riches. To some, two hours at a movie seems no longer than ten minutes, while ten minutes of Bible study drags on like an hour. To others a weekly prayer-meeting would be intolerable, but a weekly dance which debilitates spirit, soul and body and destroys one's effectual witness for Christ would be keenly enjoyed.

To "put on the new man" will mean an eager seeking after spiritual riches and setting the affections primarily and pre-eminently upon heavenly things, rather than earthly. For co-resurrection with Christ lifts one into a sphere where only Christ and the things of Christ can ever satisfy or suffice.

Col. 3:1, 2. "If ye then be risen with Christ, *seek those things which are above,* where Christ sitteth on the right hand of God. *Set your affection on things above,* not on things on the earth."

Count upon the Power of the Spirit

To claim our position in Christ and to covet our possessions in Him cannot be done by dependence upon anything in ourselves. God in His infinite wisdom and love made provision for just such impotency, and gave us the blessed Spirit of power to indwell us. He is resident within us to make Christ a living reality by conforming us to His image in every separate element of His glorious perfection of character. The Spirit will enable us to walk as He walked, in righteousness, humility, faith, obedience, lowliness, meekness, forbearance, love, patience, courage, praise and holiness. Our part is to count upon the Spirit's presence in power to keep self on the Cross and Christ on the throne of our human personality.

A Walk in Holiness

One step over the boundary line between the kingdom of Satan and the kingdom of God brings us into a new sphere and begins a walk in newness of life. This walk involves a radical change in character, what we are; in conduct, what we do; in conversation, what we say.

Holiness in Character

1:4. "He hath chosen us in him . . . *that we should be holy.*"

4:24. "Put on the new man . . . *created in true holiness.*"

5:27. "That he might present to himself a glorious church, not having spot, or wrinkle, or any such thing; but that *it should be holy* and without blemish."

In the eternity of the past the Father chose a Bride for His Son; a Church composed of those who would be united with Christ in absolute oneness of life through the eternity to come, and He Himself set the standard for their Christian character: *"that we should be holy."*

Despite all the difficulties of a walk in a thoroughly defiled and defiling world, God never lowers this standard. However, He is not unreasonable in demanding of us something which we are utterly incapable of doing by ourselves. He has made ample provision for what He requires in giving to us His Holy Spirit and His Holy Word. The Spirit uses the Word in separating us from all that is unholy and in setting us apart unto all that is holy. The way of holiness is clearly taught. A daily study of the Word under the tutelage of the Spirit, accompanied by implicit obedience to it, ensures continuous growth into holiness of life.

Christ, also, gives us fellowship with other Christians. How often the Christ-life, shining transparently and winsomely through some saint of God, has created within us a hunger and thirst for more Christlikeness for ourselves! How tenderly the Lord has responded to our heart's cry for holiness of character by sending someone who had himself thirsted and been filled to help us into the same blessed experience.

The Lord does not discourage us by demanding perfection of character all at once. But our walk should mean a step-by-step growth into Christlikeness; to keep our hearts set on perfection He keeps our eyes fixed on that day—perhaps not far distant—when He will return and the Church will be presented to Him spotless and holy, even as He is.

Holiness in Conduct

4:25. "Wherefore *putting away lying, speak every man truth* with his neighbour."

4:26. *"Be ye angry and sin not;* let not the sun go down upon your wrath."

4:28. *"Let him that stole steal no more:* but rather *let him labour,* working with his hands the thing which is good, *that he may have to give* to him that needeth."

"Wherefore." Here is another arresting word which brings us into close grips with spiritual reality. As "therefore" introduced the whole question of the new walk befitting the new sphere, so "Wherefore" indicates concrete steps to be taken immediately. Paul leaves no impression of merely speaking pious platitudes, or giving nebulous exhortations. Here is a sharp jerk of the reins to bring conduct into swift correspondence with character. *Be* what you *are,* Paul shouts from the housetop of Ephesians, so that every Christian on down through the centuries may hear. In this word "wherefore" he is insisting that holy character must be transmuted into holy conduct; that it is impossible to have the new man's desires and the old man's deeds; that it is altogether inconsistent to talk of living in the heavenlies while walking in the old haunts of the world. "Wherefore" opens the gate from principle into practice; from the abstract into the concrete; from the general into the particular.

Paul cannot enumerate all the wicked deeds of the old man. Here he takes but a few samples of conspicuous sins. Certainly they are those common to men of all centuries and climes. They are strictly up-to-date, even in the highly cultured society of the twentieth century.

"Putting away lying—speak truth." Lying and truth are placed here as exact opposites, for such they are. Lying, therefore, includes anything and everything that has any degree of falseness in it. Within its range comes deception, hypocrisy, misrepresentation, artificiality, shams, half truths, and unreality. We have limited lying to speech, but we can lie by our deeds, and by our false pretensions and professions.

A primary necessity in human relations is truth, as confidence and trust rest upon truth as their foundation. Is there anything in your life you feel compelled to cover up? Anything that will not stand the full light of day? Anything that has not its source in Him that is truth?

From babyhood those Ephesian Christians had breathed the corrupt atmosphere of heathenism. Lying had been ingrained into them. The habits and practices of the old life still had a strong hold upon them. But they had left forever the sphere of the devil. He was a liar and no truth abode in him (John 8:44). Lying was natural to life in the old sphere over which he reigned. But they had been translated into the kingdom where truth prevails and where there is no place whatever for untruth in any form. Therefore Paul calls for decisive action. Lying has been put off as one of the filthy garments of the old man. "Wherefore *speak every man truth.*"

"*Be ye angry and sin not.*" What a common sin is anger! smouldering resentment, inward irritation, hidden malice, bad temper that suddenly flames up into violent outburst and evident exasperation. All of which is very patently sin. But the wording of this command would seem to indicate that sometimes anger is not sin. We must, then, turn to our perfect Example, and ask if our Lord was ever angry. Though sinless and perfect in His human life, He was angry on more than one occasion. Once He entered the synagogue with the soul purpose of helpful service. The Pharisees entered also, but with a sinful purpose,—"to *watch* him whether he would heal on the sabbath day that they might *accuse* him." A man with a withered hand was there, and Christ healed him. The Lord challenged them to come out from under the cover of their professed sanctity, which was only professional hypocrisy, and face the issue honestly by answering His question, "Is it lawful to do good on the sabbath days or to do evil? But they held their peace." And we read, "He looked round about on them *with anger, being grieved* for the hardness of their hearts." Toward their sin of resisting His gracious work of healing while professing to love and serve God, and toward their contemptible falseness and hypocrisy in the matter, He had naught but anger; but towards them in their utter spiritual blindness and hardness of heart, He had only grief. He was angry, but He did not sin in His anger.

Is there a red-blooded Christian anywhere in the world who would not be stirred to anger to read of millions of innocent civilians bombed to death, or of other millions left homeless and penniless, or of the rape of thousands of women and girls? Would he have the right to call himself a Christian were he not angry? But coupled with that anger at such awful sin, is there grief that leads to real prayer for the nation or individuals committing the sin?

We sin in anger when its root is self, when our anger is directed not so much against the sin as the sinner, and because of some personal hurt rather than for the sake of Christ's glory and the honour of His name. To be angry and sin not, we must "be angry at nothing but sin."

"*Let not the sun go down upon your wrath.*" If we have felt the presence of anger in our hearts, let there be a strict self-examination and a severe searching of motives before the day is over, to determine whether it has been sinful or not. Let there be honest and quick dealing with every trace of anger. A walk in holiness forbids any smouldering fires of unjudged temper or the inward burning of unrighteous indignation. If the anger is sinful, let it be confessed to God; and, if it has found utterance before others, let the confession be made to them before you retire to sleep.

"Let him that stole steal no more." Lying, anger and stealing are very common sins in all lands, and are often condoned. Hence the convert to Christianity is often slow to see that they are part of the old life which must be completely abandoned. Evidently some of the Ephesian Christians not only had stolen, but were still stealers, and Paul is insisting that this filthy rag of the old life must be cast off.

Perhaps some twentieth century Christians in so-called Christian lands would dismiss this command as one which bore no relationship to them. Having never been guilty of theft, embezzlement, or such crimes, this command does not concern them. Perhaps we need to get a new angle on the word "stealing."

All would agree that obtaining something unjustly by fraud or force was stealing; also to take the possession of another without right or permission. Legally, to do these things is to steal. But would not God's standard of absolute righteousness in all dealings with others go further and place profiteering, all forms of gambling, misuse of funds, living on credit, refusal to pay debts, in the same category? A walk in strictest righteousness and holiness would also preclude other forms of dishonesty which a Spirit-renewed conscience would shrink from doing. I served once on a committee that prepared for summer conferences for Christian leaders whose travelling expenses were paid. A request came for a pastor with lung trouble to be allowed to go as a delegate. At the place where the Conference was held was also a hospital for tubercular patients, and those responsible for sending him thought this a splendid way of having his travel expense to the hospital met. At another Conference there was a bookroom. One Christian asked to be allowed to take several books to his room to decide which to buy. The books were kept many days; all apparently were read, but none bought.

Scripture shows us an even more refined form of stealing of which every one of us may be guilty to some degree. Stealing is withholding from God that which should be given Him because we wish to hoard it, or to spend it on ourselves.

Mal. 3:8. "Will a man rob God? *Yet ye have robbed me.* But ye say, Wherein have we robbed thee? *In tithes and offerings."*

In a recent revival in China, a Chinese brought to the church $600, of which he said he had robbed God in past tithes. Have any of us robbed God?

"But rather let him labour . . . that he may have to give." Every man should work toward an end—that he may have. But the getting is to be inspired by a righteous, holy aim,—that he may give. Implicit obedience to this simple injunction by every child of God would provide ample funds for every God-appointed work.

Accepting Christ as our Saviour and Lord involves the acceptance of the moral and ethical standard that governed His life on earth. The Holy Spirit, who indwells us, knows our every deflection from that standard, however great or small, and would apply the knife continually to every phase of unrighteousness in our daily conduct.

Holiness in Conversation

Our conversation is very self-revealing. What one says and the manner in which he says it gives an X-ray of the heart, "for out of the abundance of the heart the mouth speaketh." It might almost be said of some Christians that they speak out of the emptiness and dearth of the heart. So the Head of the Body sets a standard for conversation that is as high as that already mentioned for character and conduct. It calls for a sanctified tongue.

4:29. *"Let no corrupt communication proceed out of your mouth, but that which is good for the use of edifying, that it may minister grace unto the hearers."*

"No corrupt communication"—putrid, foul, unfit for use. Surely such speech should never fall from the lips of a Christian. Corrupt speech can be traced to but one source: the unclean flow from an unclean fountain. (4:19, 22) It is "the old man" speaking. Paul tells us the forms such speech may take:

5:4. "Neither *filthiness,* nor *foolish talking,* nor *jesting,* which are not convenient (befitting) but rather giving of thanks."

Utterly unbefitting the conversation of a saint are unclean stories and coarse jokes; idle, inane talk with no meaning or profit to anyone; the smart, witty remark or the facetious pleasantry, often regarding things sacred to call forth a laugh at the expense of self-respect and decency. Whatever in the slightest degree is morally tainted or destructive to faith is utterly out of place in the Christian's conversation. Someone whom God had led into a more consistently holy walk wrote me, "I think you will find me changed; my people, even my servants, say it. I seem to myself as if I have lost my joking ways, as if I have grown a bit more grave because *I have seen the sin of making a joke about everything, even spiritual things.* I've learnt to be more careful in my whole manner of living."

The context would show us two other forms of speech which are also prohibited,—that which is covetous and that which is critical. Do you know people who are always saying, "Oh, I wish I had—!"? A lust for money, possessions, or, as used in 5:3, even sensual greed. Discontent and murmuring flow freely in speech where there is a fleshly craving for more of earthly things.

Again, if we listen to our own or others' speech, how much of it one has to admit is uncharitable, unkind and unnecessary. Are any of us guilty of being gossipers, whisperers, slanderers, or back-biters? Then the Lord is speaking to us out of Ephesians. He has exhorted us to speak only that which is true; now He enjoins us to speak only what is pure and kind. And He holds us responsible for our speech.

"Let no . . . but that." These two phrases in 4:29 show us that God means for us to both control conversation so that it may not be along wrong lines, and to conduct it along those that are ennobling and edifying. When we talk it is to be for a purpose,— "to minister grace unto the hearers." This does not imply that conversation must always be on spiritual themes, certainly not just "pious" talk, nor necessarily that a complete ban is put upon good humour and wholesome wit. But it does mean that it will be conversation that "becometh saints"; more than that, it will be such as befits the presence of the *Holy* Spirit who indwells us.

God has given us a tongue which is to be used, not as "an instrument of unrighteousness unto sin," but as "an instrument of righteousness unto God" (Rom. 6:13). There are many whom we meet, even casually, who need and want instruction, encouragement, comfort, warning. There are those who hunger and thirst after righteousness, but do not know how to be filled. Conversation is a mighty power to be used for such upbuilding of the Body of Christ and for the salvation of souls. Every "hearer" of ours needs some further measure of grace. Does our conversation minister constructively to his need? A friend of mine consecrates her conversations to Christ, and constantly has the most unusual and wonderful opportunities on buses, trains, and in stores, offices and restaurants, for entering into conversations that she *conducts* so as to lead on to Christ. This is the privilege of every child of God.

The standard God has set for a walk in holiness is very high, but not unreasonable, because He has given to us the Holy Spirit to indwell and infill us for the very purpose of inworking into the spiritual fibre of our being the holiness of the Holy One.

3. A WALK IN LOVE

The third characteristic of a worthy walk is revealed in 4:31-5:2 as a walk in love. Paul constantly writes from the standpoint of two spheres, the old and the new, and shows there is a walk that befits each sphere. In the passage before us we se᷉ hate in its various shades of expression sharply contrasted with love in its different manifestations.

Sources of Hate and Love

Let us turn for a moment to the first epistle of John, where hate and love are tracked to their source in the spheres of darkness and death, and light and life; and where it is so clearly shown that the one who walks in hate belongs to the old sphere; while the one who walks in love lives in the new.

I John 2:9, 11. "He that saith he is in the light, and *hateth his brother, is in darkness*, even until now . . . *He that hateth his brother is in darkness, and walketh in darkness.*"

I John 2:10. *"He that loveth his brother abideth in the light."*

I John 3:14. "We know that we have *passed from death unto life, because we love the brethren. He that loveth not his brother abideth in death."*

Love for the brethren is one proof that we have passed out of the old sphere into the new where love is the native atmosphere. If we are in the new sphere, we inhale and exhale love.

Satan presides over the old sphere and is the fountain-head of hate. He hates Christ and all who are Christ's, and instils this same hate into those who follow him. Cain, filled with Satanic hatred, murdered his own brother Abel. Christ presides over the new sphere, and is the fountainhead of love. He loves all His Father's children, His brethren, and imparts His love to them.

Expressions of Hate

4.31. "Let *all bitterness*, and *wrath*, and *anger*, and *clamour*, and *evil speaⁿⁱⁿ⸗*, ᵇᵉ put away from you, with *all malice*."

Here we see Satan's brood hatched out in the nest of hate into concrete sins of temper and tongue. Let us note several things. First, unlove is the setting for all six sins mentioned here. Not one of them could abide in a love-filled, love-constrained heart. Secondly, there is a gradation in the expression of unlove from an inner attitude to an outward act. That root of "bitterness," canker in the innermost spirit, or secret resentment over some hurt or wrong, allowed to home itself in the heart, will one day flame into white heat in an outburst of passionate fury. That grievance nursed in the spirit, that indignation which became a settled attitude of mind, that hot feeling of injury which smoulders in the heart will one day reach the tongue and find expression in heated discussion, "clamour," and intemperate "evil speaking." A devil-touched, hate-tipped tongue will go to any length of railing, slander, insult, and abuse in giving vent to "anger." Lastly, there is an inevitable progression in unlove if left unchecked. How simple the words sound, "with all malice!" What is malice? Secret ill-will, just *thinking* evil. What does it become if allowed to remain? Spite that cannot rest until it *works* evil. Malice is the henchman of hate; a poisonous weed whose growth into "bitterness, wrath, anger, clamour, evil speaking," is absolutely assured, unless uprooted.

Unlove rooted in malice came into the heart of one Christian worker toward another, and was allowed to do its devilish work. It sent lies flowing like a putrid stream into one country after another to hinder God's message and thwart God's work. So let us face squarely what it means if we permit any one of these devil-begotten sins to remain in our heart. Let us search ourselves through a Spirit-conducted examination to discover any of this hateful brood, and be prepared to obey God's command so plainly written here.

"Let all . . . be put away from you." This word "let" places responsibility squarely on us for decision that results in action. It challenges our will to take sides against Satan in favour of Christ, and calls to definite action in regard to concrete sins and tells us exactly what to do. *"Be put away from you."* Let these sins be not merely confessed, but let them be carried out and cast off as something utterly incongruous in the life in Christ. Do it and be done with it, is the full force of the verb "put away." *"All"*—and may this house-cleaning be very thoroughly done. Let no particle of unlove lurk in the corners. This three-lettered word "all" is the biggest word in the verse, for it commands a total abstinence of hate. There is to be *no* root of bitterness, *no* symptom of wrath, *no* trace of anger, *no* echo of clamour, *no* slime of evil speaking, *no* dregs of

malice. Both the inner attitude and the outward act are to disappear entirely. "The Holy Spirit gives quarter to no evil feeling whatsoever."

But Paul never stops with mere renunciation. Sin is not merely the presence of hate; it is equally the absence of love. Christian conduct is not based on negatives. Emptying the heart of hate is only preparatory to having it filled with love. Unless a hate-emptied heart is immediately filled with God's love, "seven devils" may return to occupy it, and the latter state be worse than the first.

If someone asked you if you *hated* some fellow-Christian with whom you were evidently out of fellowship, you would hesitate, perhaps, to say, "Yes." That would seem going too far. But, if you were asked if you *loved* that person, could you honestly say you did? Did you note the wording of I John 3:14? It does not say "he that hateth," but "he that *loveth not* his brother abideth in death." There is a distinct place for hate as well as for anger in the Christian's heart. But we must be sure it is directed toward the right object. "God willeth that we endlessly *hate the sin* and endlessly *love the soul,* as God loveth it." So Paul now turns to the positive exhortation.

Manifestations of Love

4:32. "And *be ye kind* one to another, *tenderhearted, forgiving* one another, even as God for Christ's sake hath forgiven you."

"Be ye,"—"become with a perpetual becoming," like Christ until His love in all its manifold manifestations becomes your love for one another. To avoid not being hate-full, be ye love-full. To keep free from the sins of 4:31, cultivate the virtues of 4:32. Bitterness and kindness; malice and tender-heartedness; anger and forgiveness are not good bed-fellows. Where one is the other cannot be.

"Kind,"—what a homespun, simple word it is! Yet how comprehensive and beautiful! To be kind is far, far more than merely doing kindly deeds. It means that the very essence of our spiritual nature is kindness itself. The intrinsic meaning of the word will be understood only as we ponder deeply His kindness toward us through Christ Jesus (2:7). The full measure of the word will be comprehended only as we realize in experience "the kindness and love of God our Saviour toward man" (Tit. 3:4). How kind the Lord Jesus is! loving the unlovely and the unlovable with a love that took Him to Calvary's Cross! It was also a kindness that in His earthly life made Him unfailingly courteous, considerate, appreciative, and thoughtful of others.

Is it not in some of these less spectacular expressions of kindness that most of us fail lamentably? Are not many Christian workers guilty in this respect? We may give ourselves unstintedly in leading meetings and in teaching His Word to win lost souls, yet fail utterly in even common courtesy to fellow-Christians with whom we labour, or in legitimately expected appreciation and considerateness toward those who serve us anywhere.

A man, deeply taught in the Word and greatly gifted in Bible exposition, was unbelievably rude and discourteous, and so lacking in all the kindly graces of the Spirit in relation to fellow-workers that one derived most benefit from his public ministry if he did not see his private manners. Spending some weeks in a Christian home, one could not be unconscious of continuous strain between husband and wife, both truly devoted to each other. The more evident cause was the wife's temper and jealousy, but close observation could not but convince one of almost cruel silence on the part of the husband in speaking the kindly word of appreciation and doing the thoughtful *little* thing that would have revealed the heart's real love. A Bible teacher naturally hard in disposition told me that he "was afraid to be kind, for it seemed so effeminate." But here the simple word stands, "Be ye *kind.*" Oh, that in this world, which inevitably inflicts so many hard blows on most folks, we who are in Christ might be more kind one to another! How it would smooth many a rough road and sweeten many a bitter cup!

"Be ye . . . *tenderhearted.*" How strange it is that it is much easier to be harsh, uncharitable and intolerant than to be sympathetic, loving and understanding! Could we be aught but tender-hearted if we ever kept Christ on Calvary in our vision? Would our heart not be kept full of compassion toward others who have shortcomings and sins if we remembered what we were and always would have been but for the love of God manifested toward us in Christ?

"*Forgiving one another.*" Is it possible for unforgiveness to abide in the heart where kindness and tenderheartedness are dominant? The Christlike attitude results in the Christlike act. Is there any member of the Body of Christ whom you have not forgiven? If so, how can you hold out against the appeal God makes here?

"*Even as God for Christ's sake hath forgiven you.*" God has freely and fully forgiven you a life-time full of sins. He has forgiven you wrongs against Himself of infinitely greater import and degree than any wrong anyone ever did you. Can any forgiveness you are called upon to grant another compare with that which He has granted you?—a forgiveness so perfect that He forgets what He forgives. *"Even as."* Let God's measure of forgiveness to us determine our forgiveness of others.

A Walk in Love

5:1 (R.V.). "Be ye, therefore, *imitators of God,* as beloved children."

5:2. "And *walk in love,* as Christ also hath loved us, and hath given himself for us, an offering and a sacrifice to God for a sweet-smelling savour."

God is the Standard of the Love-life of His Children

God *is* love. Every thought, word and act of God is the expression of the love which is the very essence of His character. We are His beloved children, born into His family and made members of His household through love, and have become partakers of His divine nature which is love. Therefore His standard becomes ours.

"Be ye . . . imitators of God." This is an astounding demand, but a very reasonable one. As father—so child. As He is and does, so are we to be and do, for the Father rightly sets the standard for His family and His household. To love as God loves is one of the greatest proofs that we are His.

I John 4:16. "God is love; and *he that dwelleth in love dwelleth in God, and God in him."*

God Himself loves in and through the child He infills. What limit, then, need be put upon the love-life of any child of God, however cold, unfeeling and loveless his life may be in the natural?

Christ is the Example of the Love-life to Members of His Body

The Son lived up to the standard set by the Father in His love for us. In the same manner the Father loved Him, He loved us.

John 15:9. *"As* the Father hath loved me, *so* have I loved you." Then He became the example of the love-life for us.

John 15:12. "This is my commandment, that ye *love one another, as I have loved you."*

"As—so." Let us not wince under these words, but rather worship Him who thinks we have the capacity to love like that. *As* Christ hath loved us, *so* we are to love every fellow-member of the Body. Dare we so measure our love for the brethren?

"Walk in love"—Do not talk, but walk. "Let us not love in word, neither in tongue; but in deed and in truth" (I John 3:18). Some Christian workers in China strongly advocated the social

123

gospel for the amelioration of social wrongs, and in meetings discussed the wickedness of modern industry that keeps men at work seven days in the week at a pitifully low wage. But, when they themselves were engaged in building operations, they employed Sunday labour rather than give the workmen that day off with pay. To talk is *cheap:* to walk is *costly.* For it means that the whole course of one's life and every phase of his conduct, public and private, is to be in love. Love in action is to undergird every relationship of one's life, in the home, in business, in society, and in the church.

"As Christ also hath loved us." His love was self-effacing. He does not love us because we love Him. Oh no! He loved us when and because we did not love Him. While we were yet sinners, Christ loved us because of our desperate condition and utter helplessness in sin.

How far short we fall of following His example! We have our circle of friends, chosen largely because of what they can mean to us. Our choice is governed by our likes and dislikes, by prejudice or favouritism, all of which is condemned by Christ's way of loving us. How often we do not even care to have fellowship with those outside our social circle, our church affiliation, or especially with those of less educational or cultural advantages. In other words, we are not self-effacing in our love, but self-satisfying.

"And hath given himself for us." His love was self-sacrificing. The cost of our salvation was a Saviour, which He voluntarily became. The price of our redemption was the blood of the Cross, which He willingly paid. But how many Christians seem self-seeking rather than self-sacrificing. There are thousands who go to church on Sunday, who toss a coin into the offering, who fulfil perfunctorily some service for the church, but how pitifully few Christians have anything of the sacrificial in their love for Christ, for fellow-Christians, and for lost sinners! After commanding His disciples to love one another as He had loved them, He made this statement:

John 15:13. "Greater love hath no man than this, *that a man lay down his life for his friends."*

Do our hearts condemn us as we read these words? Have we ever really laid down our lives for Him, or for His own? Are we willing to-day to acknowledge the lack of the sacrificial in our love?

"Himself—for us." "Himself"—lovely, sinless, perfect. "For us"—unlovely, sinful, polluted. *Ourself—for Him.* Are you willing to-day to make it truly reciprocal? As Christ has loved me, so will I love Him and others for His sake, at any cost, however great?

4. A WALK IN LIGHT

A walk in light is the fourth characteristic of a worthy walk as unfolded in 5:3-14. No part of Ephesians reveals more strikingly the differentiation between the two kingdoms. Satan's kingdom is the manifestation of midnight darkness; God's kingdom that of mid-day light. Let us now see how vividly Paul expresses the clear-cut cleavage between citizenship in these two kingdoms:

5:8. "For *ye were once darkness,* but *now are ye light in the Lord.*"

Children of Darkness

"*Ye were once darkness.*" Way translates this, "Darkness incarnate you once were." Weymouth puts it, "There was a time when you were nothing but darkness." Paul is saying that those Ephesian Christians did not merely *do* works of darkness, but that they *were* darkness itself; that they were not only in the sphere of darkness, but they were so identified with it and so impregnated by it as to have actually become darkness. They were subjects in the kingdom of darkness, ruled by the prince of darkness, children of the father of darkness, and destined to spend eternity in the pit of darkness.

Works of Darkness

The result of such spiritual darkness was appalling moral destitution. The backward shadow of 5:8-3 is one of unrelieved moral degradation. The conduct and conversation of those who were once darkness was morally rotten. Such moral corruption was evidently common and countenanced by all circles without scruple or shame.

5:3-4. "But *fornication,* and all *uncleanness,* or *covetousness* neither *filthiness,* nor *foolish talking,* nor *jesting.*"

They were guilty not only of the performance of every form of uncleanness and impurity, but also of making these indecencies and immoralities the theme of conversation, gloating in the laughter which their coarse jests produced. Tongues and ears were steeped in vileness as well as mind and heart. No wonder Paul called it all "the unfruitful works of darkness."

Destiny of Darkness-Dwellers

5:5. "For this ye know, that no whoremonger, nor unclean person, nor covetous man, who is an idolater, *hath any inheritance in the kingdom of Christ and of God.*"

God has stated the destiny of those who prefer to remain in the kingdom of darkness and to practice the works of darkness, and further comment seems unnecessary. God's attitude towards sin remains inflexible. God and sin can never fellowship together. His love and grace ever go out toward the sinner; but He has only hatred and wrath toward sin. So every unrepentant sinner will "go to his own," even as did Judas.

Perhaps some one says, "What has this to do with us to-day? It all belongs to the paganism of olden days." But is that true? If one but scratches the surface of the veneer of our boasted twentieth century civilization he will discover all of these sins that so vitiated human society in that first century. Wherever there is a departure from God there is a consequent deterioration in ethics and morals, and the breakdown in the latter is always gauged by the depth and degree of that in the former. The further one goes from God the nearer he comes to Satan. The old Adamic nature remains unchanged on down through the centuries, and left to itself will wallow in the deepest mire of sin. If one needs proof of this he needs only to read the pages of modern literature, where the very sins mentioned in 5:3-5 are pictured with appalling frankness; and oftentimes the writer is advocating a personal liberty which is nothing less than free license to lust. Our Lord predicted that in the days preceding His coming human society would have sunk to the very lowest level such as prevailed in the days of Noah, which brought upon mankind the judgment of the Flood. Surely we are in those days, and it behooves every child of God to recognize this and to know from God's Word how to safeguard himself from the moral taint of the awful sins that vitiate the very air he breathes. Only so has he any ground of assurance that he will not be caught in this awful whirlpool of uncleanness and impurity.

Children of Light

5:8. *"But now are ye light in the Lord; walk as children of light."*

"Ye were sometimes"—a period of time now forever gone, a past that is wholly obliterated with no repetition permissible or possible. *"But now"*—a new cycle begun indicating a present that is in vivid contrast to the past and that marks the boundary line between the spheres of darkness and of light.

"Ye are light." You are so identified with light, yea, the Light so indwells you, that you have become light itself. You have been translated into the kingdom of light, made a child of Him who is light, and become a partaker of the life that is light. *"In the Lord"* —In Him we become what He is.

"Walk as children of light." Character determines conduct; therefore live, speak, act as the sons of light. "Order your lives as men native-born to the light." It is inconceivable that the walk of children of darkness and children of light should be the same in any particular. Everything in the walk of the Christian should be differentiated from that of the sinner. There is a walk that becometh sinners, but such a walk is unbefitting saints, even to its minutest details. Our conduct and our conversation betray us, for they reveal the kingdom in which we are citizens. The vile things sinners do are not only unthinkable for saints, but even to mention such things is polluting. To talk of them even in whispers or in secret is put under the ban.

5:3. "Let it *not even be named among you, as becometh saints."

5:4 (R.V.). "Which are *not befitting."

"Ye are light"—therefore become what you are and walk before men as such. Be consistent with what you are. "Nothing is purer than light." Ye are light, therefore *be as pure as you are.*

Fruit of the Light

5:9 (R.V.). "For *the fruit of the light* is in all *goodness,* and *righteousness* and *truth."*

The works of darkness are all degrading and destructive. Light generates light which is fruitful and edifying. What, then, are the distinguishing characteristics of those who are light in the Lord? Paul mentions three.

"All goodness"—beneficence in action in all things and toward all persons. There should be no action in the Christian's life that could possibly react harmfully upon another. We constantly hear one who indulges in some questionable form of amusement say, "But I can do that and it won't harm *me."* Is one's personal harm the only thing to be considered? Goodness forbids the Christian from doing anything that would be detrimental to another. He will guard his influence over others with studious care, and will gladly give up even a lawful thing if there is in it the slightest possibility of leading another away from Christ and into sin. Goodness is a most practical virtue, and exercises itself even in the realm of eating and drinking and in all of the commonplaces of daily conduct. It puts an absolute ban upon every form of selfishness, and compels the Christian not to seek his own but the other's good.

Rom. 14:15, 16 (R.V.). "For if because of meat thy brother is grieved, *thou walkest no longer in love.* Destroy not with thy meat him for whom Christ died."

Rom. 14:21. "It is good neither to eat flesh, nor to drink wine, nor anything *whereby thy brother stumbleth, or is offended or is made weak.*"

I Cor. 8:13. "Wherefore, if meat maketh my brother to offend, *I will eat no meat* while the world standeth, lest I make my brother to offend."

The divine law of love and the divine principle of goodness will not permit the Christian to seek his own pleasure and profit to the detriment or downfall of another.

"All righteousness"—a moral rectitude that is irreproachable. The applied principle of righteousness wipes off the slate every form of impurity and dishonesty, and demands an abstinence from even every appearance of evil (I Thes. 5:22). Its exercise gives the Christian a conscience void of offence toward God and toward men (Acts 24:16). The Christian's life is measured by a fixed and absolute standard of perfect righteousness—that of the incarnate Word as revealed in the written Word. Every recognized thing that deviates from that standard must go. How tragic has been the moral breakdown of even some Christian workers because they thought their position with its prestige gave them liberty to do things which they would have denounced severely in others! But a righteous God will condone no unrighteousness done under the cloak of Christian ministry.

"All truth"—severest sincerity in the most inward and hidden part of the life that countenances in one's life no pretence or sham; that allows no twilight zones; no lurking compromises; no secret alliances with evil. But, on the contrary, a life that so craves reality that it does not shrink from the most searching scrutiny of His eyes that are as a flame of fire, and welcomes every revelation of aught that displeases Him.

To walk as children of light in these days is most difficult. The difficulty is largely due to the lowered and varying standards of the Church in all lands. Satan has entered churches, and often occupies both pulpit and pew. He has dragged the world and the flesh in after him; even the missionary body has not escaped his defiling touch. May we face frankly some of the works of darkness prevalent in nominal Christianity to-day?

In a large, prominent city church there are smoking and dancing rooms for the young people, where their *worldly* amusements may be carried on in a *"Christian* atmosphere." In another magnificent church edifice a missionary meeting was held. Before the missionary spoke, the president of the society announced that at the close of the meeting an opportunity would be given to sign up for the bridge parties by which they were to raise their money *for their missionary offering!!* Exaggerated and exceptional cases, one may say. Oh it is to be hoped so, but the exception only reveals the trend toward the worldly in the Church and among Christians, both in the conduct of Church affairs and in personal life. With such a tragic mixture of darkness and light right in the Church itself, how can one walk as a child of light? In this very passage God tells us through His warning, prohibitions and exhortations. Two things will be especially necessary to those who long to shine as lights in this world (Phil. 2:15): discernment and decisiveness.

Discernment

One of Satan's greatest assets is an inconsistent Christian; one whose conduct before men belies his calling in Christ. So he will do everything possible to keep every saint sinning. His wiles are many and Paul exhorts the Ephesian Christians to be spiritually alert to these Satanic deceptions.

5:6. "Let *no man deceive you* with vain words."

"*Let.*" Subtle as the deception may be, it is not necessary to be misled or seduced, as God has given ample light on Satan's ways in the Word. "*No man.*" To accomplish his purpose Satan uses men, both unregenerate sinners and carnal Christians, who have themselves yielded to some of these temptations. "*Deceive you by vain (empty) words.*" What are some of the empty words through which Satan seeks to deceive? First, he lies regarding the very nature of sin itself. The primary tenet of his gospel is that man is ever evolving into something higher and better. But sin is too evident in mankind for him to get past altogether with this fundamental lie. So he cleverly tells another to offset it. This one he often speaks through college professors, authors and even liberal ministers. Sin is not so bad, after all, if we look upon it as "a fall upward," or "an incident of our finite nature due to the misfortune of a bad environment."

Secondly, he deceives in regard to God's attitude toward sin. He declares that the thought of the wrath of God is unbelievable, and that a monstrous wrong is done to the God of love to think He can punish sin by shutting any man away from His presence. So he urges men to have no fear of the next world, but to give themselves up fully to the enjoyment of everything in this one. His words are most attractive to the carnal Christian who has never "crucified the flesh" (Gal. 5:24), or been "crucified unto the world" (Gal. 6:44), and who has shown no willingness to co-operate with the Holy Spirit in putting off the old man and in putting on the new man. He wants to believe that he can be conformed to Christ and to the world at the same time. He prefers to think that he can walk after the flesh and after the Spirit at the same time.

So he gladly listens as Satan's emissary tells him that we in this enlightened twentieth century have outgrown altogether the puritanical standards of the past; that even godly parents who are holding to the relics of an outmoded morality are too old-fashioned for the youth of to-day; that we live in a new day of individual freedom, when everyone has the right to be a law unto himself; that even the established conventions of society regarding home life, marriage, and the upbringing of children should not be binding on us in these times. He urges not to stand aloof in self-righteousness from those who follow these modern ways, and not to make one's self unpopular by being peculiar. He reasons plausibly to come along with the crowd, deceiving the Christian by arguing that he himself will not be harmed and that by thus mixing with the worldling he may be used to make him better. Thus by his specious lies the arch-deceiver misleads many children of light in their walk.

God has clearly refuted Satan's lie regarding the nature of sin and His attitude toward sin in Ephesians. Twice He has told us that sin calls down upon the children of disobedience the wrath of God, and in 5:5 He says that those who remain in sin have no inheritance in the kingdom of Christ and of God. Then how may we know what is of Satan and what is of God? By a God-given discernment in testing every "vain word," tracing it to its source, and then rejecting it as unacceptable to our Lord.

5:10. *"Proving what is acceptable unto the Lord."*

Is this thing acceptable to Christ? This is the invariable criterion; here is stated the acid test. Not, is there any harm in this thing? Not, does everyone do it? Not even, does the Church countenance it? But, is it acceptable to the Lord as conduct that becometh saints?

The Christian who has entered into any real spiritual apprehension of what it means to be "accepted in the beloved" will have one consuming passion—that his walk step by step will be wholly "acceptable to the Lord." His loving, joyous eagerness to please his Lord will be the fitting complement to the Lord's loving, joyous eagerness to make him acceptable to His Father. He will always approach Christ saying, "What more may I give to Thee, and how may I please Thee most?"

130

To know what is unacceptable to God demands decisiveness in action. It requires a clean-cut refusal to have any partnership either with the workers or the works of darkness.

5:7. *"Be not ye therefore partakers with them."*

5:12. "And *have no fellowship with the unfruitful works of darkness,* but rather reprove them."

"Be not ye." In a recent number of the Sunday School Times there was a paragraph on the editorial page as follows:

"Forbidding is as necessary as feeding. There are child psychologists and educators to-day who would tell us that we must never use 'negatives' with a child; tell the children what to do, but never tell them, 'don't do this or that'; if we feed the child with positive truth, this is all that is necessary. God does not seem to agree with such worldly wisdom, for His Word tells us many things we are not to do, as well as many that we are to do."

5:3-14 offers ample proof of this last sentence, for in twelve verses God speaks the *forbidding* word to His children four times.

"Partakers with them." There is no kinship between light and darkness. They are mutually exclusive and aggressively antagonistic. The children of light should know where the line of division is between the two kingdoms, and should never tarry near the boundary line of the kingdom of darkness. Sin is always sin to God, and is as loathsome to Him when seen in the saint as in the sinner. So the saint cannot afford to play nor to tamper with sin.

"Have no fellowship." When once a thing has been seen to be one of the works of darkness, that settles fully and finally the question of the Christian's relationship to it. There must be an abrupt abandonment of all fellowship with it. Write in capitals that two-lettered word, *"NO."* God is light, and He has no fellowship with darkness, for "In him is *no* darkness at all." We should, then, accept our separateness from darkness and all its works as the natural consequence of our relationship with God. And "no" means "no." It prohibits any fellowship, even in moderation, or under the protective shelter of a church roof, with the works of darkness. "No" also forbids not only participation in gross and open sins, but also in all questionable and foolish conduct.

Our personal repudiation of the works of darkness does not end our responsibility toward them as those who are light in the Lord. Simply to have no fellowship with them ourselves is negative action; God never stops with a mere negation. God calls every saint to take a positive stand against the works of darkness that they may be exposed and expelled. Reproof of such works is, then, a very solemn part of the believer's responsibility.

5:11. "But rather *reprove them*."

God does not ask us to become moral detectives or spiritual spies, always on the scent of evil in others, nor does He permit us to become self-appointed judges of their actions. But He does mean that the children of light should not close their eyes to the evil about them, nor even their mouths. To be silent may be tantamount to approval. We bear a definite responsibility, that should not be shirked, to lay bare the real character of sin. There is so little of real militancy and so much of softness in the spiritual soldiery of to-day that often the enemy triumphs. We need never fear active aggressiveness against the works of darkness if we follow the directions of our Captain, for there was never One as gentle and tender as He, yet as militant and aggressive against sin. His open rebuke of the hypocritical Pharisees, recorded in Matthew 23, almost makes one hold his breath.

It is light shining upon and into darkness that reproves. Light has within itself the power both to reveal and to reprove.

5:13. "But *all things that are reproved are made manifest by the light;* for whatsoever doth make manifest is light."

The saint is light in the Lord, so his life shining upon and into the darkness about him should expose the foulness of every bit of evil he contacts and be its sharpest reproof. Unsaved ones are often convicted of sin through the light and life of Christ in His own, as is shown by this letter from a dear Christian friend in a neighbouring country:

"Some souls have been saved. One of my older brothers confessed to receive Christ. But his life continues almost the same, and we do not see much signs of life in him. His wife heard the gospel most eagerly and searched the Scriptures for a month, but said she does not want to submit and has rejected it all. *The Bible, our testimony and our life have condemned her and she is pricked to the heart.* She loves too much the world and its pleasures and would not let go."

But sometimes God asks of us the very difficult thing—the reproof through the lips. The works of darkness must be openly denounced that they may be defeated and destroyed. Peter had to expose the underground deceit and the black lie in the heart of Ananias and Sapphira by an open rebuke, that the purity and power of that newborn Church might be preserved. The pierced arrow of the spoken word from Stephen's lips to the stiff-necked, Spirit-resisting Jews was required, as well as the purifying aroma of his Spirit-filled life, to bring conviction of sin, as it apparently did, to Saul of Tarsus. And Paul himself, filled with the Spirit, faced Elymas, the sorcerer, filled with Satan, who was working to keep Sergius Paulus from receiving the Lord Jesus as his Saviour. Paul spoke publicly such scathing words of rebuke and denunciation as to make one tremble (Acts 13:10). But the authoritative, denunciatory word and act of Paul convinced the deputy of the presence in power of the Lord, and he believed.

Perhaps there was never a time in the history of the Church when there was greater need of men like Peter and Stephen and Paul, who themselves filled with the Holy Spirit and walking consistently as children of light, will faithfully expose the works of darkness within the Church and in the world, both by the spoken and the written word. The black cloud of apostasy with its trail of moral and ethical darkness hangs low over the Church, and is in itself a clarion call from God to every Christian to awake from his stupor and arise from out of his spiritual deadness to let the light of the Lord shine upon, in and through him to dissipate the darkness.

5:14. "Wherefore he saith, *Awake thou that sleepeth, and arise from the dead,* and Christ shall give thee light."

In the light of this searching bit of God's Word will you, dear friend, answer a few questions in the secret presence of your Lord?

Are you permitting any sin that is unbecoming to you as a saint?

Have you been a partaker with evil-doers in their evil works, and thus the light that is in you has become darkness?

Are you willing for the unpopularity that would inevitably come if you faithfully and decisively separated yourself from both the workers and the works of darkness?

Are you ready to obey your Lord's command to reprove them under the Holy Spirit's control and guidance?

5. A WALK IN WISDOM

The fifth characteristic of a walk that glorifies the Lord is a walk in wisdom. While in 5:15-17, the word "circumspectly" is used in immediate connection with the verb "walk," yet the content of the passage centres largely around the words "unwise" and "wise." So let us take the larger view to be an exhortation to walk in wisdom.

All through this section of Ephesians which deals with the Christian's walk Paul has but one appeal, reiterated again and again, *"Be what you are."* The ground of his appeal is also invariably the same, that the walk of the saint must be in correspondence with his position in Christ. *"Ye were sometimes—but now ye are,"* therefore walk "as becometh saints." The sinner walks "as fools," but the saint walks "as wise." Naturally a walk in wisdom follows a walk in light. So 5:15 resumes the appeal of 5:8.

Walk in Wisdom

5:15. "See then that *ye walk circumspectly, not as fools but as wise.*"

"See then"—take heed to your walk; be severely strict with yourself about your whole manner of living; check up on your walk with the deliberate purpose to correct every wrong move. "Stop, look, listen." If you are standing before the world as "light in the Lord," be very sure that the light that is in you be not darkness (Matt. 6:23). "The story is told of a lighthouse off the coast of Florida, which became the instrument of death and destruction rather than of preservation and safety. A window in the lamp room had broken, there was no time to repair it, and a piece of iron was substituted. That night, during a furious storm, a vessel beating up the coast was sent astray by *the one part dark,* with results fatal to the crew."

How absolutely consistent in every smallest detail the Christian's life must be! When giving a series of messages on the life of victory in a mission station in China, I was very conscious of the eyes of one missionary upon me in closest scrutiny every moment while in her presence. She did not believe such a life of victory was practicable or possible. When the meetings were over she came to confess that she had watched me like a detective to discover even an expression of the face or tone of the voice, or something in the manner of speaking and acting, however great or small, to prove her point. How true and timely are Bishop Moule's words just here:

"The appeal is again for a grave remembrance that a walk in the light is no mere promenade, smooth and easy, but a march, resolved and full of purpose, cautious against the enemy, watchful for opportunity for the King, self-controlled in every habit, and possible only in the power of the eternal Spirit."

"Walk circumspectly." Literally, it means exactly, accurately. Walk "looking around, watchful on every side." A walk is made up

of steps, taken one at a time. One wrong step may prove fatal, and lead into backsliding and sin, or into terrible sorrow and suffering. What a lifetime of sorrow some Christian women have had because they disobeyed God's command to marry "only in the Lord." What disgrace and shame a Christian man brought upon the name of the Lord and upon himself and family by stealing money from his employers to tide him temporarily over a crisis, expecting, of course, to repay it as times grew better.

All about us are the devil's snares and pitfalls. We walk in danger constantly. Then watch your step and know where the next step will lead you. We need to be scrupulously careful about every detail of our conduct, for nothing is trivial or unimportant. Our manner of speech, fashion in clothes, companions in pleasure, use of time, choice of magazines and books, expenditure of money, are all indicative of the degree of supremacy of light over darkness in our lives. Strictest consistency in common things is obligatory, for we are taught to avoid every appearance of evil. We are to refrain from doing both that which could give rise to scandal and evil-speaking, and that which belies the sanctity of our life in Christ.

"Walk—not as fools, but as wise"

We walk as pilgrims in an unregenerate world. All around us is gross spiritual and moral darkness, the more awful because it exists alongside the dazzling light of the twentieth century wisdom of man. We walk as Christians in the midst of an apostate Church, wherein the world, the flesh and the devil have been allowed great liberty in dictating its plans and in the control of its programs. In no period of Church history was God's exhortation in 5:15 more needed than to-day.

"Not as fools." Do not walk as an unthinking person; going with the crowd; taking the easy way of least resistance; doing something because everybody does it, with no thought of the consequences, fearing otherwise to be thought peculiar; voting with the majority, even if the action is a direct departure from the plain teaching of God's Word and a violation of one's own conscience.

"But as wise"—as one with eyes, mind and heart open Godward to see and to seize upon the light Christ promises to give (5:14); alert and eager to follow it, whether you travel alone or in the company of other saints. Countless Christians are lax and careless in their walk because they have no definite purpose. They never get anywhere because they never had a goal in mind. The wise Christian has a definite goal and purposes to have every step take him

nearer to it. He has taken the one which God has so clearly set for him and for the Church in 1:4 and 5:27, and he walks steadily toward it with unwavering fixity of purpose.

Perhaps one of the greatest difficulties of the earnest Christian to-day is how to "walk as wise." He faces baffling and perplexing problems relating to his family, his business, his country and his church. How is he to walk before some member of his family who wilfully rejects the Lord, and because of this hates him and will have nothing to do with him? What is he to do if he has become a partner in business with one who professed to be sound in his Christian faith and yet practices dishonesty in business? What is to be his attitude toward war, and how is he to vote in these times when political corruption is rampant everywhere? What is to be his attitude toward those in his church who have filled the house of prayer with the tables of money-changers? How can he take the holy communion from the hands of a man who denies the deity of Christ and does despite to the precious blood of which the wine he offers is the symbol? If He believes God has shown His Church the one and only way to finance it, can he give consent and co-operation to the prevalent scheme of money-raising by suppers and sales and even by gambling? How are Christian parents to keep the confidence of and fellowship with their children, and yet uphold the divine standard of separation from the world and of chastity of life when even so much in the teaching received in school and college cuts directly across home training? What is to be the answer of every truly Christian woman to the wholly unscriptural propaganda for birth control? How is a completely yielded young Christian to have any social life in a town where there is nothing going on but the movie, the dance, or the petting party? These are but a few of the innumerable problems earnest Christians face in present-day life. How are they to be solved? When one seeks counsel from others, he often receives quite contradictory advice from equally trusted friends. Does God give us no light on these problems and no clue to their solution? He surely does, and in I Corinthians 1 and 2 gives us a working basis for a walk in wisdom.

He speaks there of two kinds of wisdom which are exact opposites. There is a wisdom which belongs to the sphere of the world, the flesh and the devil. It is "the wisdom of this world" (I Cor. 1:20; 2:6); "the wisdom of men" (I Cor. 2:5); "the wisdom of the princes of this world" (I Cor. 2:6, 8). God shows us the utter worthlessness of such wisdom, for He says it is foolishness, ungodly, antagonistic to Christ crucified and to His Cross, and that it will come to naught (I Cor. 1:18, 20, 21, 23; 2:6). Sad and tragic is the truth that the *control* of the present-day Church is largely in the hands of these worldly-wise men, and its program, being planned according to their worldly-wise methods, is as far from the eternal purpose of God which He purposed in Christ, as revealed in Ephesians, as the heavens are from the earth. This is the primary reason for the powerlessness and fruitlessness of the Church in this tremendous world crisis and for the closing down of so many churches and forms of Christian work.

But there is another wisdom which belongs to the heavenly sphere of the triune God. It is "the wisdom of God" (I Cor. 1:21; 2:7); Christ Himself (I Cor. 1:24, 30; hidden and eternal (I Cor. 2:7); revealed and taught by the Spirit (I Cor. 2:10, 13); can be known only by the spiritual man (I Cor. 2:15). This wisdom is of infinite worth. The first century Church was under the control of men "full of the Holy Ghost and wisdom" (Acts 6:3) of this heavenly nature. Knowing the purpose of God, having the mind of Christ, and depending upon the guidance of the Spirit, the Church of Christ was multiplied and edified under their ministry. Inspired and guided by this divine wisdom—a spiritual remnant within the present-day Laodicean Church dares to take a courageous stand for both the truth and the standards of the divine Word regarding the creed and the conduct of the affairs of the Church.

God shows us that this heavenly wisdom is for us in Christ and is made ours by the Spirit.

I Cor. 1:24. "But unto them which are called, both Jews and Greeks, *Christ* the power of God and *the wisdom of God."*

I Cor. 1:30. "But of him are ye in *Christ Jesus, who of God is made unto us wisdom."*

I Cor. 2:12. "Now we have received not the spirit of this world, but *the Spirit which is of God;* that we might know things that are freely given us of God."

So God has made ample provision that every step of the walk of His child may be in wisdom.

Manifestation of the Walk in Wisdom

5:16. "Redeeming the time, because the days are evil."

"Redeeming the time"—translated "to buy up an article out of the market in order to make the largest profit out of it"; or as another has put it, "Grasp at each opportunity like merchants who eagerly buy up a scarce commodity." A casual reading of this verse would leave the impression that it was a strange thought to introduce

here, and that it has no vital connection with a walk in wisdom. But study and meditation upon it will convince one that in a brief epistle where only essential things are mentioned, this is one of the most necessary exhortations. For surely a walk in wisdom does not just happen; it is not a thing of chance. It requires study, prayer, meditation, consideration of every problem from every angle, above all an intimate knowledge with practical understanding of the Word of God. So this short phrase is worthy of the place given it, and should be committed to memory, pondered and obeyed by every Christian.

"Time." How do you consider time? Is it such a valuable thing, or such a scarce commodity that you feel the need of guarding every moment, and of giving most careful thought to the use of every hour? Do you eagerly grasp every opportunity to employ it so as to bring the largest profit to God, to others, and to yourself? Or, perchance, are you one of those murderers who kills time, hour upon hour, day after day, with no consciousness of the enormity of such sin?

"Redeeming"—what an amazing word to use here! Can it be that even time has not been in our own control, but in that of another who has caused us to misuse it, and to neglect countless opportunities to better our own life and to help others? If time is such an extremely precious thing in the sight of God that He exhorts us to redeem it, then the waste of time must be a real sin, to be recognized and confessed. Someone has truly said, "You can utilize almost any kind of waste except waste of time."

Time is short. Every moment counts. The saint who lives in Christ in the heavenlies will value time as a link with eternity, and will measure the passing hour with an eternal yardstick. *"Because the days are evil,"*—appallingly, fearsomely evil. Moral corruption in all its hideous forms grows apace, filling the whole world with a black cloud that threatens the very destruction of humanity. What a challenge to the Christian to seize upon every fitting occasion and to avail himself of every opportunity to let the light that is in him flood the darkness around him!

Maintenance of a Walk in Wisdom

5:17. "Wherefore be ye not unwise, but *understanding what the will of the Lord is."*

"Wherefore be ye not unwise." The days may be evil and the difficulties of a wise walk may be very great, but that is no excuse for folly or carelessness or neglect of duty on our part. We need

not walk as those without sense or intelligence, for God would never require a walk in wisdom without making full provision for it.

"But understanding what the will of the Lord is." This is the supreme necessity and the fundamental secret of a walk in wisdom. God has made His will known to us, as we have already seen in Part I, and He has not kept us in the dark regarding His eternal purpose and plan. His will has been revealed and unfolded to us in His Word. To walk in the whole will of God requires us to walk in the whole truth of God's Word. In that Word He has given either principles or precepts to cover every step of our walk in wisdom, and has accompanied them with commands, warnings, exhortations and examples, so that we may know His will with certainty. But there can be no thorough understanding of God's will without a systematic, prayerful study of God's Word under the tutelage of the Holy Spirit, whose task it is to open the eyes of our understanding and to enlighten us (1:7).

Dear friend, have you been neglecting the study of the Bible, and in consequence have you deviated from a walk in God's ways and been deflected from the doing of His will? If so, it needs to be confessed as a very real and serious sin that has opened doors of your life to the devil and given him place (4:27). To "redeem the time" will mean for you some portion of your day set apart deliberately and purposefully for the study of His Word, to understand His will. Then, and only then, will you be enabled to walk in wisdom.

6. A WALK IN PRAISE

While Paul does not use the word "walk" in 5:18-20, yet he is describing a life habitually filled with praise as a direct result of being filled with the Spirit. So we have seen in these verses the sixth characteristic of a worthy walk to be one in praise.

The passage opens with another of Paul's vivid contrasts:

5:18. "And *be not drunk with wine,* wherein is excess; but *be filled with the Spirit.*"

Counterfeit Pleasure

No pleasure that derives its satisfaction from the gratification of the desires of the flesh, or from the stimulation of the excitements of the world, can ever be beneficial. One such fleshly appetite Paul specifically denounces: *"Be not drunk with wine."* Drunkenness robs the drinker of all self-control; stimulates every part of his life with a false excitement; animates his entire nature with a counterfeit pleasure; throws his entire personality out of adjustment; destroys the power of his mind and will to function normally, and leads to moral, mental and physical disorder.

As we consider the contrast made, surely Paul's reference is broader than to drunkenness only, and includes every form of indulgence that stimulates falsely and detrimentally. There is a legitimate place for real re-creating pleasure in every one's life. But to-day people, old and young, seek "a good time" through the kind of pleasure that produces a momentary thrill, but often leaves one dejected in mind, jaded in body, reproached in conscience, and leaves a tragic trail of sorrow and heartache in its wake. Just this week I listened to an extremely pitiable tale of a highly respectable school teacher from a good home who in a public place drank her first cocktail, not knowing that through that one drink she would be robbed of her personal purity and bring sorrow and disgrace to her family.

Christian Joy

Over against such a travesty of pleasure Paul places this blessed experience: *"But be ye filled with the Spirit."*

But—one need never live on any plane but the highest. God does not offer the once confirmed drunkard something a bit less harmful or a bit more beneficial, nor does He suggest mere reformation in regard to drunkenness. But He offers him *the best* in exchange for *the worst;* the true in place of the false. God does not wish His children to live just on a *higher plane,* but on the *highest* plane.

"Be filled with the Spirit."—The fulness of the triune God, Father, Son and Spirit, is the Christian's heritage. This is the keynote of Ephesians (3:19; 4:13; 5:18). To make us possessors of this fulness is the work of the Holy Spirit. To do it He must have absolute sway over us through complete control. We must be filled with the Spirit. Fulness imparts to the Christian the power of self-control; animates his heart with pure joy; invigorates his whole being with newness of life; brings his spirit, soul and body into right adjustment; enhances the power of mind, heart and will to fulfil the divine purpose, and leads to spiritual, moral, mental and physical wholeness.

Drunkenness with wine and the filling with the Spirit are two contrasted states that produce visible results that are extraordinary. A drunkard is so intoxicated by wine that he is incapacitated for normal life and work, while the man who is filled with the Spirit is thereby made normal and prepared for any kind of fruitful ministry. When a man is drunk he has lost self-control and given himself over completely to the influence of wine, while the Spirit-filled man has gained self-control by voluntarily placing himself under the control of the divine Spirit. The drunken man cannot hide his drunkenness, for his walk and his talk disclose his condition. So the fulness of the Spirit cannot be concealed, for the Spirit-filled man attracts attention by his truly separated walk and sanctified talk. Not only will his life be in marked distinction from that of the unregenerate man, but it will also be manifestly different from that of the worldly, carnal Christian. To be drunk implies a craving for wine that will not be satisfied with anything but wine. The drunkard has but one consuming desire—to drink wine; to satisfy which he will sacrifice everything else in life, however precious. To become filled with the Spirit implies thirst on the part of the Christian for the living water, the Holy Spirit, that will not be content with anything less than fulness, and that makes him willingly yield all for the sake of this priceless treasure. The drunkard to remain drunk must keep on craving and drinking wine. So the Christian to remain Spirit-filled must keep on thirsting and drinking the living water.

A Twofold Command

"Be not drunk." This was a command spoken to every Christian in that Ephesian church, from the deacons and elders on down to the newest, weakest convert just out of paganism. No one was exempt, and disobedience to this command would have been considered gross and glaring sin.

"Be ye filled." This also was a command spoken with equal authority and insistence to every member of the church at Ephesus. By the giving of this twofold command God would seem to be saying that He even expected the one who had been habitually drunk in the old life to be now habitually filled in the new. So He would teach us that being filled with the Spirit is not optional, but obligatory; that it is not the privilege of a favoured few, but the perogative of every saint.

Paul then proceeds to show what is the outworking of a Spirit-filled life. Being filled with the Spirit is not an emotional, ecstatic experience which makes one abnormal and fanatical, but it is a sane, joyous experience which makes for a sound mind, a radiant heart, and a poised spirit. The fruit of the Spirit is joy. It is only when filled with the Holy Spirit that one experiences purest pleasure. The whole being of the Spirit-filled Christian is flooded with radiant joy that exhilarates, but at the same time invigorates. The inflow of joy will find its outlet in praise.

Walk in Praise

Praise involves outward expression as well as inward enjoyment. It will find expression in speech, in song and even in silence.

5:19 (R.V.). *"Speaking one to another in psalms and hymns and spiritual songs, singing and making melody with your heart to the Lord."*

In social fellowship one with another praise to the Lord will flavour even our conversation. Murmuring, complaining, discontent, will find no place, for praise to the Lord deep-rooted in our life will bubble up from our hearts through our lips. How feebly most of us have capitalized our opportunities in ordinary conversation to thus glorify the Lord! How the enjoyment of any social gathering of saints would be enhanced by reading together from the Scripture and by worshipping Him in song!

At a summer Conference for students, one young woman gifted with a beautiful voice refused stubbornly to yield her life to the Lord. She left the Conference at its close in a miserable state. One car on the train was filled with delegates from the Conference, and the joy of some hearts burst forth in spiritual songs. One after another joined until everyone was singing but the one with the most beautiful voice of all. She could not open her mouth to sing until she opened her heart to yield. But the Lord conquered, and she yielded herself to Him. Oh, the joy that then poured forth in song, such as she never before had realized!

"Singing to the Lord." Does this not rule out every silly, worldly song? Does it not forbid jazz and all forms of music that foster unwholesome revelry? Is not the motive of the Christian's song to please the Lord and not to entertain himself or others? The new heart will have a new song.

"Making melody in your heart." Perhaps some of us cannot sing, and, if we did, it could hardly be called melody. But there is a song without words that catches the ear of our listening Lord,—the song of praise silently voiced in the heart of a Spirit-filled Christian. Every Christian should be a singing Christian.

5:20. *"Giving thanks always for all things unto God and the Father, in the name of our Lord Jesus Christ."*

"Giving thanks unto God, the Father."—How many times a day do you say "Thank you, Father"? Such a spirit of thankfulness and such an expression of thanksgiving is one of the surest ways of victory over the devil. In olden days when a great multitude of Moabites and Ammonites came against Jehoshaphat to battle, the king first prayed and then appointed singers unto the Lord who, as

they went out before the army, were to say, *"Praise the Lord;* for his mercy endureth forever." And *"when they began to sing and to praise,"* the Lord gave them victory over the enemy.

"Always."—Every real Christian gives thanks sometimes, but who gives thanks *"always"? "For all things."* Every true Christian gives thanks for some things, but who could give thanks for all things, including, as it may, sickness, financial loss, sorrow and trouble of various kinds? It seems an impossible standard. But, if we know of even one life in which there is perpetual thangsgiving in the midst of unceasing suffering, then that proves the possibility. Last night I read a page in the August *Moody Monthly* which told the story and showed the picture of the radiant face of "Lloyd Jensen of Sunshine Corner." I quote from the story hoping it will interpret to you, as it did to me, the meaning of the word "always." Dr. Lockyer writes:

"I was shown into a room of indescribable physical anguish, which I have elected to name, 'Sunshine Corner.' And I shall never cease to praise God for what that visit meant to my soul. Lloyd Jensen, one of God's heroes, has discovered the art of turning a bed of pain into one of the brightest spots on earth. Healthy and active for the first twelve years of his life, at the age of thirteen, a mysterious illness overtook him. The trouble was ultimately diagnosed as the worst form of arthritis, which has since developed into Still disease, a fearful malady resulting in the hardening of the members.

"For over eleven years now, Lloyd has lain in one position on his back. During the last six years, this hero has been perfectly helpless, and cannot move any part of his emaciated frame. All his joints are set. His hands, corrupt and distorted, rest upon a pillow of cotton wool. Exposed, these rock-like, ugly lumps have been fixed upon his chest for almost six years. His legs and feet are gruesome. The mouth cannot open beyond the width of a cracker, and yet it is in this way that his patient mother feeds him with small pieces of food.

"When he first took sick, Lloyd was not a Christian. His young heart was somewhat rebellious at being kept in bed when others of his age could walk and play. The prayers of a godly mother prevailed, however, and through the influence of a radio program, Lloyd became a born-again soul. Two years ago, a very severe heart attack almost sent Lloyd home to heaven. Rallying, he determined to read the Bible through. He felt that shame would be his if he met his Lord without having meditated upon His Word from cover to cover. His Bible rests upon a small music stand and with his head half turned, its only position night and day for years, he reads the open pages, then Mother comes and turns the leaves.

"Of his sufferings Lloyd has nothing to say. If visitors take him sympathy, they soon have to pocket it or expend it upon themselves for having grumbled over little troubles and ailments. To all who come Lloyd smilingly testifies of a Saviour's love."

Lloyd Jensen lives on "Giving-thanks-always-for-all-things" Avenue. Where do you make your home? If you have been living in the slums of murmuring, complaint and discontent, won't you move to-day at least into "Praise" Alley? And soon you will be living way uptown on "Joy" Street or "Thanksgiving" Boulevard, in the precious fellowship of the Spirit-filled Christians of the earth.

"Unto God and the Father."—Unto the One who in infinite wisdom and love has permitted "the all things," whether of joy or sorrow; of pleasure or pain; of gain or loss; and who has permitted them for the very purpose of enabling us to walk worthy of our high calling of "being holy even as he is holy." Not one thing can ever come into the life of one who is called of God that does not work out for his good. God has said so, therefore it is true, and He asks us to believe it and give thanks.

Rom. 8:28. "And we know that *all things work together for good to them that love God, to them who are the called* according to his purpose."

"In the name of our Lord Jesus Christ." As we claim the power and the merit of that blessed Name in offering our petitions, so may we also in offering praise. He who always gave thanks unto His Father for all things will enable us to do it also as we rely upon Him for it.

7. A WALK IN HARMONY

The social order of to-day is disjointed by frightful maladjustments. Government, business, school and home are all being rocked by revolt; lawlessness runs riot over the earth; anarchy grows apace; and everywhere the utter collapse of civilization is feared. Frantic efforts are being made to produce harmony by social legislation and governmental action, but the result is negligible. Ephesians teaches God's way of harmony.

Human Relationships—Harmonized in Christ

The Christian's life can never be isolated. Incorporation into Christ's Body as a member brings organic relationship with every other member.

5:30. "For *we are members of his body.*"

4:25. "For *we are members one of another.*"

Then we should treat fellow-Christians as we would treat ourselves. As there is mutual co-operation of eye with eye, hand with hand, and foot with foot, so should there be mutual co-operation between fellow-members of the mystical Body.

A Walk in Harmony

Paul gives a simple but very workable basis for harmony in all the varied relationships between believers.

5:21 (R. V.). *"Subjecting yourselves one to another* in the fear of Christ."

"Subjecting yourselves." Is it a "hard saying" from which we instinctively turn away? Let us face it courageously as a direct word of the Lord to us personally, and gladly, as one of the first-fruits of a Spirit-filled life. Therefore we know that what seems to us bitter is in reality sweet. *"Subjecting"*—a present participle, indicating a continuous process, an attitude governing every act. *"Yourselves"*—voluntary self-negation rather than to assert one's rights; true humility which esteems others better than one's self, and looks not upon his own things but upon the things of others.

"One to another"—not a one-sided subjection by which some truly lowly-minded, unselfish, retiring Christian becomes the prey of one who is imperialistic, selfish and domineering, but a mutual subjection which demands selflessness and Christlikeness of each alike. One human will does not yield to another human will, but both wills are mutually yielded to the will of God in every matter relating to both persons. Mutual subjection is a voluntary meeting on the common ground of mutual desire to do the will of God in the love of Christ through the guidance of the Spirit.

"In the fear of Christ." There must necessarily be a strong, motivating reason and incentive for such mutual subjection, which is quite foreign to the flesh. Paul finds it to be a reverential fear of displeasing and dishonouring Christ. Paul now turns from the general to the particular, and applies the principle of mutual submission in the Christian home.

Harmony in the Home

The home is the first divine institution. From it human society is replenished. Human society is the home and the family projected and amplified. It is there that the individual is prepared, disciplined and trained to take his place and fulfil his responsibilities in human affairs. Because the home is the unit around which the social structure is built, its importance cannot be over-estimated.

Never were there so many enemies of the home as now which seek to bring about both its degeneration and disintegration. Forces are at work either to destroy it or otherwise to empty it of its occupants, or to rob it of its character-making qualities. There is very little of the old-time cultural home-life. In fact, much of the time of both parents and children is spent outside the home in the auto, at the cinema, the bridge party, the club, the camp. And frequently when the family do gather together for meals, no conversation is possible because the radio does all the talking. One trembles at the increasing number of curbstone homes, and one shudders at the stark tragedy so many of them shelter. Recently a wife was enjoying herself at a bridge party, while her husband at home committed suicide.

Nothing on earth is more beautiful than a truly Christian home where Christ reigns and brings a heavenly harmony, proving that "the greatest gift of Christianity to the social fabric is the Christian home."

The Christian Home

5:22-6:9 pictures a Christian home in its threefold, all-inclusive relationships:

| Husband | Parents | Masters |
| Wife | Children | Servants |

The members of this earthly household are first members of the heavenly. The picture is of a dual family life, the heavenly and the earthly, with the former the pattern for the latter. The standard for the human is determined by the divine. This is made clear in such phrases as "unto the Lord," "even as," "so—as," "in the Lord," "of the Lord," "as unto Christ." Christ is both the Lord and the Life of the Christian home.

Thus in the heavenly relationship all are on the same footing. In Christ all members of the Christian family are one. The wife, child and servant are in Christ as truly as the husband, parent and master. In Christ all are equally possessors of the unsearchable riches of Christ. The wife, child and servant are as truly heirs of God and joint-heirs with Christ as the husband, parent and master. In Christ their spiritual standing is exactly the same; they are spiritual equals in God's sight.

But on the human side of the relationship there is a Scriptural distinction in status which is typical of the vast differences existing between members of human society. Position, age, education, gifts, ability, training, all play a part in determining one's position. To bring about a right adjustment so that harmony reigns in the home is a very necessary thing, and merits the large place given to it in this epistle.

Let us get clearly in mind that such a standard could only be maintained in a Christian home. Paul is writing by inspiration of a harmony produced by Christ as the creator and centre of the Christian home.

Harmony between Husband and Wife

When God sets a standard that seems especially high and difficult, He usually gives us a divine pattern to be followed. This is just what He has done here.

The Divine Prototype

In the first three chapters of Ephesians we saw the Church as the Body of Christ. In Chapter five we see it as His Bride. In one of the most beautiful and profound expositions of the relationship of the heavenly Bridegroom to His Bride, God sets forth the pattern for that of the earthly.

Let us consider the relationship of Christ to the Church, His Bride: Christ first wooed and won the Church through His sacrificial love as the Saviour. He gave Himself to the uttermost for it.

5:25. "Christ *loved* the church and *gave himself* for it."

5:23. "Even as *Christ is the head of the church,* and he is the saviour of the body."

As Head He began to make the Church worthy of His companionship. Having been made a very part of Himself, the Bride must now become like Him, that she might enter into all His life, His purposes and plans. A holy Christ must have a holy Bride, separated from all that pertained to the earthly, and sanctified wholly unto the heavenly. It was the Bridegroom's responsibility to prepare the Bride here and now for presentation unto Himself at that marriage feast in heaven, arrayed in the garments of spotless holiness and glory.

5:26. *"That he might sanctify and cleanse it* with the washing of water by the Word."

5:27. *"That he might present it to himself a glorious church,* not having spot, or wrinkle, or any such thing; *but that it should be holy and without blame."*

As Head it is His responsibility also to provide everything needful for the well-being of the Church. As He knows its trials and troubles, its difficulties and dangers, its material and temporal needs, with perfect devotion and faithfulness He provides all needed to nourish and sustain it (5:29).

Only one thing is stated here concerning the relationship of the Church to Christ:

5:24. "The church is subject unto Christ."

In the divine prototype we may reverently say there is a mutual submission between Christ and the Church. Christ submitted Himself in self-denying, self-sacrificing love, even unto death, for His Bride, whom He cherishes and cares for in the most tender manner. The Church, the Bride, responds with the submission of absolute loyalty in yieldedness and obedience. It is the mutual submission of a pure love for a perfect Lover.

The Human Product

With this high and holy pattern before us, let us now weave the threads of the earthly relationship according to it. The basis for harmony is in the knowledge and recognition of the divinely-appointed relationship between husband and wife, with its resultant responsibility for obedience to God's commands on the part of both. Paul begins by stating the wife's part in making and keeping harmony with her husband:

5:22. (R.V.). "Wives, *be in subjection* unto your own husbands as unto the Lord."

"Be in subjection." Let no Christian wife shrink from this plain statement, nor from its implications. God is speaking and commanding, and this truth should be as readily and gladly received as any other. Let us divest ourselves of all resentment and rebellion as women, and be open-minded and open-hearted to every line of God's holy Word. We shall see shortly that there is nothing to fear from any husband who lives up to his responsibility. God gives both a sufficient incentive and a reason for obedience to this command.

"As unto the Lord." If the submission is made gladly because God asks and expects it, He accepts it as a personal service unto Himself, and our joy will be accordingly. Then the Lord gives the reason for asking for subjection and puts it upon a very high plane:

5:23. "For *the husband is the head of the wife,* even as Christ is the head of the church."

5:24. "Therefore *as the church is subject* unto Christ, *so let the wives be* to their own husbands in everything."

The headship of the husband is by divine appointment. Scripture shows that there is a headship within a headship which is but the shadow of the relationship between Christ and God. The husband's headship over the wife has its roots in Christ's headship over him, while in turn Christ's headship over the husband is rooted in God's headship over Him.

I Cor. 11:3. "For I would have you know that the head of every man is Christ; and the head of the woman is the man; and the head of Christ is God."

Our Lord when on earth did nothing of Himself. He sought only to know and to do His Father's will. In such subjection there was nothing stultifying or degrading. So the subjection of the wife to the headship of her husband, when placed upon such a lofty plane, can in no wise degrade her.

"As the church is subject unto Christ." The nature and extent of the headship now is shown to be in everything that pertains to the life of the home and the family. It is not a slavish obedience to every whim and fancy of unreasonableness and selfishness on the part of the husband, but the loving and joyous subjection of loyalty to love. For the one to whom she is united as "one flesh" she will have only respect and reverence.

5:33. "And the wife see that *she reverence* her husband."

In worldly society to-day one of the most degenerating and degrading factors is the growing and excessive mannishness of women as expressed in clothing, in hair-dress, and in such habits as smoking and drinking. It is also manifested by the entrance of women into fields of work which more properly seem to belong to men. Sad to say, this spirit of usurpation of the privileges and responsibilities of the husband, as head of the family, has invaded many a Christian home, where one sees a masterful wife assume the headship of the home, and where husband and children are quite under her dictation. God is teaching us in Ephesians that this is not His plan, and that it cannot make for harmony in the family life.

Let us now turn in thought to the position and responsibilities of the husband. Five things are stated in regard to it:

5:23. *"The husband is head of the wife,* even as Christ is the head of the church."

"The husband is head of the wife." This may sound very distasteful to modern ears. It may seem to give the husband undue and unfair rights in the marriage relationship. However, if we study this passage with an unbiased, open mind, all such objections should be removed. Let us remember two things. The headship of the husband is by divine appointment. Therefore it is not only right and just, but it is the best and wisest plan for the home. Secondly, let

us remember that the heavenly is the pattern for the earthly. *"Even as Christ is the head of the church."* The marriage of a Christian man and woman is the holy counterpart of the heavenly wedlock. What Christ is in His love-relationship to the Church, the husband is to be to his wife. It does not allow him to be either a bully or a brute. It does not grant him uncontrolled license to do his will or unrestrained liberty to have his way. The responsibilities of such headship are clearly defined.

Christ loves the Church as a very part of Himself. Paul now uses this heavenly pattern to press home still further the husband's responsibility to his wife:

5:28. *"So ought men to love their own wives as their own bodies.* He that loveth his wife loveth himself."

"So ought"—a divine compulsion that exempts no husband. The divine standard can never be lowered. The "ought" of the wife's loyalty is complemented by the "ought" of the husband's love. *"Men to love their wives as their own bodies"*—the very highest human standard of which man is capable of reaching, which, when reached, means that the husband loves his wife as he loves himself.

The husband's headship entails upon him yet one more responsibility: He is to protect and provide for his wife in the same tender and loving way that Christ does for the Church.

5:29. "For no man ever yet hated his own flesh; *but nourisheth and cherisheth it,* even as the Lord the church."

For a man to hate his own flesh would be wholly abnormal and imply serious mental disorder. So there is moral disorder when a husband does not love his wife with a love that makes him self-forgetful in the desire to supply her every need.

5:25. "Husbands, *love your wives, even as* Christ also loved the church and gave himself for it."

"Husbands," put your ear close to this bit of God's Word, and get the full force of these words. Yours is the submission of love which partakes of both the nature and the manner of Christ's love for the Church, His Bride. Christ loved with a love that was utterly selfless and self-sacrificing. He loved, not thinking of what He could *get,* but of what He could *give.* And He gave all that He is and has; He gave Himself unto the uttermost, even of death. Christian husband, "love your wife, *even as."* Then subjection to you on the wife's part will be only a joy and a delight. Then she will reverence you for what you truly are.

We admit readily that such harmony between husband and wife is very beautiful as an ideal and very desirable, but as a standard to be lived out it seems impossible. To be sure, a price must be paid for it on the part of both. And may it not be that a down-payment needs to be made at the very start of married life? In a little sea-side cottage at Peitaiho, China, two missionaries were united in mar-riage at 9:30 one summer morning. The bride-to-be was up at five o'clock, and had one hour in fellowship with her Lord down by the sea. After breakfast she dressed for her wedding, and then for one hour just before the ceremony she and her lover were togther in communion with the Lord Jesus, who Himself united them in a spiritual union which has been unusually harmonious and happy. Should not every Christian home be started with His blessing and benediction if harmony is to prevail?

Harmony between Parents and Children

The harmony in many a home is broken by the maladjustment between parents and children, due very largely to a twofold failure, —disobedience and lack of discipline.

Much is said and written to-day of the revolt of youth. The attitude and the acts of many children show a reckless disregard for parental counsel; a spirit of lawlessness that will suffer no correction or rebuke and brook no interference with their plans; and a restive-ness under restraint, all of which threatens the very foundations of family life. One has seen several times recently accounts of suicide or murder by boys or girls simply because their will was crossed on some matter and they could not have their own way.

To-day there is very little respect for authority or deference for the experience of elders. The tendency in the modern home is for an undue freedom and familiarity which counts it a smart thing for a child to call the parent by his given name, and to tell the parents what to do, instead of listening to the advice of the parents. One of the most difficult and dangerous factors in the situation is that schools and colleges are encouraging this revolt of youth, and their teaching seems purposely aimed at making anarchists and Bolshe-vists of youth. The Satanic lie taught in so many circles, that a child's will is never to be crossed, but only guided, and that every child must be left quite alone to work out his own way in life, is bearing fruit in a ruinous waywardness and an unprecedented flood of lawlessness.

How necessary it is, then, for the Christian youth to go first-hand to the Word and read what God says of his responsibility in making the home harmonious.

6:1. *"Children, obey your parents in the Lord;* for this is right."

"Children" are recognized by God as an integral part of the home. They are placed next to parents in importance in human relationships, for they are not only the fruit of marriage, but are also the future home-makers. Therefore, though treated as children now, they should be trained to be the parents of the next generation.

"Obey"—no stronger word could be used to show that God's command to parents is to exercise parental authority, and to children to practice implicit obedience. In two places in Scripture God reveals His estimate of the heinousness of disobedience to parents when he places it in the list of the most degrading sins of the godless, heathen world (Rom. 1:29-31), and of the sins of lawlessness that characterize the perilous times of the last days (II Tim. 3:1-5). The child that has never learned to obey parents in the home will not find it easy to obey the law of his government or the commands of his God. The obedience God requires is not merely that of action, but also of attitude, which makes a child ready to listen to his parents, willing to heed their advice, and to follow the guidance of more mature minds.

"Your parents." Though the headship of the family resides in the father, yet the plural form of the noun implies that Christian parents should be agreed and united in the discipline of their children, so that the child knows there is no possibility of appeal from one to the other, or for interference on his behalf. The mutual support and strengthening of parents in discipline is absolutely essential if obedience from the child is expected.

"In the Lord." The atmosphere of a Christian home, which is surcharged with the mother's loyalty to and reverence for the father, and the father's love for and tender care of the mother, will inspire in the child the desire to emulate their example of mutual submission by an obedience that does not spring from compulsion or fear, but from love and respect.

"For this is right." From the standpoint of both the human and divine, such obedience is right. Obedience is a fundamental law in all God's universe, so of course it must be in the most intimate of relationships. From every angle it is right; for God's glory, the home's harmony, and the child's good.

Obedience may be given grudgingly and ungraciously because there seems nothing else to do to avoid the penalty of punishment. So another command is given which calls the child to still higher ground:

6:2. *"Honour thy father and thy mother;* which is the first commandment with promise."

To honour parents implies genuine deference to their wishes, respect for their judgment, and trust in their love. Willing, heartfelt honour is instinctively given. Such obedience and honour are enjoined first, because they are right, and then because they reap a rich reward of definite blessings.

Paul now turns to parental responsibility toward children, and gives two definite commands, one negative and the other positive:

6:4. "And ye fathers, *provoke not your children to wrath;* but *bring them up* in the nurture and admonition of the Lord."

"Ye fathers." While the mother has her own definite responsibility for the discipline and development of the children because of her more constant and more intimate companionship with them in the formative period of their lives, yet here again the father is recognized as the head of the family, and especial responsibility is placed upon him for the parental government and the spiritual growth of the children.

"Provoke not your children to wrath"—do not irritate or exasperate or discourage by unreasonable demands, by unnecessary interference, by irritable nagging, by perpetual faultfinding, by harsh criticism, by unceasing "don'ts," by a dictatorial manner, by unjust commands. In the exercise of authority there is great need for understanding, love, justice and self-control. The parent should guard against anything either in the method or the manner of discipline that repels the child, destroys confidence, or wounds his spirit. Parents sometimes wound a child's self-respect by openly and jestingly speaking of faults, or by alluding to personal defects about which the child is keenly sensitive; or they distance the child from them by unreasonable or selfish demands. As a result the child regards home with fear and abhorrence and desires to get away from it as soon as possible.

But the trend of to-day on the part of parents is not toward severity in discipline, but rather of laxity; in many cases even of criminal neglect. A letter recently from one in charge of a Children's Home had this statement: "Each one of these fifty or more children has a case against his parents. Two or three out of the number are orphans; the others have parents who have handed their responsibility over to the state. Awful!" Parents have turned their children loose upon the public for their education and recreation; they are too often either in an auto or a cinema while the parents follow their own pursuits and pleasures. Even many Christian parents sadly fail in the oversight of the social and recreational life of their children. A mother was heard to say to her small boy in a movie theatre: "You must come home, you have been here seven hours." And what had he seen? Let me quote from published reports:

"The Committee of Child Welfare of the League of Nations analyzed two hundred and fifty American films and found in them: 97 murders, 51 cases of adultery, 19 seductions, 22 abductions, 45 suicides. Of the characters in these 250 films there were: 176 thieves, 25 prostitutes, 35 drunkards. Also the Censorship Board sometime ago eliminated from 788 pictures 1811 scenes of assault with guns with intent to kill, 175 scenes of assault with knives, 231 scenes of hanging, 757 scenes of attacks on women for immoral purposes, 929 scenes of nudity and semi-nudity, 21 scenes of jail-breaking. And 115,000,000 people attend the movies every week."

Christian parents, are you allowing your children to attend this school of crime? Worse still, are you setting them an example by going yourself? If so, will you prayerfully consider this matter in the light of God's clear command to you in Ephesians?

"Bring them up." To bring up children is a Scriptural way implies a serious and enlightened assumption of responsibility for their spiritual, moral, mental and physical well-being. This requires wise counsel and guidance in regard to the books they read, the pleasures they seek, the friendships they form, the school or college they attend, and all other matters that relate to character-building. Children are God's gift to parents, and they are also a trust. Will not God one day require Christian parents to give an account of their stewardship of parenthood and of the guardianship of their children? Will you have failed in this most sacred trust?

"In the nurture and admonition of the Lord." The parent needs to be taught and trained of the Lord for the task of teaching and training the child. Many parents, feeling their own incompetency, shirk their responsibility and entrust the spiritual nurture of their children to the minister and the Sunday School teacher. But here in Ephesians, God places squarely upon parents the responsibility for the instruction and training of the child in those things which make for a well-rounded, full-orbed Christian character and service. Such bringing up will include discipline, warning, admonition, correction, above all the teaching of God's Word and fellowship in prayer around the family altar. God tells clearly how it is to be done and to what end:

II Tim. 3:14, 15. "But *continue thou in the things which thou hast learned and hast been assured of,* knowing of whom thou hast learned them; and *that from a child thou hast known the holy Scrip-*

tures, which are able to make thee wise unto salvation through faith which is in Christ Jesus."

A college student once came to me in great perplexity. She was taking a course in Bible which was absolutely destructive of faith in God and in His Word and the exact contradiction of all she had been taught by her parents in family worship since childhood. Her question was, "Shall I continue taking Bible in college?" I asked, "Which teaching do you believe is true, that of your parents or your professor?" She replied, "My parents lived the most godly lives I have ever seen. I believe the Bible as my parents taught it." Christian parents, wouldn't you like to have *your child* say that about you when he gets away from the old home and faces the terrific temptations of modern life that are sweeping so many young men and women into atheism, immorality and crime?

Harmony between Masters and Servants

In the social order of Paul's day, as in our own, there were conditions utterly wrong and unjust. Slavery was prevalent, and among those Ephesian Christians some were slaves and some were slave-owners. Paul, an ardent advocate of righteousness and justice, did not attempt to remake the social order, nor did he counsel rebellion against it on the part of those who suffered from it. Instead of attempting to make a "Christian" social order in a non-Christian world, he taught Christians how to live in a Christian way in the social order of which they formed a part. What he says here to slaves applies equally to all kinds of employees whose labour is sold to another.

6:5. "Servants, *be obedient* to them that are your masters according to the flesh."

"Servants"—a name of honour in that the Lord Jesus Christ Himself was called Jehovah's "servant." *"Be obedient."* Obedience is a rightful obligation of those who are in the employ of another. The secret of harmony within the relationship between servant and master depends upon two things on the servant's part.

The Manner of Service

"With fear and trembling"—with a true eagerness to perform every duty conscientiously and honestly and with a sincere anxiety lest he fail in measuring up fully to his task. *"In singleness of heart"*—with the sincere desire to give undivided loyalty to his master. *"Not with eye-service as men-pleasers"*—not working faithfully merely when the master is on a tour of inspection and for the

sake of gaining his favour. *"With good-will doing service,"* free from resentment and rebellion, and working with the interest of the master at heart and with a real desire to see him prosper.

The Motive in Service

"As unto Christ"—for the sake and the glory of the heavenly Master, remembering that in faithfully serving the earthly master, Christ receives it as service done unto Him. *"As servants of Christ, doing the will of God from the heart."* Their real servitude is to Christ, and in doing His will in whatever circumstances they are placed, they can rejoice even in the most menial service. Such a motive sanctifies all work and enables one to put his whole soul into it. *"As to the Lord, and not to men"*—conscious that his earthly service takes on a heavenly character, so he is able to work motivated by the one desire to please his Lord. *"Knowing that whatsoever good thing any man doeth, the same shall he receive of the Lord, whether he be bond or free."* His earthly master may deny him just recompense for his labour, but not so his heavenly Master whose "Well-done, good and faithful servant," one day he will hear. The rewards withheld on earth will be conferred with certainty in heaven.

Such motives lift service to the highest possible plane and take the sting even out of slavery. It enables the servant to live and work "far above all" in the most difficult and provocative of circumstances, and to do his part to make and keep harmony in the home or place of business.

After a revival in a mission station in China during which many of the Christians had received the fulness of the Holy Spirit, one missionary wrote, "Our hospital is no more like it used to be. There is *perfect harmony* among all the hospital workers from servants on up. All do faithful work. I never have to reprove any of them. I even never have to tell servants what to do. All know their work, and do it faithfully." Filled with the Holy Spirit, both the manner and the motive of every servant's work will be such as to make for harmony.

Paul, then, turns to the Christian master:

6:9. "And, *ye masters, do the same things unto them, forbearing* threatening, knowing that your Master also is in heaven; neither is there respect of persons with him."

"Ye masters"—whoever is in a position which gives him the right to command and control the activities of others. *"Do the same*

things unto them." The general principle of mutual subjection in Christian relationships is here again applied. The master should do unto the servant as he wants the servant to do unto him. As the servant has given himself over to serve his master faithfully and to work only for the master's best interests, so the master in turn should with equal abandon look after the welfare of his servant. The application of this Scriptural principle of mutual subjection of master and servant, to effect mutual benefit and blessing, would solve the baffling and entangling problems of to day between employer and employee. *"Forbearing threatening."* Harsh, violent language intended to intimidate may win a temporary submission to authority, but it will not have won the servant into giving willing and trustworthy service. *"Your Master also is in heaven."* You, too, are a servant. Your Master is your servant's Saviour as well as yours, and in His sight you are no better than he is, though you occupy a higher earthly position. You are His bond-servant, and of you He expects the same manner and motive in service to Him and to others that He has taught your servant to render you. *"Neither is there respect of persons with him."* Christ does not judge by earthly, but by heavenly standards. So the external differences of position, possessions, prestige and power between masters and servants in the flesh mean nothing to Christ in His estimate of the two. As He looks upon the quality of the inward, spiritual life, He may regard the servant even more highly than the master.

Perhaps the thought dominant in some minds is "Are there any homes of the Ephesians' type in the world to-day. Mine is not like that, though I wish it were." One loves to believe there are such homes in different lands where love and loyalty reign and where sweet harmony is the result. But one can be absolutely sure such Scripturally-enjoined harmony is possible when one has seen it and felt its radiant warmth and joyousness. It was my joy once to spend several days in a missionary home in China which sheltered a husband, wife, daughter and son. Love pervaded the home and the hearts of its occupants to an unusual and evident degree. Sweet harmony prevailed. Recently a letter was received from the wife and mother in that family.

The war had devastated the city in which their mission was, and their house had been looted and burned, causing the loss of all their earthly possessions. But their *home,* built upon the enduring foundation of 5:22-6:9, was indestructible, and the *harmony* of it lives on in those four hearts though now unsheltered by brick and mortar, as this quotation from the letter so beautifully proves:

"It is Scriptural to call one's friends together to rejoice with one, is it not? So rejoice with us, for while seventeen out of our twenty buildings in ——— are in ashes, we have gained more than we lost. And, if to-day I could have the brick and mortar back, being minus the precious lessons and the loving, tender watchcare over us through homelessness, I would not want it. Anyway, the ——— home cannot be burnt, it is safe in four hearts for time and eternity. And I am hoping that one day the lad and the lass will establish two homes where they are 'hopelessly in love with each other,' as ——— and I are to this good day, with all praise for said blessings at His feet where they do most surely belong; for two quick tempers, but for His tempering grace, would not have had the home we have had and now have. Then, too, we have thanked God that when the children were small, in fact, as long as they needed it, they had the home, and now both have gone on their way with such memories as humble us before the God who is love."

Part III

THE WARFARE OF THE CHRISTIAN

———————

THE WARFARE OF THE CHRISTIAN

EPHESIANS begins with the Christian in Christ in the heavenlies abounding in his exhaustless wealth as an heir of God and joint-heir with Christ. It continues with the Christian walking worthily of the Lord in loving and joyous fellowship with fellow-Christians, and in the strength and peace of a harmonious home. This would seem to be a suitable place to end the epistle.

But what a change of scene and of atmosphere when we come to 6:10! We are suddenly transplanted from the restful shelter of the home to the rigorous warfare of a battlefield, where we see vast hosts mobilized for conflict; we hear the call to arms, and we smell the smoke of battle. 6:10-18 pictures the Christian facing a foe, forced into warfare. Does this present an anti-climax, and is it a bit disappointing? By no means. It is the inevitable consequence of a life lived in Christ in the heavenlies, filled with the Holy Spirit, and walking as a foreigner through a world "that lieth in the evil one" (I John 5:19 R.V.) and is under his domination. So here we have a clarion call to arms to which every Christian should respond courageously.

1. A CALL TO ARMS

6:10, 12. "Finally, my brethren, *be strong—for we wrestle.*"

"Finally" indicates the close of the epistle, implying also a climax. *"My brethren."* Note that Paul does not call only fellow-apostles, or fellow-pastors, or fellow-evangelists, to arms, but summons fellow-*soldiers*. The arch enemy of Christ is attacking His Body of which the "brethren" are members. Therefore no one of them is exempt from the conflict. God has no place for a spiritual pacifist. Every Christian is conscripted for both defensive and aggressive warfare. He calls every saint to arms. "Not into a religious playground or sports field, but into grim, terrible, bloody conflict are we called."

2. THE ANTAGONISTS

6:12 (R.V.). "For *our wrestling* is not against flesh and blood, but *against the principalities, against the powers, against the world rulers of this darkness, against the spiritual hosts of wickedness* in the heavenly places."

"*Our wrestling against.*" The warfare involves powerful antagonists in terrific, desperate, hand-to-hand battle. Tremendous issues of life and death, defeat and destruction must be at stake, for it is no ordinary combat. The word "against" stands out five times upon the page. We have an out-and-out adversary who is actively and aggressively warring against us, assisted by powerful and wicked allies. "*Not against flesh and blood.*" This negative statement clarifies the atmosphere immediately regarding the nature of our foe. The conflict is not with the human and the visible, but with the superhuman and the invisible. We do not belong to the same order of being or to the same plane of life as our foe.

The Antagonists

Let us marshal the antagonists and their allies before us, and then study their method of warfare.

THE LORD 6:10	"brethren" 6:10 "we"—the saints 6:12
	vs.
THE DEVIL 6:11	"principalities" "powers" 6:12 "world rulers darkness" "spiritual hosts wickedness"

6:10-18 reveals a battlefield where the empowered, energized hosts of the Lord are pitted against the demonized, mobilized hosts of the devil. It is a mass organization of the supernatural forces of heaven against the subtle fiends of hell. One necessity in victorious warfare is to know the enemy. So let us see what Scripture teaches regarding the devil.

Our Adversary—His Person

Scripture everywhere shows Satan as the bitterest enemy of God and His people; the implacable foe of Christ and the Christian. It distinctly warns us against him as a cruel adversary seeking whom he may devour.

I Pet. 5:8. "Be sober, be vigilant, because *your adversary, the devil,* as a roaring lion, *walketh about, seeking whom he may devour.*"

The names given him indicate personality; Satan, spelled with a capital S, deceiver, liar, murderer, accuser, tempter, prince, Apollyon (destroyer), the evil one, Beelzebub. Every name is repulsive and repellent, and discloses his nature. God speaks also of "the working of Satan," and every one of his works, which are defined as "wiles" (6:11), "devices" (2 Cor. 2:11), "snares" (1 Tim. 2:24), reveal personality. He beguiles, seduces, opposes, resists, deceives, sows tares, hinders, buffets, tempts, persecutes, blasphemes. Every work of Satan is diabolical and destructive. Our Lord spoke of Satan many times, and every time in a way and by a name that confirms his personality. Our adversary, then, is personal, aggressive, intelligent, cunning and destructive, who is to be reckoned with seriously, vigilantly and intelligently.

Our Adversary—His Position

He occupies a very superior position which is twofold. In governmental authority he is a "prince" in two localities—in the earth and in the air; and rules over both evil men and evil spirits. Christ never acknowledged Satan as king, but three times he calls him *"the prince of this world,"* thereby acknowledging his governmental authority. Ephesians teaches that he is the ruling spirit over "the children of disobedience," which includes all unregenerate mankind.

2:3. *"The spirit that now worketh in the children of disobedience."*

Satan also has control over the nations and is the master mind behind the whole system of world government dominated by lust for power, greed, ambition, intrigue, hatred, lies, aggression, rivalry, and brutality. Satan offered Christ all the kingdoms of this world with their power and glory if He would but worship him. Christ did not dispute his claim to their control. Moreover, Christ plainly says there is a kingdom of Satan (Matt. 12:26). Ephesians teaches that the devil heads the rulers of the darkness of this world.

6:12. "Our wrestling is against *the world rulers of this darkness.*"

Satan has governmental authority, also, over a vast host of demons and evil spirits. The devil has his angels (Matt. 25:41). Ephesians teaches that he rules as prince over hosts of evil spirits in the aerial heavens.

2:2. "Wherein in time past ye walked according to *the prince of the power of the air*."

6:12. "Against *the spiritual hosts of wickedness* in the heavenly places."

There is, then, an evil one (6:16) presiding over a Satanic government composed of powerful potentates of exalted position, with tremendous authority, who have in their employ hosts of evil spirits with ability and power to control and govern human affairs. It is a perfected mass organization of hellish forces working secretly and subtly against heavenly forces.

6:12. "Our wrestling is against {
principalities
powers
world rulers darkness
spiritual hosts wickedness"

Scripture accords Satan another title and position which shows that he has gone to the utmost limit of revolt against God in seeking and getting the worship of men. He trespasses upon the most sacred in the spiritual realm and becomes the god of this age.

II Cor. 4:4. "In whom *the god of this age* hath blinded the minds of them which believe not, lest the light of the glorious gospel of Christ, who is the image of God, should shine unto them."

Satan has set up within his kingdom what someone has aptly called "a state religion." It is *an exact counterfeit* of true Christianity. Satan has his "synagogue" (Rev. 2:9); his gospel which is "a different gospel" (Gal. 1:6 R.V.) from that of God's grace and redemption through the precious blood of Christ; his "ministers" who pose as ministers of righteousness (II Cor. 11:14); his "doctrines" (I Tim. 4:1), though his ministers decry creeds, while having a well-defined creed of their own which is a denial of all the fundamentals of the Christian faith; his "sacrifices," "communion," "table," and "cup" (I Cor. 10:20, 21), all devoted to Satanic worship; his "depths" (Rev. 2:24), for there is no extreme of imitation and deception to which he does not go to satisfy the innate religious instincts in man as long as it stops short of true, living faith in Christ. Satan will even permit his followers to have the Cross as a symbol hung on the wall, made into a bookmark, worn as an ornament, worshipped even as a thing. In lands where one is constantly confronted with the Cross as a symbol two persons said, "I love the *Cross*, but I hate the *blood*." Only a Satanic counterfeit has a *bloodless* cross. Behind all false systems of religion, ancient and modern, all cults, by whatever name, all error, however garbed, is this arch-heretic and supernatural apostate. Satan presides as "god" over the apostate Christendom of all centuries.

Our Adversary—His Power

The power of the devil is very definitely acknowledged in Scripture, so, for us to deny it when God admits it, is sheer folly. In fact, men are held captive by the power of Satan until delivered from it by the power of the Saviour.

Acts. 26:17. "The Gentiles unto whom I now send thee, to open their eyes, and to turn them from darkness to light and *from the power of Satan unto God.*"

The power of Satan is "the power of darkness"—malign (Col. 1:13); "the power of the air"—invisible (2:2); "the working of Satan with power and lying wonders"—supernatural (II Thes. 2:9); "the power of death"—destructive (Heb. 2:14). It is the power of that awful, "great red dragon" (Rev. 12:3) and like unto that of the king of beasts, "a roaring lion" (I Pet. 5:8).

Satan is not only powerful in himself, but he is mightily equipped and strongly entrenched for this warfare. He is "the strong man armed" (Lk. 11:21). He has his "strongholds" (II Cor. 10:4); his "palace" (Lk. 11:21); his "armour" (Lk. 11:22); his "hosts" (6:12); and he has carried from the battlefield mighty "spoils" (Lk. 11:22).

Our adversary is a supernatural person occupying a superior position and exercising supernatural power. He is supreme dictator over the kingdom of evil; a pastmaster in every phase of diabolical deception and deviltry to be used in the seduction and destruction of human souls, and the instigator of all hatred and rebellion toward God and His Son. In the light of such a revelation, what utter folly for anyone to underestimate or ignore the power of the devil!

Our Adversary—His Purpose

From Genesis through Revelation Satan is revealed as an archtraitor in open revolt against God. Was he always thus? He could not have been so, for among his many names are two very beautiful ones: "Lucifer, son of the morning, the shining one" (Is. 14:12), descriptive of his person, and "the anointed cherub" (Ez. 28:14), indicative of his position. Evangelical scholars believe that Ezekiel 28:11-19 reveals Satan as he was originally in person, position and power. As Lucifer, son of the morning, he was God's noblest and most beautiful angelic creation. "Perfect in beauty and in all his ways" and "full of wisdom," he was a being gifted with marvellous intelligence and glorious in holiness (Ez. 28:12, 15). In position also he surpassed all other created beings, being nearer to God Himself and in closer relationship to His throne. He was entrusted with the exalted position of "the anointed cherub," which probably gave him governmental authority over the angels of God and may also have made him a prince over the primeval creation. Possibly he also led the worship of the angelic hosts. Such a position gave him power second to that of God alone. This perfect creature in that exalted position with this mighty power was called by God "Lucifer, son of the morning," meaning "daystar."

But, incredible as it seems, his heart was lifted up with pride, which led to self-exaltation, ending in rebellion (Ez. 28:15-18). Open revolt against God followed, and Lucifer, son of the morning, became Satan, father of the night, and king over the kingdom of darkness, Satan would no longer be second in position and power, but first. So he purposed to dethrone God in His own universe as sovereign and to displace Him in the worship of angels and men by becoming their god.

Is. 14:12, 13. "How art thou fallen from heaven, O Lucifer, son of the morning! For thou hast said in thine heart, I will ascend into heaven, I will exalt my throne above the stars of God; I will sit also upon the mount of the congregation, I will ascend above the height of the clouds, I WILL BE LIKE THE MOST HIGH."

When Lucifer said "I will," sin began in God's universe. How awful was the fall of heaven's greatest and most glorious archangel! Satan's sin was high treason, and brought down upon him the immediate condemnation and punishment of God. He was cast out of heaven and the immediate presence of God and deprived of his position.

Ez. 28:16. Thou hast sinned: therefore *I will cast thee as profane out of the mountain of God."*

Is. 14:12. "How art thou *fallen from heaven."*

He was ultimately to be deprived of all power and brought down to hell.

Is. 14:15. *"Yet thou shalt be brought down to hell."*

Hereupon his hatred of God began to be crystallized into a well-defined plan with a definite objective.

Our Adversary—His Plan

Satan's revolt against God precipitated a rebellion among some of the angelic host in heaven, who transferred their allegiance and worship to him and became his obedient servants.

II Pet. 2:4. "For if God spared not *the angels that sinned,* but cast them down to hell, and delivered them into chains of darkness, to be reserved unto judgment."

Matt. 25:41. "Then shall he say unto them also on the left hand, Depart from me, ye cursed, into everlasting fire, *prepared for the devil and his angels."*

As soon as God created man and placed him in the garden of Eden, Satan was there seeking to extend his kingdom and establish it on earth by tempting Adam and Eve into self-will and disobedience to God. He succeeded, and they became the first human subjects in the kingdom of darkness and the first slaves of the devil. With this beginning, he began to build up a world-system that holds captive all of mankind that refuses to accept God's way of redemption and to obey and worship God. As "prince of the power of the air" and as "prince of this world," Satan now had the beginning of his spiritual and human hosts of wickedness, through whom he would work to establish a kingdom that would overthrow and supersede God's kingdom in heaven and upon earth.

To understand his plan of accomplishing this, we must never lose sight of his declared objective, which was to be *like* the Most High. Then Satan would make himself as near a counterfeit of God as possible and his plan of action would imitate that of God. God had a Son whom He had appointed heir of all things and by whom He had made the worlds: who was the brightness of his glory, and the express image of His person, who upheld all things by the word of his power, (Heb. 1:2, 3). Did Lucifer, who was "full of wisdom," know this, and was it perhaps one cause of his revolt in heaven? Could it account in part for his implacable hatred of the Son of God? However that may be, the plan of this arch-traitor will one day culminate in "the man of sin," "the son of perdition," who is the Antichrist, who will appear on earth claiming to be God and taking the place of God.

II Thes. 2:3, 4. "That *man of sin* be revealed, the *son of perdition, who opposeth and exalteth himself above all that is called God, or that is worshipped;* so that *he as God sitteth in the temple of God, showing himself that he is God."*

"That man of sin,"—the very incarnation of sin in its highest development of treachery and apostasy, the man in whom sin will have found its most comprehensive expression and in whom Satan will have his most perfect tool. As the Christ is the Representa-

tive man of redeemed and holy humanity, so the Antichrist will be the representative of unregenerate mankind which refuses redemption.

To this man of sin Satan will give power, his throne and his authority, and place him as his own personal representative in the warfare against the Lord and His saints.

Rev. 13:2-4, 7, 8 (R.V.). *"The dragon gave him his power, and his throne, and great authority* . . . and the whole earth wondered after the beast; and *they worshipped the dragon,* because he gave his authority unto the beast; and they worshipped the beast, saying, Who is like unto the beast? and who is able to war with him? . . . And it was given unto him to make war with the saints, and to overcome them; and there was given him authority over every tribe and people and tongue and nation. And all that dwell on the earth shall worship him, everyone whose name hath not been written from the foundation of the world in the book of life of the Lamb that hath been slain."

Satan, then, is a self-constituted sovereign over a rebel government. A deep-dyed traitor is in the midst who is ruler over a kingdom of darkness whose subjects are all moral intelligences, angelic or human, celestial or earthly, of all centuries and climes, who are in revolt against God and therefore are outside of His kingdom. To his Satanic activities are due the present awful state of world affairs, the appalling apostasy in Christendom, the growth of multitudinous false religions and counterfeit world movements, all of which are devised and used by him to prepare the world to receive "the lawless one," to believe his lie, and to worship him as its deliverer and God.

The Result of Satan's Revolt

The high treason of Satan, which knew no bounds in its perfidy and proved capable of no repentance, made two demands upon God. Just retribution must be meted out to Satan and all angels and men who followed him in revolt against God, and a place must be prepared for them outside of God's domain. In the sublime statement of Genesis 1:1 we read that "In the beginning God created the heaven and the earth." But God did not create an underworld. It was Satan who necessitated the lake of fire for rebels like himself. So God prepared a place for the devil and his angels, and all men who refuse the redemption offered in His dear Son will go there.

Matt. 25:41. "Depart from me, ye cursed, *into everlasting fire prepared for the devil and his angels."*

Satan's revolt had caused a terrible disarrangement in God's ordered universe, requiring a reconciliation unto God of all things both in heaven and in earth (Col. 1:20). Adam's fall made a third demand upon God—a way of redemption for sinners who desired to escape from the servitude of Satan. With the fore-knowledge of Deity God was prepared for this revolt, and a way out to perfect victory was made "according to the purpose of him who worketh all things after the counsel of his own will" (1:11). He willed that His kingdom must be freed of every rebel and of every trace of rebellion; every enemy must be put under His feet, and everything must be brought into subjection to Him, and He must become all and in all as He was at the beginning. This was to be accomplished through His Son.

I Cor. 15:24, 25, 28 (R.V.). "Then cometh the end, when he shall deliver up the kingdom to God, even the Father; when he shall have abolished all rule and all authority and power. *For he must reign, till he hath put all his enemies under his feet.* And when all have been subjected unto him, then shall the Son also himself be subjected to him that did subject all things unto him, *that God may be all in all."*

God's Eternal Purpose

We meet this eternal purpose of God at the very threshold of Ephesians, and its outworking in part is unfolded to us in the epistle. In the eternal counsels of the triune God it was determined to carry out God's purpose of retribution, redemption and reconciliation through *the Son,* who by stages covering many millenniums of human history would become *the seed, the Saviour* and *the Sovereign.*

3:16. "According to the eternal purpose which he proposed in Christ Jesus our Lord."

The SON—
  { Christ —the seed of the woman
  { Jesus —the Saviour of sinners
  { Lord —the Sovereign of heaven and earth

Three cords run through Scripture which mark the trail of God's eternal purpose. There is the *black* cord that starts with the treason of Satan in heaven, blackens the entire course of human history, and ends in the torment of Satan and all his followers in hell. There is the *red* cord of salvation according to the riches of His grace that begins in heaven with "the Lamb slain before the foundation of the world," leads to the Cross of Calvary on Golgotha, and ends in heaven with the adoring worship of the redeemed. Then there is the *golden* cord of sovereignty, with its beginning in heaven in the eternal Son made heir of all things, which runs the whole length of humiliation and suffering of the incarnate, crucified Son on earth, and ends in the throne in heaven of the risen, exalted, sovereign Lord.

God's All-inclusive Plan

God's eternal purpose eventuated in a three-fold plan.

Conquest over Satan

Satan's apparent victory in the garden of Eden was in reality his death-knell. The sin of Adam and Eve gave opportunity for the manifestation of God's grace. "For where sin abounded grace did much more abound." God made a way of salvation from sin for Adam and Eve and for all men who wish to escape from the sovereignty and slavery of Satan. In that dark hour at the very dawn of human history, God gave the promise of a Saviour, who would defeat and destroy Satan, and nullify his work through the redemption of man. The coming Conqueror would be Christ, *the seed* of the woman.

Gen. 3:14, 15. "The Lord God said unto the serpent . . . *I will put enmity between thee and the woman,* and *between thy seed and her seed*: it shall bruise thy head, and thou shalt bruise his heel."

The enmity between Satan's seed and the woman's seed results in a double bruising. Here the very heart of God's eternal purpose is revealed—the Cross upon which hangs a bleeding Saviour made Victor over a fatally-bruised Satan.

It is most fascinating to trace the two seeds through the Old Testament. The overshadowing of the seed of the woman is most beautiful as one sees how God chose an elect nation—the Jewish, through which the Messiah should come: then a tribe,—Judah; then a king,—David; until finally the time approaches for the Virgin Mary to bring forth a Son. Side by side all through the prophecies run the two cords, the red and the golden, as we see Christ, the Messiah, a suffering Saviour as in Isaiah 53, and a triumphant Sovereign as in Isaiah 11. The black trail of Satan's seed is seen everywhere, as he seeks by every conceivable cunning to destroy the seed of the woman. But God frustrates every crafty plan of Satan, and defeats him stage by stage.

The day long promised dawned and "the seed royal" was born of a virgin. His name was called JESUS,—*the Saviour* of sinners.

Matt. 1:21. "And she shall bring forth a son and *thou shalt call his name JESUS, for he shall save his people from their sins.*"

Luke 2:10. "For *unto you is born* this day in the city of David, *a Saviour,* who is Christ, the Lord."

It is the finished work of this Saviour that we find in Ephesians I-II, where we see Christ made HEAD of the Church, which is His Body, composed of the redeemed out of every race, nation, people and tribe. In this present age of grace the HEAD works through the Body, carrying out to its fruition God's redemptive plan. The supreme task of the Church is to preach and teach the gospel of full and free salvation through a Saviour by which sinners are delivered out of the kingdom of Satan and are made saints in Christ. The whole force of Satan's implacable hatred for Christ is now lashed like a hurricane against the Church and the Christian who are the Lord's faithful witnesses and wrestlers. This is the warfare of 6:10-18.

Reconciliation of all things in heaven and upon earth

God's eternal purpose will not be fulfilled until all things in heaven and upon earth are brought into reconciliation through subjection to the Son. Ephesians speaks of a double headship. He, who in this age as the risen Saviour is Head over the Church, in the age to come will gather all things together in Himself and exercise headship as the Sovereign Lord over all things.

1:10. "That in the dispensation of the fulness of times *he might gather together in one all things in Christ,* both which are in heaven, and which are on earth; even in him."

We have considered our adversary, the devil, who is one of the two antagonists in this spiritual warfare; we have also briefly reviewed God's purpose in His Son, who is the other opponent, and His plan of campaign through Him for Satan's overthrow and destruction. Let us now turn to consider the person, position and power of Satan's antagonist. If in victorious warfare it is necessary to know the enemy and to estimate aright his resources and power, it is even more essential to know the greater prowess and power of the Conqueror, and thus be assured of our own invincibility in Him.

Satan's Antagonist—His Person

Who is the One who is mentioned sixty-six times in the six short chapters of Ephesians? Let His names tell us Who He is. Twenty-seven times He is called "Christ"; thirteen times "the Lord"; six times each "Christ Jesus" and "the Lord Jesus Christ"; five times "Jesus Christ"; and once each "Jesus," "Lord Jesus," "Christ Jesus our Lord," "Son of God," and "Master." Could anything tell us more clearly that the One with whom Satan has to reckon is the God-man. And God told us this in matchless language centuries ago through the prophet Isaiah.

Is. 9:6, 7. "For *unto us a child is born, unto us a son is given;* and the government shall be upon his shoulder; and his name shall be called Wonderful, Counsellor, The mighty God, The everlasting Father, The Prince of Peace. And of the increase of his government and peace there shall be no end, and upon the throne of David, and upon his kingdom, to order it, and to establish it with judgment and with justice from henceforth even forever."

"Unto us a child is born"—a Babe lies in that Bethlehem manger, born as no other child ever had been or ever would be born. Mary, his mother, "was found with child of the Holy Ghost" (Matt. 1:18), and the angel said unto her, "that holy thing which shall be born of thee shall be called the Son of God." "They shall call his name Emmanuel, which being interpreted is, *God with us.*" No wonder He is called "Wonderful!" The Son of God born of woman! The God-man! *"Unto us a son is given."* The child is *born*; the Son is *given.* The Babe of Bethlehem is none other than the eternal Son, who was with the Father before the world was (John 17:5); the only begotten Son in the bosom of the Father (John 1:18); The Word, that in the beginning was God (John 1:1); which was made flesh (John 1:14); the Lamb slain from the foundation of the world (Rev. 13:8); Christ, the Messiah, foretold by the Old Testament prophets as the Lord, the mighty God, the everlasting Father, The Prince of Peace, who would rule the world in righteousness and peace. What names He bears! revealing Him to be God's beloved Son and Servant and man's beneficent Saviour.

Satan's Antagonist—His Position

A child is born. To what end? To die. A Son is given. To what end? To reign. To fulfil the eternal purpose of God, the eternal Son became the incarnate, crucified, risen, ascended, exalted Son. God Himself tells the story in a matchless way:

Phil. 2:6-11. "Who, being in the form of God, thought it not robbery to be equal with God; but made himself of no reputation, and took upon him the form of a servant, and was made in the likeness of men: and being found in fashion as a man, he humbled himself, and became obedient unto death, even the death of the cross. Wherefore God also hath highly exalted him, and given him a name which is above every name: that at the name of Jesus every knee should bow, of things in heaven, and things in earth, and things under the earth."

The Incarnate Son

Out of eternity into time, out of heaven to earth, came the Son of God to become the Son of man. He took the body supernaturally prepared for Him (Heb. 10:5), in which He lived a perfect life fulfilling every demand of the law for righteousness and holiness; doing beneficent works that manifested the love, compassion and mercy of His holy nature; doing the Father's will from the largest to the smallest thing in life. Then He voluntarily laid down that body in death (Heb. 10:10). Satan, who, until our Lord's resurrection, had the power of death, tried in every possible way to destroy the human body of Jesus; to overthrow it through Herod, to overcome it in the wilderness, to overstrain it in Gethsemane, that he might keep it from the death of the Cross. But He was born to die on Calvary's Cross, and no power of Satan could frustrate the redemptive death of the Saviour.

The Crucified Son

Thwarted in his attempts to keep Christ from going to the Cross, Satan tried through the voice of priests and people to persuade Christ to come down from the Cross before those triumphant words "It is finished" could be spoken. But our blessed Conqueror was "obedient unto death, *even the death of the Cross*," for through *that death alone* could He destroy the devil and his works, and gain an eternal victory for God and for man over their adversary, the devil. The whole outcome of the age-long conflict, yea, the fulfilment of God's eternal purpose and His prophecy-promise of Genesis 3:15 hung upon the death of the crucified One. When the anguished cry "My God, my God, why has thou forsaken me?" came from the lips and heart of the dying Saviour, it seemed as though Satan had triumphed. But another moment passes, and with the strong voice of One consciously achieving His long-promised mission of conquest and deliverance, the Saviour cried, "It is finished."

Satan's destruction was accomplished through the death of Christ.

Heb. 2:14, 15. "Forasmuch then as the children are partakers of flesh and blood, he also himself likewise took part of the same; *that through death he might destroy him that had the power of death,* that is, the devil; and deliver them who through fear of death were all their lifetime subject to bondage."

Satan's works also were destroyed.

I John 3:8. "He that committeth sin is of the devil; for the devil sinneth from the beginning. *For this purpose the Son of God was manifested, that he might destroy the works of the devil."*

Satan's workers also were included in Christ's conquest over all the foes of God and the forces of evil.

Col. 2:15. "And *having spoiled principalities and powers,* he made a show of them openly, *triumphing over them in it."*

Weymouth's translation of this verse is very telling and throws light on 6:12. "And the hostile princes and rulers He shook off from Himself and *boldly displayed them as His conquests, when by the Cross He triumphed over them."* Through the death of the Cross the victory is the Lord's. The enemy and all his forces were routed. The principalities and powers were disarmed and so completely conquered that a public spectacle could be made of them with great boldness.

The Risen, Ascended Son

Satan well knew the prophecy of Genesis 3:15 had been fulfilled. The Son lived and died as Saviour. But the dead Christ must be kept dead, that God's redemptive purpose might yet be frustrated and Christ might not reign as Conqueror. So the resurrection was opposed by all the forces of the evil one. The sepulchre was sealed. A watch was set over it. But by the working of the mighty power of God Christ arose (1:20) and, ascending, passed triumphantly through Satan's realm as "prince of the power of the air," and was seated at the Father's right hand in the heavenlies, *"far above all"* the spiritual hosts of wickedness arrayed against Him.

The Exalted Son

As we enter Ephesians we are ushered immediately into the throne room where we meet the triumphant Conqueror, the Victor-Son, the supreme Lord of the universe, the Head over the new race of redeemed men. During our whole stay in Ephesians, whether we walk before men on earth or engage in warfare with the powers of Satan, we never leave this throne room, nor are out of sight of the victorious Lord.

The Lord Jesus Christ now occupies the very highest position possible in God's universe. As it relates to governmental authority, God has exalted Him to be Lord of the universe, a position of supreme authority and power. In position He is far above all angelic and celestial beings, both good and evil (1:21; 6:12), and has been given sovereign control over all things which were put under His feet (1:21). As it relates to worship, Christ has been made the Head over the host of the redeemed out of every race and nation. Over them also He was given supreme control and direction. As Head of the Church, He has His holy temple (2:21); His gospel (1:13), which is the gospel of a full and free salvation from sin and perfect deliverance from the bondage of Satan; His ministers, called "apostles, prophets, evangelists and pastors" (4:11); His doctrines, which are all summed up and included in the "one faith" (4:5) and "the faith" (4:13); His "sacrifice," the precious blood of Calvary's Cross (1:7), His "table" and "cup," around which His Church gathers to have communion with Him in adoring worship. So our blessed Lord presides as High Priest over His true Church.

Satan's Antagonist—His Power

Satan is powerful, but the Lord is *all*-powerful. Ephesians speaks repeatedly of God's mighty power and of its effectual working (1:19; 3:7; 6:10). But all God's power He manifests in and through His Son. Satan has authority within his realm over fallen angels and evil men, but the Lord has authority over Satan and his hosts. All authority has been given to the Victor-Son, as He Himself said:

Matt. 28:18 (R.V.). *"All authority hath been given unto me in heaven and upon earth."*

In the light of this statement let the limitations of Satan's power be noted:

Satan's Power is a Permitted Power

Rom. 13:1. *"There is no power but of God."*

So Satan's power is only what God permits him to exercise and which must inevitably be subordinated to the carrying out of God's eternal purpose. Satan virtually admits this when he offers Christ the kingdoms of this world, in saying, "All this power will I give thee, *for that is delivered unto me.*"

Satan's Power is a Limited Power

Job 1:12. "The Lord said unto Satan, Behold all that he hath is in thy power; *only upon himself put not forth thine hand.*"

Job 2:6. "The Lord said unto Satan, Behold he is in thine hand; *but save his life.*"

Satan was permitted to afflict Job, but his power was restricted. Job's sheep, camels, oxen, asses, even his sons and daughters, were in Satan's power, but not Job himself. God set a boundary line beyond which Satan could not touch or harm Job.

Satan was permitted even to tempt Jesus. But God set a time limit to the temptation and, when God's moment came for its ending, the devil had to depart (Lk. 4:13). Just so the God who knows the exact proportion of our strength and endurance will not allow Satan's temptation to proceed a whit beyond what we are able to endure (I Cor. 10:13).

Satan's Power is a Resisted Power

Lk. 22:31, 32. "The Lord said, Simon, Simon, behold Satan hath desired to have you, that he may sift you as wheat: *but I have prayed for thee, that thy faith fail not.*"

Heb. 7:25. "Wherefore he is able to save them to the uttermost that come unto God by him, *seeing he ever liveth to make intercession for them.*"

Acts 12:5, 11. "Peter therefore was kept in prison: *but prayer was made without ceasing of the church unto God for him* . . . And Peter said, The Lord hath sent his angel and hath delivered me out of the hand of Herod."

Satan does not have a smooth path nor an easy time, for his power manifested for harm against God's people is met by a barrage of prayer both from the faithful High Priest in heaven and His prayer warriors on earth.

Satan's Power is a Broken Power

Lk. 11:21, 22. "When a strong man armed keepeth his palace, his goods are in peace: but *when a stronger than he shall come upon him, and overcome him,* he taketh from him all his armour wherein he trusted, and divideth the spoils."

The stronger man has already overcome the strong man. Since Calvary Satan is a defeated foe. He has no claim whatsoever upon any child of God, and no power to touch him beyond what God permits for the outworking of His own purpose in and through that child. Satan was permitted through his emissaries to stone Stephen to death, but God without doubt used Stephen's triumphant martyrdom as one factor in robbing Satan of one of his most successful warriors, Saul of Tarsus.

Satan's Power is a Doomed Power

A day is coming when Satan will be shorn of all power and sent to the bottomless pit for a thousand years.

Rev. 20:2, 3. "And he laid hold on the dragon, that old serpent, which is the devil, and Satan, and *bound him a thousand years. And cast him into the bottomless pit, and shut him up, and set a seal upon him,* that he should deceive the nations no more, till the thousand years be fulfilled."

The Reigning Son

The warfare begun in the holy mountain of God in heaven; extended to the garden of Eden on earth; waged against "the seed of the woman" through the Old Testament times; focused on the human body of Christ in His earthly life; concentrated upon His mystical Body, the Church, in this age, will end in one climactic, catastrophic war after the translation of the Church and at the end of the tribulation period. The eternal purpose of the Father is coming nearer and nearer to its final fruition. The time is near at hand, we believe, when the usurper-prince and the apostate-god is to be deprived of all power and even of all freedom, and the Victor-Son and pre-eminent Lord is to come to His own throne to reign as King of kings and Lord of lords. So all the hate of all the ages of the great red dragon, the devil, toward God and His Son is summed up and expressed in the Antichrist, who will reign during the brief tribulation period as a civil and political potentate over the whole world, and in the false prophet who will act as head of the religious apostasy. It will be Satan's final attempt to wrest from Christ His right to govern His own universe and to have and hold the worship of men for whom He laid down His life. The issue will then be settled once for all. With all the cunning and wisdom of a master mind he will summon his human and hellish hordes from the ends of the earth for the decisive combat. The Lord will descend to earth: the battle of Armageddon will be fought, and Scripture records the result. Will you not pause just here to read it in Revelation 19:11-20:3.

He who becomes King of kings and Lord of lords will set up His kingdom upon the earth, where He is to rule for one thousand years. During this time Satan will be in the bottomless pit. Released at the end of the millennial imprisonment, which has wrought no slightest change in his diabolical nature, surcharged with venomous hatred of Christ, he will start again the role of a deceiver of the nations. And marvel of marvels, there are still men on earth who will follow him even though the end be the lake of fire.

Rev. 20:10. "And the devil that deceived them was cast into the lake of fire and brimstone, where the beast and the false prophet are, and shall be tormented day and night forever and ever."

Rev. 20:15. "And whosoever was not found written in the book of life was cast into the lake of fire."

The warfare between heaven and hell; between darkness and light; between the devil and the Lord, is ended at last; every enemy has been subjected and cast out; and the kingdom is delivered up unto God. The eternal purpose of God through Christ Jesus our Lord has been perfectly fulfilled, and God is all and in all.

3. THE BATTLEFIELD

It is most important to know where this warfare takes place, as its location determines our position in relation to the enemy, the nature of the warfare, and the kind of weapons to be used. The battlefield is definitely located.

6:12. "Our wrestling is against spiritual hosts of wickedness *in heavenly places.*"

Where, then, do we find Satan's opponent? The Captain of the Lord's host is twice located in Ephesians.

4:10. "He that descended is the same also that ascended up *far above all heavens,* that he might fill all things."

1:20, 21. "In the heavenly places, *far above all principality,* and *power, and might, and dominion.*"

Two localities seem to be mentioned here. One the "heaven of heavens," the dwelling-place of God, and the other a yet lower heaven, the atmospheric heavens, where Satan and his forces have their seat of operation. This places the enemy in a distinctly lower and disadvantageous position.

Then where are the Lord's wrestlers? As they are none other than the members of His Body, they must be where He is, and this is just where Ephesians locates them.

2:6. "Us—*in heavenly places in Christ Jesus.*"

From this superior, advantageous position on the battlefield we may approach the enemy with an absolutely confident attitude. We will never be terrified unless we have allowed ourselves to get beneath, but we may always be triumphant because we know our position to be "far above." The position from which we face the powers of evil determines our defeat or victory.

Prof. H. S. Miller makes this illuminating suggestion regarding the place of warfare:

"Where, then, is the wrestling, this hand-to-hand encounter? In the heavenlies, surely, but which heavenlies? It is difficult to see that Christ sends us down, or even permits us to go down to the level of these demonized, spiritual powers to fight there with them. The alternative is that they have access to the spiritual place where we are, and that their suggestions are such as would, if successful, at least bring us down to their level."

The location of the battlefield determines, also, the nature of the warfare. If in the heavenly realms, it is a spirit-warfare. May not our defeat be that we have fought with human rather than spirit foes, and that we have encountered the enemy on an earthly rather than a heavenly plane?

The place of warfare decides, also, the kind of weapons that must be used. As the old-time bayonet or even more modern hand-grenade avails little against mechanized, motorized tanks and fleets of air bombers, so the carnal weapons we so often employ have no power against the cunning "wiles" and "fiery darts" of the wicked one.

II Cor. 10:4. "For *the weapons of our warfare are not carnal,* but mighty through God to the pulling down of strongholds."

Satan contests the Lord's victory and fights to retain sinners in his kingdom and to regain control of saints. But he wrestles as an already defeated and therefore desperate foe. Satan knows the manifold wisdom and mighty power of God as he sees Christ and His Church "far above all" in the position of invincible, unconquerable power and authority; the already determined position of full and final victory.

4. THE WRESTLERS

6:12. "For *we wrestle.*"

"*We.*"—This is the "we" traced through Ephesians as those redeemed through Christ's blood (1:7); identified with Christ in His death, resurrection and exaltation (2:4-6); His workmanship (2:10); who have access unto the Father through the Son by the Spirit (2:18); who are members of His Body (5:30) and members one of another (4:25), and it is synonymous with "the brethren" of 6:10. The wrestlers are the Church in its corporate capacity and each Christian within its fellowship.

On what ground do we become wrestlers against these terrible forces of evil mobilized under Satan's leadership? If the conflict is between the two seeds, the supernatural antagonists, Christ and Satan, how do we become involved in it? Ephesians unfolds a three-fold reason, the positional, the personal and the prophetic.

The Positional Reason

2:6. *"In heavenly places in Christ Jesus."*

Before the risen, exalted Lord lay the task of continuing and consummating His redemptive ministry. The eternal purpose of the Father must go steadily on to full fruition. As truly as Christ needed a human body through which to accomplish His redemptive work, He needed a mystical Body to make the fruit of that work available to all men everywhere. So on the day of Pentecost, ten days after His ascension, the Holy Spirit descended to form the Body of Christ. From that day to this everyone redeemed by the precious blood of Christ has been baptized into His Body as a living member of Christ Himself.

Satan recognizes that organic union, so now the venomous hatred and the vicious attacks of the evil one are directed against the Church as they were vented against Christ in His earthly life. It is Christ in the Christian and the Christian in Christ that Satan hates and would destroy.

The Church is the most damaging evidence of Satan's defeat on Calvary, for it is the greatest proof of Christ's resurrection. The Church, the Body of Christ, is a reminder to Satan, not only of his own personal destruction, but also of his works, for every saint was a sinner taken from Satan's kingdom. The Church reminds him further of his broken power and of the mighty power of Christ, for all the unsearchable riches of Christ, His wisdom, strength, power, even His authority, have been given to the Church through the in-dwelling of the Holy Spirit. So the devil sees that with Christ in the Church and the Church in Christ he has no less to cope with now than he had when Christ was upon earth. All the resources of Christ which proved too much for even his most cunning wiles then, and led him each time of an attack into ignominious defeat, have now been made the riches of the Church, which constitutes it a truly formidable foe.

Even in the beginning of the apostolic Church Satan sought its destruction. For this purpose he used many cruel rebels, but his most fanatical warrior was Saul of Tarsus, who fairly breathed out threatenings and slaughters against the Christians, and, according to his own testimony, was committed to the persecution unto death of both men and women. That Satan was striking at Christ in the Christians through Saul was revealed so clearly when from the glory Christ spoke, saying, "I am Jesus *whom thou persecutest.*" The devil suffered a tremendous defeat when Saul turned "from the power of Satan unto God," and all the fanatical fury once poured out against Christ and the Christians was changed into the most skilful strategy against Satan and his hosts. Who can estimate the damage done to Satan's cause by this wonderful epistle to the Ephesians, setting forth as it does the way of complete and continuous victory over Satan and all his evil forces?

According to the faithfulness of the Church in revealing the standing and state of the sinner in Satan's bondage, in preaching the gospel of full salvation through Christ alone, in indoctrinating the Church in the fundamentals of "the faith," which has the atoning sacrifice upon the Cross as its very heart and the coming reign of the King as its blessed hope, will be the fierceness of the fury which Satan will pour upon it. In Christ we inherit not only all the love of God but all the hate of the devil.

The Personal Reason

3:17. "That *Christ may dwell in your hearts* by faith."

4:15. "*May grow up into him* in all things, which is the head, even Christ."

5:18. "*Filled with the Spirit.*"

The Church on earth is the fulness of Christ. Its presence proves the ascension of our Lord and the descent of the Holy Spirit to indwell the Christian that the life of the living, glorified Christ may be manifest on earth to an unbelieving world.

We should not marvel, then, that "we" are drawn into the warfare. Who is the devil's greatest hindrance? Who menaces the carrying out of his plan in greatest measure? Most assuredly it is the Christian who lives "far above all," who "walks worthily," who is "filled with the Spirit" and so is "able to stand against all the wiles of the devil," and "to withstand in the evil day." To so appropriate our wealth in Christ that we are enabled to walk worthily glorifies Christ; reveals the beauty and desirability of the new nature; advertises the privileges and possessions of the new life in Him; manifests the superiority of life in the Spirit over life in the flesh; furnishes an open testimony to Satan's subjects that the advantages of citizenship in the kingdom of Christ far exceed those in the kingdom of Satan.

This is a distinct check on Satan. It impedes and imperils his work, arousing and angering him. No testimony is stronger against the devil than that of a consistent Christian walk. When the Lord Jesus becomes an inward reality by the indwelling of and infilling with the Holy Spirit, then the life of the glorified Lord is reproduced. The saved, separated, Spirit-filled saint is Satan's greatest enemy on earth. The Church, "the fulness of him that filleth all in all," and the Christian, "filled unto all the fulness of God," arouses all "the fury of the oppressor." Hence we wrestle.

The Prophetic Reason

1:10. "That he might *gather together in one all things in Christ.*"

Rev. 3:21. *"He that overcometh, I will give to him to sit down with me in my throne,* as I also overcame, and sat down with my Father in his throne."

Rev. 5:10. "And hast made us unto our God kings and priests; and *we shall reign on the earth.*"

I Cor. 6:2, 3. "Do ye not know that *the saints shall judge the world?* Know ye not that we shall judge angels?"

The prophetic reason is not emphasized in Ephesians, but a slight hint is in 1:10, which refers to Christ's future headship over all things. The Christ of Ephesians is seated at the right hand of the Father on His throne. But in the millennial age the Son will be upon His own throne reigning over the kingdoms of this world, which will have been wrested from the control of Satan and his world-rulers and given to Him who has become King of kings and Lord of lords. As we are now seated with Him at the right hand of His Father's throne, so then, as overcomers, He will give us the right to be seated with Him on His throne and to share with Him His reign over the earth.

But what relationship has this future glorious task to our present warfare with Satan? Much, every way, both from Satan's viewpoint and ours. Will it mean nothing to Satan that his rule over the world for so many millenniums is wrested from him and conferred upon Christ and the Christians whom he hates with such violent hatred? Can he be indifferent to the prospect of those very saints whom he persecuted and sought to destroy on earth becoming the judges of the world that belonged to him and the fallen angels? Does he not know that his time is short (Rev. 12:12), and that the age-long conflict between the two seeds is nearly over, that the armies of the Lord are being especially prepared for the last campaign? Could this not account for his especial hatred toward the Christians of the present time who believe in and teach the imminent return of the Lord, and who "press toward the mark for the prize of the high calling of God in Christ Jesus?"

Would any ruler on earth place wholly untrained and inexperienced men in positions of great leadership and authority? Then surely the saints who will be reigning and judging conjointly with Christ in the millennial age must now be trained for such a task. Those who will reign over the world must now overcome the world rather than be overcome by it, and must overcome Satan from whose control that world must be wrested.

I John 5:4. "For whatsoever is born of God *overcometh the world; and this is the victory that overcometh the world,* even our faith."

I John 2:14. "I have written unto you, young men, because ye are strong, and the word of God abideth in you, and *ye have overcome the wicked one.*"

The Lord will permit severe testings which will be part of this training, and the devil will challenge every step onward and upward of God's saints with such diabolical assaults as they have never known before. But the outcome is assured, and our eyes must ever be upon Him in whom we overcome and with whom we are made worthy to reign.

5. THE TACTICS OF THE ENEMY

If in warfare the first necessity is to know the enemy's position, surely the second is to know his tactics. "Satan's empire is ruled with a settled policy. His warfare is carried on with a systematic strategy." No wrestler, then, should be ignorant of his "devices" (II Cor. 2:11) in so far as Scripture reveals them, nor unintelligent concerning his objective. In the light of Ephesians Satan will attempt three things:

> To Despoil the Christian of his Wealth.
> To Decoy the Christian from his Walk.
> To Disable the Christian for his Warfare.

To Despoil the Christian of His Wealth

The wealth of the Christian is deposited in a Person, and is dependent upon a position. Our riches are Christ Himself, made ours by our organic union with Him. In Christ we possess Christ. So to despoil us from our wealth Satan seeks to distance us from Christ and to dislodge us from our position in Him, on that highest plane, "far above all."

Let it be clearly understood that once really in Christ through the baptism with the Holy Spirit, the Christian is forever there. No power of Satan or of hell can ever break the vital union between Christ and any member of His Body, but that union can be weakened. Having had his own works destroyed through the redemptive ministry of Christ, Satan will do all within his power to deprive Christ of the fruitage and the enjoyment of His work.

Satan would first wean the Christian away from Christ through coldness of heart, and then he is prepared to weaken his belief in Christ's Word through blindness of mind. Satan would first rob Christ of the Christian's love and then of his loyalty.

Is not this order in Satan's studied strategy revealed with unmistakable clearness in the messages of the glorified Lord to the seven churches, recorded in Revelation II and III? Read if you will Revelation 2:1-7, which pictures the church of Ephesus at the end of the apostolic age. There is very much that the Lord finds to commend. This church was still absolutely evangelical and sound in "the faith," so much so that it hated all forms of error and evil, and tried those who were false apostles and judged them as liars. From the record it is certain the church at Ephesus was a beehive of activity, much commendable work being wholeheartedly done in the name of the Lord. But the Lord makes one very definite and most damaging charge against it:

Rev. 2:4 (R.V.). "But I have this against thee, *that thou didst leave thy first love.*"

Christ forgotten in the defence of and devotion to *the Church!* Love for Christ Himself waning while loyalty to His work and to His truth waged with ever greater intensity! From the church at Ephesus to the Laodicean church, where Christ is so little loved and so completely forgotten that He is outside the door, even seeking entrance, *there are but six steps downward.*

Oh, what a word of warning this is to the Christians who have smothered their Lord in a dead orthodoxy and in hectic activity that leaves no time for quiet communion over His Word; for fellowship in prayer; for adoration and worship of Christ Himself! Dear fellow-Christian, have *you left your first love?* Has the love of your heart waxed cold? Has it lost the lustre of the warmth, intensity, fervour, constancy, depth, and faithfulness of the first days and years you knew Him as Saviour? Is He still the pre-eminent Lover and Loved One in your heart? Oh, if not, for His sake and for yours will you not return to your first love to-day? For it is Satan who, because of his hate against Him, has weakened your love for your Lord.

To be in Christ in the heavenlies is to enjoy marvellous privileges. There every spiritual blessing is ours. There one experiences liberty, victory, peace, rest, assurance and security. There one is conscious of sharing in Christ's victory over sin and Satan and of being "more than conqueror through him that loved us." As long as that position is taken and maintained by faith, we are invulnerable to both Satan's allurements and attacks. This he knows, so seeks desperately to dislodge us from our position by undermining our faith. Let us study his method, for certainly he uses a systematic strategy here. Who he is enables us to know what he will do.

Satan is a *liar* and the father of lies. John 8:44. "Ye are of your father the devil, and the lusts of your father ye will do. He was a murderer from the beginning, and *abode not in the truth, because there is no truth in him. When he speaketh a lie, he speaketh of his own; for he is a liar, and the father of it."*

Satan is *a deceiver.* Rev. 12:9. "That old serpent, called the devil, and *Satan, which deceiveth the whole world."*

Let us keep ever in mind Satan's purpose—to take God's place. Therefore his ruling passion is to draw men away from God unto himself. To achieve this end will he come out into the open and frankly say, "I am the great red dragon, the devil, Satan by name, come follow me, fall down and worship me!" Did he approach any truly reborn child of God in that way, he would run from him in terror. Satan depends upon his power to lead us away from God through lies. The underlying principle of all Satan's tactics is deception. It will well repay you to study the emphasis Scripture puts upon this word in relation to the devil's work. Satan does not purpose to be unlike God, but to be as like God as possible. Therefore he is a crafty, clever camouflager. He designs to counterfeit everything God is and does. Satan's last deception and his masterpiece will be the Antichrist, such a skilful imitation of Christ that almost the whole world will be prepared to worship him. This duplication of God's Christ will be a great humanitarian, working for the welfare of mankind.

185

But for his deceptions to be successful, they must be so cunningly devised that his real purpose is concealed by wiles. So he works subtly and secretly, always with duplicity. He would deceive even the very elect, and no Christian, however spiritual or strong, is beyond his seductive assaults. Satan is an adept at deception, for he began that work in the garden of Eden 6000 years ago and has practised the art ever since.

Gen. 3:13. "The woman said, *The serpent beguiled me* and I did eat."

In Eden Satan used a serpent as his mouthpiece. Since then he has used men. Satan has in his constant employ seducers.

II Tim. 3:13. "But *evil men and seducers* shall wax worse and *worse, deceiving and being deceived.*"

Ephesians warns us of these seducers, unveils their deceptions, and shows how necessary it is for us to grow up into spiritual maturity that we may not be ensnared.

5:6. *"Let no man deceive you* with vain words."

4:14. "That ye henceforth be no more children, tossed to and fro, and carried about with every wind of doctrine, by *the sleight of men, and cunning craftiness, whereby they lie in wait to deceive.*"

Let us now see in what guise these deceivers come, that we may be able to recognize them and discern their works.

Satan uses men as *false teachers.*

Paul warned the Ephesian elders that such men would arise from among themselves, speaking perverse things to draw away disciples unto themselves (Acts 20:30). They would be the false teachers of whom Peter writes:

II Pet. 2:1-3. "There shall be false teachers among you, *who privily shall bring in damnable heresies, even denying the Lord that bought them,* and bring upon themselves swift destruction. And many shall follow their pernicious ways; by reason of whom the truth shall be evil spoken of. And *through covetousness shall they with feigned words make merchandise of you:* whose judgment now of a long time lingereth not, and their damnation slumbereth not."

"False teachers."—There is no truth in Satan, the liar. Second only to his hatred of Him who is the truth is hatred of "the word of truth, the gospel of your salvation" (1:13). It follows naturally that he hates all those who "walk in the truth" (III John 3). So there is no length to which Satan will not go to dislodge the saint from his faith-position in Christ. To do so he has counterfeited the entire system of God's truth, and has trained men as teachers of this cleverly designed religious system, with the distinct ob-

jective of causing God's people to believe *what is false* and to lead them into error and delusion. Sometimes his doctrines are a flat denial of all the essentials of the Christian faith; sometimes they are half-truths—a clever admixture of truth and error; the truth furnishing the bait, the error the poison that kills the one who takes the bait.

"Among you."—Note particularly that Satan does not build a church of his own out of his own funds and put a sign upon it: "First Church of Satan." Oh no; he calls it the "First Church of Christ." He goes even to the uttermost limit of devilish deception and places his teachers in the pulpits, Bible classes and Sunday Schools of evangelical churches. It may be the man or woman who teaches you or your children in your church is one of these false teachers, and you do not know it.

"Privily," "creeping along under some sort of cover." Under cover of the prestige of a church or institution that for generations has stood for evangelical truth; under cover of the name of some theological seminary or Bible school in which the false teacher once studied, but from whose teachings he has wholly departed; under cover of the vocabulary of orthodoxy these false teachers deliberately and intentionally "bring in damnable heresies," to turn men away from the Lord, *"even denying the Lord that bought them."* This unmasks them and stamps their teaching as Satanic, for Satan's deepest hatred—the one that inspires all other hatreds—is for the gospel of redemption through the shed blood of Christ. Had it not been for that shed blood of the Redeemer, every man, woman and child since Adam's day would still belong to him.

"Many shall follow their pernicious ways"—not knowing that in gulping down and feeding upon what these false teachers say they are taking the devil's poison into their spiritual life. Thousands of uninstructed Christians are so deceived to-day. Recently in the Sunday School of a church belonging to one of the largest denominations, a very earnest young woman gave a talk which was absolutely contrary to the truth of God's Word. A friend of mine who heard it spoke to the young woman afterward, expressing grief that she should have given such a message. "Why," said she, "I got it *out of the S. S. Quarterly.*" And so she had—a Quarterly filled with these same "damnable heresies."

How could that truly earnest young woman be so deceived? *"They with feigned words make merchandise of you,"* and again in vs. 18, "For when *they speak great swelling words of vanity,* they allure through the lusts of the flesh." Their use of high-sounding words, which seem like the epitome of scholarship, culture and oratory, are a part of the trickery so cleverly designed to beguile unthinking and untaught souls.

How can we know these false teachers are Satanic? Is it unrighteous judgment, or is it spiritual discernment that places them as Satan's emissaries? They *"bring upon themselves swift destruction"* and *"their damnation slumbereth not."* God Himself has thus judged them, and so exonerates every child of His who not only has discernment to distinguish between the false and the true, but the courage to expose the false.

The Holy Spirit has taken special pains to warn us of these apostate teachers in the days preceding our Lord's return, and has Himself disclosed their Satanic origin.

I Tim. 4:1, 2. "Now the Spirit speaketh expressly, that in the latter times, *some shall depart from the faith, giving heed to seducing spirits, and doctrines of devils,* speaking lies in hypocrisy."

These false teachers have departed from "the faith" which God has given as His revealed truth for the Church in this age of grace. The Spirit distinctly states that the reason for their turning away is that they gave heed to Satan's lies and deliberately chose to accept the doctrines of devils rather than the truths of God. So they themselves become the mouthpiece of Satan, speaking lies with his own duplicity and hypocrisy.

Satan uses men as *false prophets.*

In the early Church God chose His own prophets, and bestowed them upon the Church as His gift (4:11), yet even in the beginning of church history false prophets arose.

II Pet. 2:1. "But *there were false prophets* also among the people."

Our Lord told His disciples that in the end of this age many false prophets would arise to deceive many.

Matt. 24:11. "And *many false prophets shall rise,* and shall deceive many."

There is ample proof of the fulfilment of this prophecy. False prophets have arisen in such numbers that thousands of Christians have been utterly confused and led astray. Back of all such false systems as Christian Science, Unity, Russellism, Ballardism, Mormonism, Bahaism, Spiritism, Theosophy, and all others where men or women claim to have received some special revelation from God, or to be His special messengers, is Satan, the arch-deceiver.

Satan even uses men as *false Christs.*

Again our Lord in His Olivet discourse, where He answers

the disciples' question concerning the signs of His coming, states first of all that there would be many false Christs.

Matt. 24:4, 5. "Take heed that no man deceive you. *For many shall come in my name, saying, I am Christ;* and shall deceive many."

Incredible as it seems, now in our time this prophecy is being fulfilled; some men actually claim to be divinely appointed liberators of the oppressed,—in other words to be "The Messiah." It seems still more incredible that men and women by the tens of thousands are deceived into following such persons. Is it not indicative of the gnawing unrest, uncertainty and dissatisfaction that fill men's hearts to-day? Everywhere there is perplexity and bewilderment. Men have lost faith in their fellow-men. Nations are truce-breakers: men are liars. Who is trustworthy enough to be trusted? The prestige and power of even the greatest nations is gone. The whole world is looking for a superman; men are crying out for a deliverer, and they are ready to accept self-constituted Messiahs, false Christs, who pose as saviours of the down-trodden. All this is but Satan's preparation for his Antichrist.

"False teachers, *false* prophets, *false* Christs!" One would think this word "false" would be enough to establish their origin as Satanic and quickly reveal them to us as deceivers. Why is it, then, that so few of God's children detect them as such? It is because of the very falseness of the way in which they approach God's people. Not only is what they teach and profess to be false, but their method is the very acme of deceit. This is God's own indictment of them. He says these powers of darkness mask as angels of light.

II Cor. 11:13-15. "For *such* are false apostles, deceitful workers, *transforming themselves* into the apostles of Christ. And no marvel; *for Satan himself is transformed into an angel of light.* Therefore it is no great thing if *his ministers also be transformed as the ministers of righteousness;* whose end shall be according to their works."

Let us study the method of approach of Satan and his present-day satellites who seek to dislodge the saints from their faith-position in Christ.

To Dislodge through Doubt

The arch-deceiver entered Eden as an angel of light. He was there as the great humanitarian who would excel God as a benefactor to man. True, God had placed Adam and Eve in a perfect garden and had given them all needful for spirit, soul and body, in overflowing abundance. A single commandment had been given—one reservation made, and that for their greatest good.

Then comes this Satanic "angel of light" with his insidious question, "Yea, hath *God* said, Ye shall not eat of *every tree* of the garden?" (Gen. 3:1). For, if He did say that, then can God be called good? So argued the serpent who "beguiled Eve through his subtilty" (II Cor. 11:13). To distance Eve from God Satan bores into her heart through doubt, with the diabolical intent of weakening her love for and trust in God. Having won such a signal victory in Eden by this "angel of light" method, Satan has not departed from it.

He comes to-day through his apostate teachers, asking the same insidious question, "Hath *God* said" that every man is a sinner, and that the soul that sinneth it shall die? "Hath *God* said" that there is no other way of salvation but through faith in the shed blood of Jesus Christ? "Hath *God* said," that all men who do not believe upon and receive Jesus Christ as Saviour shall be eternally separated from Him? If so, then, can such a God be a God of love?

To Dislodge through Disobedience

Having instilled doubt regarding God's goodness into Eve's heart, then Satan, the liar, comes out with a bold, blatant denial of God's Word with the studied intent to break their relationship with God through disobedience. In commanding Adam not to eat of the tree of the knowledge of good and evil, *God said*, "For in the day that thou eatest thereof *thou shalt surely die." "The serpent said* unto Eve, *Thou shalt not surely die."* The issue was perfectly clear. Would they believe and act upon Satan's lie, or upon God's truth? They believed Satan's lie, and were immediately dislodged from their position of fellowship with Him, and hid from His presence. They became the first "children of disobedience" (2:2).

Satan comes to-day with the same lies and the same denial of God's Word. God has said that all have sinned, and that the wages of sin is death. Satan through one set of false teachers says that no one sins, for there is no such thing as sin; and no one dies, for there is no such thing as matter. God has said that sin is lawlessness, and that the very core of sin is enmity toward Him. Satan through another set of false teachers says that sin is not at all the heinous thing God declares it to be, nor does it need the kind of salvation which He requires. Sin is rather a "fall upward," and, if only man's environment and circumstances were made perfect, then man will fall backward into a personal righteousness which a truly loving God would accept. So in a thousand different forms this intelligent, versatile apostate sets his lies over against God's truth, and misleads people as to plainly-stated fact, thus beguiling them into error.

To Dislodge through Delusion

The world to-day is flooded with Satanic cults. All kinds of new movements are coming on to the arena which are suited to the temperament and circumstances of the ones Satan seeks to ensnare. He has one kind for the elite and another for the common run of folks. Some of these are such clever counterfeits that even saintly souls are being deceived. Sometimes the vocabulary used is that of Scripture, but with a private interpretation given to it. Then again the language of the Word is studiously avoided, and that used is capable of diverse meaning. But it all sounds so fair and enticing that it makes the counterfeit even more dangerous.

Earnest children of God are often taken unawares by Satan's craft in times of sickness, suffering or sorrow, when they seek for healing, relief or consolation. The devil takes advantage of the physical, mental or spiritual condition to ensnare them through his "lying wonders." Many of God's children, longing for health, and not knowing that Satan has power to perform miracles, have been drawn away from the pure gospel of Christ to the cult of Christian Science. Other thousands of God's people, sorrowing over the loss of loved ones, and longing for touch with them again, have been ensnared by the "lying wonders" of Spiritism. But God shows us clearly the origin of all such perversion of truth, which has deluded such large numbers of people.

II Thes. 2:9-11. "Even him whose coming is after *the working of Satan with all power and signs and lying wonders, and with all deceivableness of unrighteousness* in them that perish; because they received not the love of the truth, that they might be saved. And for this cause God shall send them strong delusion that they should believe a lie."

To Dislodge through Deflection

No child of God will be left untempted by Satan's snares. Those who would not be deceived by these grosser errors he tries to deflect from the whole truth of God's Word by the admixture of error with truth; of law with grace. He will do all he can to strike a deadly blow at the gospel of salvation by grace so marveilously set forth in

Ephesians and to seduce men from trust in Christ alone for salvation and for sanctification. In Paul's day Satan tried to deflect the Galatian Christians from this gospel of grace. They were saved, and were running well, but they wanted to go further and know the power of fulness of life in the Spirit. Just there Satan sought to dislodge them from their position of liberty and to entangle them again in a yoke of bondage. For this purpose Satan used *false brethren*.

Gal. 2:4, 5. "And that because of *false brethren unawares brought in* who came in privily to spy out our liberty which we have in Christ, *that they might bring us into bondage;* to whom we gave place by subjection no, not for an hour; *that the truth of the gospel might continue with you.*"

How manifold are such deflections from the pure gospel to-day, and how watchful every saint should be that he is not taken unawares by them! If Satan cannot get us to believe too little of the gospel, then he will attempt to get us to believe too much and to go beyond what the Word teaches.

From this brief study of Satan's deceptions we see he is doing two things in the minds of Christians in relation to the truth. He would, first, corrupt their minds to turn them from the simplicity of the gospel.

II Cor. 11:3. "But I fear, lest by any means, as the serpent beguiled Eve through his subtilty, *so your minds should be corrupted* from the simplicity that is in Christ."

Failing in this, Satan then tries to confuse the minds of earnest Christians. An illustration of such devilish work is seen in Satan's attempt to confuse the minds of those devoted Christians at Thessalonica over the precious truth of the Lord's return. In the first epistle to the Thessalonians Paul had written of this blessed hope that it might bring them "comfort" (I Thes. 4:18). Satan tried to pervert the truth to bring confusion.

II Thes. 2:1, 2. "Now we beseech you, brethren, by the coming of our Lord Jesus Christ, and by our gathering together unto him, *that ye be not soon shaken in mind, or be troubled,* neither by spirit, nor by word, nor by letter as from us, as that the day of Christ is at hand."

Satanic deceptions began in the first days of the apostolic Church. Paul, Peter, John and Jude discerned them and warned against them. Our Lord declared that Satanic deceptions would be a special sign of the growing apostasy leading up to His return. To-day such deceptions abound on every side and are increasing. The question that confronts every true Christian is how to stand against these wiles of the devil. We need not be deceived. God exhorts us repeatedly in Scripture to take heed.

Lk. 21:8. *"Take heed* that ye be not deceived."

Our faithful Lord has made ample provision for every child of His to meet Satan, the deceiver, victoriously and to discern his deceptions.

Through the Abiding of Christ.

I John 3:24. *"He abideth in us,* by the Spirit which he hath given us."

I John 4:4. "Ye are of God, little children, and have overcome them; *because greater is he that is in you,* than he that is in the world."

It is this Christ in us, who calls Himself the truth, who will meet Satan, the liar and the deceiver, and overcome him.

Through the Anointing of the Spirit.

I John 2:20. "But *ye have an unction from the Holy One,* and ye know all things."

I John 2:27. "But *the anointing which ye have received of him* abideth in you, and ye need not that any man teach you: but as *the same anointing teacheth you of all things, and is truth,* and is no lie, and *even as it hath taught you,* ye shall abide in him."

Under the teaching of the Holy Spirit the tests of Scripture will be applied to these Satanic deceptions, and every lie will be exposed as a lie, and God's eternal truth will shine in our minds, giving the light of God for clear discernment.

To Decoy the Christian from His Walk

The Lord Jesus offered a very significant prayer for His disciples:

John 17:15, 16 (R.V.). "I pray not that thou shouldest take them from the world, *but that thou shouldest keep them from the evil one.* They are not of the world, even as I am not of the world."

"They are not of the world." The saints are an other worldly company, a people who are now citizens of heaven, even though they walk as pilgrims on earth. Though in the world they are not of it. *"I pray not that thou shouldest take them from the world."* But how very difficult to live an other-worldly, heavenly life in such a world as this, which Christ and His apostles declared would grow worse and worse until it reaches such a state of appalling wickedness that God has to act again in judgment as He did in the days of Noah

(Matt. 24:37-39). Look upon the picture of the state of the world in the last days, and see if present-day conditions warrant one in thinking we are nearing this stage.

Matt. 24:6, 7. "Ye shall hear of wars and rumors of wars; For nation shall rise against nation, and kingdom against kingdom."

Luke 21:12, 16, 25, 26. "They shall lay their hands upon you, and persecute you, delivering you up to the synagogues, and into prisons, being brought before kings and rulers for my name's sake. Ye shall be betrayed both by parents, and brethren, and kinsfolks, and friends; and some of you shall they cause to be put to death. And ye shall be hated of all men for my name's sake. . . . Upon the earth distress of nations, with perplexity; men's hearts failing them for fear, and for looking after those things which are coming on the earth."

II Tim. 3:1-4. "This know also, that in the last days perilous times shall come. . . . For men shall be lovers of their own selves, covetous, boasters, proud, blasphemers, disobedient to parents, unthankful, unholy . . . without natural affection, truce-breakers, false accusers, incontinent, fierce, despisers of those that are good, traitors, heady, highminded, lovers of pleasure more than lovers of God; having a form of godliness, but denying the power thereof."

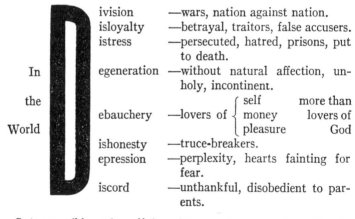

	ivision	—wars, nation against nation.
	isloyalty	—betrayal, traitors, false accusers.
	istress	—persecuted, hatred, prisons, put to death.
In	egeneration	—without natural affection, unholy, incontinent.
the		⎧ self more than
	ebauchery	—lovers of ⎨ money lovers of
World		⎩ pleasure God
	ishonesty	—truce-breakers.
	epression	—perplexity, hearts fainting for fear.
	iscord	—unthankful, disobedient to parents.

It is a terrible and terrifying picture, yet we must honestly admit it is all too true of the world in which we are now living. We witness to-day a world-wide revolution to destroy governments through anarchy, society through debauchery, and Christianity through apostasy. We live in a world whose civilization is on the brink of utter collapse, literally rotting to pieces through its own corruption. Moral restraint has been cast to the winds. Growing indecency permeates every phase of life, manifesting itself in speech, in clothing, in amusements and in relationships. The very atmosphere is charged with unwholesome and unclean suggestions which pollute both eye and ear. The evils of Noah's day, with all their demonized, degrading influences, seem rife in our midst. The very foundations of even the nations built upon the fear and the love of God are being destroyed. Those things that ministered to the finer and nobler things in human life are largely discarded. The cultural side of life has declined. There is little time to read or think or converse. Sadder still, there seems no sense of loss in the passing of those things that in other days were the charm of many homes. The modern-day person is a bundle of nerves, accurately described as without self-control.

Perhaps the most hopeless thing is the abandonment of the standards that safeguarded the moral, ethical and religious life of human society. The standards of our forefathers are not only scoffed at by the world, but are ridiculed also by the Church. Students in a Bible class were asked to define sin, and one person said, "That is a very difficult thing to do, for what was considered sin twenty-five years ago is not sin to-day." Alas! how true; and this lowered evaluation of sin accounts for the moral deterioration of the past generation. God describes the attitude of men in the last days toward godliness and holiness, "blasphemers, unholy, despisers of those that are good."

Yet from such a defiled and defiling world Christ does not pray for the Christian to be taken. Nor does He lower the standard of life expected of the saint. The journey from 1:13, the day we first heard the Word of truth and believed in Christ, to 5:27, when we shall be presented to Him without spot of blemish, is long and difficult. But God chose us to be holy, started us walking on the highway of holiness, and expects us to go steadily on to the goal. Satan will dog our footsteps along every bit of our pilgrim journey. This our Lord knew, so prayed *that thou shouldest keep them from the evil one.* The devil came to Christ as "the tempter," and he will come to the Christian in the same way.

Matt. 4:3. "The tempter came to him."

Lk. 4:12. "Jesus, being full of the Holy Ghost . . . was led by the Spirit into the wilderness, being forty days *tempted of the devil.*"

I Thes. 3:5. "When I could no longer forbear, I sent to know your faith, lest by some means *the tempter have tempted you,* and our labour be in vain."

I Pet. 1:6. "Wherein ye greatly rejoice, though now for a season, if need be, *ye are in heaviness through manifold temptations.*"

Throughout the earthly life of Christ the devil sought to tempt Him to swerve from the path divinely marked out for Him—the pathway to the throne by way of the Cross. By enticing words, by threats, by every conceivable subtilty, Satan tempted our Lord, but found nothing in Him (John 14:30). Knowing the fierceness of the devil's temptations and that there is within us a sinful nature that responds to such enticements, our Lord faithfully prays that we may be kept when these temptations assail us. Let this be great comfort and strength to us.

Throughout the pilgrim journey of the Christian, Satan will seek to decoy him from the sevenfold walk so clearly unfolded in Ephesians, by tempting him to yield to these demonized influences of his worldly environment and circumstances, and to the evil desires of the flesh. His temptations will come from without and from within, and each has its definite objective. Let us note how cunningly he adjusts the temptation to each phase of the walk.

Unity—Division

Satan's first diabolical work was to destroy the unity among angels, and then among men. He brought division into the first home and family, causing brother to murder brother. He began this deadly work in God's habitation, the Church, in its very beginning, and has continued through the centuries to cause schisms and splits, until to-day the Church is divided into hundreds of camps of Christian soldiers often fighting against each other rather than uniting all their forces against the one common foe. This is Satan's masterstroke against Christ, to discredit before a hostile world the testimony of the Church, of which He is the Head.

Satan divides Christian from Christian by injecting poison of unwarranted suspicion, unloving intolerance, intense dislike, corroding jealousy, and acrimonious criticism. These poisons go through the system and find an outlet through the tongue. An unbridled tongue, "full of deadly poison and set on fire of hell" (Jas. 3:6, 8), becomes the devil's instrument and the poison spreads to other church-members until "Behold, how great a matter a little fire kindleth!" A full-fledged church quarrel is started with the membership taking sides and dividing into factions.

Satan is especially active in fostering misunderstanding between Christians who are in the front ranks of valiant warriors for the faith, and are united in soul-winning and in building up Christians in Christ. In this morning's mail came a letter from one working with others for a prayer retreat for revival, saying, "I am expecting great things from those two days. Ever since we settled to have this week-end difficulties have come. Untrue things are being said by other Christian workers. We can expect Satan to work now and we must be above everything. But these attacks come from such unexpected corners, that it is like a thunderstorm suddenly bursting loose, when nothing has happened. Such things do bring us to our knees more than ever." Is that not exactly the victory the Lord would gain in such an attack? He would keep us very humble and dependent; reminding us to be very watchful of our own attitudes, and very vigilant in guarding our hearts against every Satanic temptation to separate us from fellow-Christians.

Holiness—Degeneration

What has been the result upon the Church of the crumbling of the foundations of civilization and the collapse of standards in modern life? Sad to say, instead of withstanding these deadening, degrading influences emanating from the powers of darkness, too often the Church has succumbed to them and become the devil's prey. Everywhere there is a lamentable deterioration in the very warp and woof of Christian principles and standards. There is such an appalling ignorance of God's Word on the part of most Christians that they know little of God's ways and still less of Satan's, so they follow the path of least resistance, that of the world and of the flesh, both of which tend toward the unrighteous and the unholy.

Satan would lure the Christian away from the high ground of heavenliness to grovel in the dust and dirt of earth. He would have us interested in and satisfied with the things of earth and time and sense. Satan wars against daily growth into the image of Christ, and will go to any length to hinder a continuous, consistent walk. The devil ever trails the saints to decoy them away from the highway of holiness, and to detour the heavenly pilgrim into the haunts and habits of sin. He argues with the Christian that Christ is no joy-killer and that Christianity is not narrow. "Does not Bypath Meadow always seem to lie close by the King's Highway? Does it not always promise the easiest going?"

Doubtless all of us have somewhere a blind spot, and just there Satan concentrates his temptation to inconsistency. He will make some fall forward in worldliness while they bend backward in orthodoxy, as the militant fundamentalist who smoked and played bridge, seeing no discrepancy between her orthodoxy and unspirituality. Often-times Satan trips us at our strongest point. Manifestations of the self-life that had been counted crucified appear again in the same hideous form. In the measure the Christian seeks to advance and to live habitually on the highest plane he will be the target for Satan's fiercest fury.

Love—Disloyalty

"The brother shall betray the brother to death, and the father the son; and the children shall rise up against their parents, and shall cause them to be put to death." These words almost take away our breath, for they seem so terrible. Yet they describe conditions already existing in some countries. A friend of mine visited her aunt in one of the totalitarian countries of Europe and, when questioned as to the difficulties observed, she said that one dared not speak with freedom, even within one's own home, for fear there might be a spy in the family.

But in many homes in all lands a more refined but scarcely less cruel form of disloyalty is often manifested by unsaved members of the family toward a real believer. Several days were spent in the home of one greatly used in teaching God's Word. One daughter would not eat at the table with us, and even the most charitable person could not truthfully have called the husband polite. Later the wife was forbidden to have Bible classes in the home. *"Without natural affection.* How Satan delights to separate good friends! Oftentimes it is accomplished by a fiery dart of misunderstanding allowed to lodge in the heart; then it is easy for motives to be misconstrued; words to be misinterpreted, and actions to be misrepresented.

Oh, how often the heart of the missionary or minister is well-nigh broken by disappointment through the disloyalty of someone for whom he had willingly poured out his life. Did not our Lord know something of the suffering of disloyalty when all His disciples forsook Him and fled? When Peter, who had avowed allegiance to Him even if all others deserted Him, denied Him three times? The tragic note of such suffering is found more than once in Paul's epistles. How each of us needs to have the Spirit of love shed abroad in our hearts, the love of God, that we may never yield to Satan's temptation to jealousy, envy, malice, dislike, slander, backbiting, or misunderstanding.

Light—Distress

"Upon the earth *perplexity,* for *it is a day of trouble."* And no person is left untouched by this environment that is surcharged with fear and foreboding; with dread of what even a day may bring forth.

Within the past weeks a whole continent was held in the grip of the fear of war. To-day a letter came from a French friend showing how the awful atmosphere filled with the aerial hosts of darkness oppressed her.

"During the past weeks we have had a strenuous life, full of work and worry. We feared even to be obliged to go South, far from a possible war. But, worst of all, *we felt this wave of hatred, fear, war, around us;* everywhere there is persecution, oppression, war in one form or another, and nobody seems able to find a right solution for all the problems of the world. But God reigns! If we did not believe that, life would not be worth living."

In China the greatest migration of all human history has been made by whole villages and families who sought greater peace of mind through deliverance from the fear of death or atrocities worse than death. Everywhere to-day there is a haunting sense of insecurity engendered by fear, which Satan capitalizes to bring believers as well as unbelievers into a state of bewilderment, keeping one from seeing issues clearly and from being able to pray through problems.

Satan delights to torment God's saint through injecting his own filthiness into the mind. The experience quoted is one all too common to-day.

"I am a woman of many years' experience and service in the Christian life. In my younger years I never indulged in unclean thought, conversation, reading or stories; the suggestive joke is an abomination unto me, and the picture shows have little or no attraction for me because of their suggestiveness of the impure. Now for some time evil, obscene, unholy thoughts have been flashing unbidden through my mind, vile words (and I have seldom even allowed myself to indulge in slang), enter my thought and the simplest thing will suggest impurity. I realize this is from Satan. Last night when at prayer unholy thoughts flashed up and I felt prostrated with fear and shame and almost despair."

Such distress of mind that torments even to despair has but one source, the devil, and should be refused and resisted as from him.

Wisdom—Distraction

"Men's hearts failing them for fear and for *looking after those things* that are coming upon the earth. Satan first busies himself with working havoc in our circumstances and then in us by getting us "to look after" those things which he has wrought, thus filling our hearts with anxiety, worry, care and fretfulness. The Holy Spirit would have us always looking *up*. Satan would keep up looking *around.* The Spirit would fix our eyes upon Christ, whatever our circumstances. Satan would keep our gaze upon our circumstances to obscure Christ. If we *look up,* we shall be enabled to *live above* and get clear guidance on all the perplexing problems confronting us; but, if we *look around,* we shall surely *be beneath* and wholly unfit for the decisions and actions required.

Praise—Depression

The human spirit is the headquarters of the Holy Spirit in the believer, and the vantage ground from which He works to carry the abundant life of Christ to the uttermost part of the human personality. So it is very necessary to keep it untrammelled, joyous, assured, thankful. For this very reason Satan assails it and tempts to depression.

The devil not only tempts us to look around, but to look *in,* and for the same purpose—to keep our eyes off of Christ. He will make us wrongly concerned over our spiritual condition in order to create doubt of God and disbelief in the work of the Holy Spirit within us. One of the saintliest men I ever knew suffered acutely at times through the Satanic temptation to doubt his own salvation. Beyond most men he exalted the Lord in his life and magnified the Word in his preaching and gloried in the grace of God toward man. Yet the devil periodically cast over his life a baneful cloud of doubt regarding his own acceptance with the Lord and God's goodness to him, robbing his heart of all peace and his face of a glory that shone with marvellous beauty.

The lengths to which Satan is going is unthinkable, even at times successfully tempting some of God's choicest ones to suicide or to such depression as ends in insanity. He cruelly commandeers the pains of illness and the sufferings through disaster to serve as his vassals in robbing the saint of a thankful, praise-full heart. One should ever recognize any torment of spirit through depression as from the devil and instantly refuse it.

Harmony—Discord

In all the relationships of life to-day one has to be constantly on guard against the discordant dart, for the devil can make such big chasms out of such little cracks. Fretfulness, irritability, nagging, incompatibility, indiscreet behaviour, can result in estrangement between husband and wife. Disaffection between parents and children can disrupt the home. Satan thinks of hundreds of ways to cause friction and irritation between members of a family which make it almost impossible for them to live in the same house.

How, then, are these manifold temptations to be met and overcome? First of all by recognizing the tempter and refusing to yield to the temptation. Christ knew it was the devil speaking through Peter and said, "Get thee behind me, *Satan*." So must we go behind the flesh and blood instrument to the Satanic instigator of every temptation and definitely resist him. Secondly, we must follow the clear instructions given in Ephesians IV and V to put off the old man; to put on the new man; to yield no place to the devil, and not to grieve the Holy Spirit. The devil will constantly seek place in us through the uncrucified flesh. If yielded to him, the Holy Spirit is grieved and rendered powerless to enable us to resist the devil. To live with an ungrieved Spirit is to have the secret of victory over the temptations of Satan.

To Disable the Christian for His Warfare

The great objective of Satan now is to delay the final consummation of God's eternal purpose, that his own ejection from the earth and imprisonment in the bottomless pit may be projected into the future as far as possible. For this age of grace it is God's purpose to complete the Body of Christ and to prepare His chosen ones to be presented to Christ, purified and perfected in His likeness. To this end He would have the gospel carried to the ends of the earth that every person might have an adequate opportunity of hearing the Word of truth and of believing upon the Saviour; and He would have the spiritual life of the Church enriched, deepened and vitalized by the continuous infilling and energizing of the Holy Spirit.

To-day there is felt everywhere a desperate attempt to thwart God's plan of world-wide evangelization and of real revival within the Church. When the last soul needed to complete the Body of Christ has been won from Satan's kingdom, the Lord will come for His own to take them unto Himself, and then to return with them to reign on the earth. So the final battle of the ages comes on apace. The devil knows full well it is no mere skirmish or sham battle in which he is engaged. The issue for him is destruction, so the warfare is desperate. Satan will do everything within his power to side-track and to hinder the work and to lay low and wear out the worker. There is no method he will not employ to intimidate or to intrigue into folly. He draws upon every resource within himself to disable God's wrestler. So let us see who he is in order to know what he does.

Satan is the Accuser of the Brethren

Rev. 12:10. "Now is come salvation, and strength, and the kingdom of our God, and the power of his Christ: *for the accuser of our brethren is cast down, which accused them before our God day and night."*

To win others to the Lord one must have both the liberty and the power of the Spirit. There must be the inward consciousness that there is no known, unconfessed sin, or any deliberately permitted inconsistency of life; that one is himself living obediently according to the Word he preaches and teaches to others. As the apostle Paul said, he must exercise himself to have a conscience void of offence toward God and toward man (Acts 24:10).

To disable for soul-winning, Satan will pour into or upon the worker a stream of accusations, whether true or false. From within he will torture with the remembrance of past sins and present sinfulness, pressing home the realization of failures, defeats, mistakes, shortcomings, and weaknesses, until we feel utterly incapacitated to speak to others of salvation. Satan will turn our thought in upon ourselves in self-reproach, so that we will think it hypocritical and futile to witness to others. From without through his emissaries, animated by jealousy, prejudice, hatred or dishonesty, he will often flood a community with lies, false accusations, slander, against some devoted, innocent, unoffending Christian, to besmirch his reputation and to nullify his witness. The object of the accuser is to create within the worker a sense of his own personal unworthiness and unfitness before the Lord, and to make him cringe in fear before the devil.

Satan is the Hinderer and Great Adversary

I Thes. 2:18. "Wherefore we would have come unto you, even I Paul, once and again; *but Satan hindered us.*

I Cor. 16:9. "For a great door and effectual is opened unto me, and *there are many adversaries."*

From every mission field to-day, and even from other countries, these very words are heard, describing the hindrances to God's work by the great adversary. Every fresh opportunity to preach the gospel in hitherto untouched fields is challenged; every true and powerful work of the Spirit in revival is crosscut or counterfeited; efforts are being made to close the door to the gospel in one country after another and to compel missionaries to leave. The number and kind of adversaries are many indeed. Sometimes it is the leaders of a false or pagan system of religion; again, it is the government of the land; while in some cases it is individuals or movements.

Why and how Satan hinders is described by a missionary on a far-flung mission frontier:

"When the child of God, yieldedly and wisely, attacks sin, preaching the Cross, and redemption from sin through blood alone, then let him confidently anticipate opposition. Trouble will surely come, and very generally from some most unexpected source. Great spiritual awakenings have occurred, quietly, with no excitement, like unto deep-flowing water. And every time such outpourings of the Holy Spirit have been followed by difficulty. The very powers of evil have been marshalled. Satan invariably gets busy. Everything goes badly. Seriously needed supplies do not arrive with the coming of the annual ship, that which does arrive is very generally ruined by sea water, our preserved meats mouldy, our eggs spoiled, our drugs and medicines not as we had expected, furniture broken. We are misunderstood, our motives questioned, and our best efforts maligned. Programs go awry and our earnest endeavours seemingly go for naught."

Satan will resort to countless ways to keep us from fruit-bearing service. He will hinder us from going to prepared places and people; will dissipate our time and strength, putting upon us such pressure that Christ's power is lacking, and we become strained and feverish in too many activities; he will occupy us with secondary and secular concerns; will tempt us to use carnal instead of spiritual weapons; will intrigue us into worldly alliances and the acceptance of worldly counsel instead of seeking to know and follow the counsel of God.

Satan is the Persecutor and Murderer

John 8:44. "Ye are of your father, the devil, and the lusts of you father ye will do. *He was a murderer from the beginning.*"

Satan would ever seek to kill God's Gideons, those stalwart wrestlers, the "called, chosen and faithful" ones (Rev. 17:14) who would gladly lay down their lives in martyrdom, if need be, or in an even more tortuous daily dying through days and nights, months and years of lengthened persecution, rather than make any compromise with God's truth or be disloyal to God's Son.

This very day there are ministers of the gospel languishing in concentration camps and prisons, others are enduring terrible torture and barbarous persecution because of refusal to worship at pagan shrines. Every Spirit-filled wrestler is open to Satan's murderous attacks and death ambuscades through disease and disaster.

There needs to be a definite committal of the body to the Lord for protection from every such danger.

How, then, is this accuser, adversary and murderer to be met? With fear or with faith? If with faith, upon what solid ground does our faith rest for the power to overcome such a powerful enemy?

Rev. 12:11. "And they overcame him *by the blood of the Lamb,* and *by the word of their testimony: and they loved not their lives unto death."*

"They overcame him."—Victory is absolutely assured. No child of God need or should ever fear the devil. The way of victory over all his accusations, hindrances and murderous attacks is clearly outlined in this verse, *"By the blood of the Lamb,"* or on the ground of the blood. We may have been guilty of every sin of which the devil accuses us; we may even be guilty this moment of the accusation he brings, but the precious blood of Christ was shed to redeem us from the guilt, penalty, and power of sin, and we may trust in the blood of Christ to answer every indictment the devil may bring against us. Instead of his holding over us the fear of our own guilt, we may hold over him the fact of his own defeat as our accuser by the already accomplished victory of the Cross.

"By the word of their testimony." To overcome the enemy he must be silenced and his power to hinder must be thwarted. Next to the power of the blood is the power of the Word spoken in the power of the Spirit. A deep, genuine experience of the truths of salvation and sanctification, wrought in one through the indwelling, infilling Spirit, and then witnessed to by one empowered by the Spirit, is a mighty weapon against the adversary.

"They loved not their lives unto death." What can the murderer do but acknowledge himself overcome before such a sacrificial spirit as this? To save us and to destroy Satan our Lord was "obedient unto death, even the death of the Cross." When for love of Him, or for those to be won to Him, we are willing even to lay down our lives in death, or "to fill up that which is behind of the afflictions of Christ in your own flesh for his body's sake," through long-drawn-out persecution, then Satan, the murderer, has been truly overcome.

6. THE CHRISTIAN WRESTLER'S VICTORY

We have not shrunk from declaring the power of the devil, which is clearly stated in the Word and seen in the world. While it is foolish to underestimate his power, it is fatal to overestimate it. However great and powerful he is, he has been overcome by the mighty Lord, whose victory is our victory (I John 4:4). Let us now see how that victory is made ours:

The Assurance of Power in Christ

6:10. *"Be strong in the Lord* and in the power of his might."

"Be strong."—Never fear nor falter nor faint, but always be prepared through an enduement with fresh strength which enables you to be victorious from the start to the finish. The devil says, "Be fearful, look around at difficulties and dangers. Be cowardly and give up, for you can never win out against such hindrances and opposition. Be discouraged, look in at your own weakness." But God says, *"Be strong!"* Victory is ours when we realize that strength lies first of all in our inward attitude. To assume power we must be assured of power. But that assurance will never come if we look in at ourselves or out at the enemy. If we try to match our power against his, we will succumb in ignominious defeat. We may raise up all kinds of sandbag defences of our own making, but the master strategist will make a surprise attack on our blind side, or drop a fiery dart from the air, and we are overcome.

"Be strong *in the Lord.*" Our strength lies in a Person, and Oh, what a Person! Note His name. THE LORD. Ponder that name until it stands out before you in all its singular glory and solitary grandeur. Not "Jesus," his personal, human name that indicates His Saviourhood, sweet and precious as that name is. Not "Christ," His official, mediatorial name, The Anointed One, indispensable as that is to us. But "LORD," His sovereign, kingly name that stands for His rulership over the universe and all in it. "The Lord, the mighty God, the blessed and only Potentate, the King of kings and Lord of lords."

"IN." Yes, capitalize, italicize and underline this two-lettered word. But why give it such emphasis and importance? Because herein lies hidden the secret place of victory over the devil. Where we are determines our victory, because it determines our strength and power of resistance. *"In the Lord"* we are both strong and secure. Our Victor envelops us, for "we are hid with Christ in God." So, as someone has said, "Before the devil can touch you, he must get through God and Christ."

"And in the power of his might." Our strength lies not only in what He is, but in what He has. Our power is in a Person whose power is extraordinary, for "it is the power of *his might.*" This is exactly the same word used in 1:19, when describing the quality of the power used in raising Christ from the dead. In the strength of the

mighty power of the Lord we are equipped to fearlessly meet Satan and all his hosts, confident that we shall be "able to stand," "able to withstand," and "able to quench all the fiery darts of the wicked one." Our part, then, is calm, confident assurance of power over all the power of the enemy. We enter the warfare victors through faith in the victorious Lord, upon whom we keep our eyes fixed. Dear reader, do you know in your daily experience the conquering power of His might?

The Assertion of Our Position in Christ

6:11. "That ye may be *able to stand* against all the wiles of the devil."

6:13. "Having done all, *to stand.*"

6:14. *"Stand therefore,* having——"

6:13. "That ye may be *able to withstand.*"

"That *ye.*"—Every Christian, even the least and the lowliest, is included. Not one need fear the enemy, for there is victory for every Christian who has heard the call to arms and offered himself as a warrior. *"May be able."* What intense relief and courage these words, used three times in this passage on warfare, bring to the warrior! They are God's pledge of perfect provision for victory. God cannot lie and will not mock us, therefore, "ye *shall* be able."

"To stand."—Do not fear, falter, faint, fall nor flee before the foe. Never expect defeat or plan retreat, but wait to see the devil depart from you as he did from Christ in the wilderness. Do not even fight. The battle is not ours, but the Lord's. Our part is to *"stand still* and see the salvation of the Lord, *for the Lord shall fight for you,* and ye shall hold your peace." *"Stand"* in the perfection of Christ's finished work and in your divinely-appointed position in Him. *Seated* in Christ in the heavenlies, far above all principality, power, might and dominion, we are able to *stand* against Satan. In Christ the enemy is under our feet. We do not wrestle *for* a position of victory, but *from* one. Therefore standing in Christ we may reckon on the battle won before it is begun. Calmly, confidently, take your position in Christ and assert it courageously. Stand *unafraid.*

"Stand against *the wiles of the devil.*" Note it does not say "the power," but "the wiles" of the devil. He is a practised strategist who has been in warfare against God and His people for many millenniums, and there is no art, no craft of cunning, no machination in warfare of which he is not the master. He can out-manœuvre us completely by his deceptions and devices. But Christ, the *wisdom* of God, is Victor over Satan, the master of *wiles*. So in Christ we stand *undaunted*.

"Having done all, to stand."—Having fully equipped ourselves according to God's directions, and having nothing more we can do to prepare ourselves for battle, then during an especial attack of the enemy we must stand unmoved. However fiery the trial of faith may be, however long it may last, we must stand in faith, refusing all doubt and depression, knowing that all is by the Father's permission and in the fulfilment of His purpose. The Lord of hosts anticipates no cowards nor deserters in His army. It is not enough for us to resist sometimes and to gain occasional victories, then, when some peculiarly hard trial or severe affliction comes, to go under in defeat. However fierce or often the attack, or however many the forces massed against us, let us never give in, nor retreat one step, but in the thickest of the fight and in the darkest hour, let us see the enemy overwhelmed and overthrown, the battlefield covered with victor's spoils, and ourselves standing in the midst as overcomers. Stand *unconquered*. "Stand your ground in the day of battle, and having fought to the end, *come off victors on the field.*"

"Stand, therefore, having—." After one attack, do not be worried or worn out, but stand firmly holding your ground, fully equipped for the next assault. Stand without flinching or faltering, but joyously and peacefully when all is pitch-dark before you, when you cannot see a step ahead, when the enemy seems to be in the ascendant and to have complete control over your circumstances. Stand with a victor's spirit, faith, courage, assurance, conviction. Stand *invincible*.

"That ye may be able to withstand." The believer's exalted position in Christ is not one only of high privilege, but also of great responsibility, for Christ shares with him His authority over all the power of the enemy, as well as His victory. So it is not enough that, as a member of Christ's Body, we stand in victory in our personal conflict with Satan. We must also resist his attacks against the corporate Body and against individual members of it. We must withstand Satan in his efforts to block world evangelization and the deliverance of individual souls from his kingdom, and in his opposition to revival within the Church. There is an offensive as well as a defensive warfare to be waged. Christ's victory over Satan must be enforced and the spoils must be claimed. We rejoice exceedingly that on Calvary's Cross the Lord spoiled the principalities and powers and triumphed over them. But the practical part of that victory involves stripping these evil powers of all the authority they

previously exercised over us and, instead, exercising authority over them.

Just before our Lord's ascension He said, *"All authority* hath been given unto me in heaven and on earth." He assumed that authority when He sat down at the right hand of God in the heavenlies and was exalted as Lord over all created things and beings. He shared that authority with the Church, His Body, when He was made Head over it. Therefore, every saint in Christ is the possessor of the authority of Christ. This is a staggering fact, which we hesitate to accept, and from which we consciously shrink. The responsibility for such a possession is simply overwhelming, and most of us would gladly shirk it. The failure of the Church to assume and exercise this divinely-imparted authority accounts in large measure for its impotence to-day before the massed hosts of evil.

Let us understand clearly just what this authority is and involves. Authority should not be confused with power. The distinction is made clear in the following quotations:

"Authority is not power, it is only *the imparted right* to bring the power of another into operation."

"One stands at the crossing of two great thoroughfares. Crowds of people are surging by; multitudes of high-powered vehicles rush along. Suddenly a man in uniform raises a hand. Instantly the tide of traffic ceases. He beckons to the waiting hosts on the cross street, and they flow across in an irresistible wave. What is the explanation? The traffic officer has very little 'power.' His most strenuous efforts could not avail to hold back one of those swiftly-passing cars. But he has something far better. He is invested with the 'authority' of the corporation whose servant he is. The moving crowds recognize the authority and obey it. *Authority, then, is delegated power.* Its value depends upon the force behind the user."

Having authority defined, now let us have it illustrated. Paul was an ambassador of Christ, sent into Satan's domain to rescue sinners from his power and kingdom. On his first missionary journey he met two men in Paphos. One was Sergius Paulus, deputy of the country; the other, Elymas, the sorcerer, a false prophet. The deputy desired to hear the Word of God through Paul, but the sorcerer *withstood* Paul, "seeking to turn away the deputy from the faith." Here is the picture of a man, filled with the devil, *withstanding* a man filled with the Spirit. One has behind him the authority of Satan, the other of the Lord. Which would be the victor? Let Scripture answer:

Acts 13:9-12. "Then Saul, (who also is called Paul) filled with the Holy Ghost, *set his eyes on him,* and *said,* O full of all subtilty and all mischief, *thou child of the devil, thou enemy of all righteousness,* wilt thou not cease to pervert the right ways of the Lord? . . . And now, *behold the hand of the Lord is upon thee, and thou shalt be blind, not seeing the sun for a season.* And immediately there fell on him a mist and a darkness; and he went about seeking some to lead him by the hand . . . Then the deputy, *when he saw what was done,* believed, being astonished at the doctrine of the Lord."

Note the three-fold expression of authority. In Paul's *look;* "set his eyes on him." Did not Elymas know he was defeated the moment his eyes met Paul's? Did he not see in every expression of Paul's face fearlessness, conviction, courage, victory? In Paul's *words:* "Thou child of the devil, thou enemy of all righteousness." What man would dare or would have the right to say such words to another man? Paul was only bringing the power of the Lord into operation against the power of Satan. In Paul's *act:* "Thou shalt be blind." How awful for one man to inflict such a punishment upon another! But no; a man did not do it. "The hand of the Lord is upon thee." Paul was the Lord's agent in the administration of punishment. But, even acknowledging that the authority is the Lord's and Paul was merely the channel for its exercise, who is sufficient for such a task? Only he who is "filled with the Holy Spirit."

Satan sought and found entrance into the early Church through Ananias and Sapphira, through whose sin he aimed to destroy the purity and power of the Church, thus dishonouring and defeating Christ, its Head. Peter used his God-given authority in discipline and in the destruction of Satan's work (Acts 5:7-14). The spiritual condition of the Church would be vastly different to-day if such authority had been exercised during its history by those responsible for its leadership. God calls his warriors fearlessly to bind the strong man and his spiritual hosts of wickedness and of darkness in all parts of the world, as through the Spirit's enlightenment they are made aware of their working.

The Acceptance of Our Protection in Christ

As our power and position are in a Person, so also is our protection. This is fully consonant with the whole truth of Ephesians in that all our wealth which is deposited in Christ is sufficient for the requirements both of our walk and our warfare.

God gives persuasive reasons why we should accept this protection: *"For* we wrestle against" a foe so powerful in himself, in the hosts united with him, in the strength of his organization, in the cleverness of his wiles that, if unprotected, we will meet certain defeat. *"Wherefore"* we need an armour that is sufficient to protect our whole being and that will equip us for both defensive and offensive attacks. *"Therefore"* be prepared, either in an emergency or in ordinary circumstances, for any kind of an attack. Never knowing where, how or when Satan will attack us, we should never be unprotected or unprepared. His attacks may come at the most unexpected time and from wholly unlooked-for quarters. There will not be time when the attack comes to put on our panoply. "Therefore" it is well to anticipate that "evil day," and to stand every moment fully protected by our divinely-provided armour.

6:11. *"Put on the whole armour of God* that ye may be able to stand against the wiles of the devil."

6:13. *"Wherefore take unto you the whole armour of God,* that ye may be able to withstand in the evil day, and, having done all, to stand."

"The whole armour."—There are six pieces of armour, each of which is a source of strength and security in warfare. Five are for defensive and one for offensive warfare. No part of the life must be exposed, for even one vulnerable place would mean defeat. So we cannot pick and choose what parts of the armour we wish to wear. We need to wear the whole armour all the time. *"Of God."* What a relief to know that we do not need to provide the armour! How ignorant we are of the strength and the stratagems of the enemy! How inadequately we gauge our own inability and impotence! But our omniscient God, who knows all about our foe and about us, has provided an armour both suitable and sufficient.

"Put on"—clothe yourself with this armour for defensive protection against every wile of Satan to despoil you of your wealth, to decoy you from your walk, and to disable you in warfare. The armour is not a museum piece, but for the battlefield. *"Take unto you"* the whole armour as protection in offensive warfare. God makes the armour, but we must take it. Note that God has provided no protection for the back, for He expects no deserters.

"Stand—having your loins girt about with truth"

We have seen that Satan comes to us first as the liar and deceiver, so we can understand why God provides first of all the girdle of truth for our protection. Christ, the Truth and the true God, is our armour against the attacks of Satan, the liar and deceiver.

John 14:6. "I am *the truth.*"

Rev. 3:7 "These things saith he that is holy, *he that is true.*"

The soldier's girdle was no mere ornament. It went around the body, holding other pieces of armour in place and giving the soldier freedom in movement. So this divine girdle of truth must encompass our whole life. The whole circle of truth should wholly encircle us, leaving no gaps. This will really mean the two prayers of Ephesians answered in us; the revelation of God's truth to our minds through the Spirit's enlightenment, realized in our experience through the Spirit's enablement. Truth apprehended will be applied. This involves a very intimate dealing of truth with every department of our lives, which the apostle John described as "a walk in truth."

III John 4. "I have no greater joy than to hear that my children *walk in truth.*"

Such a walk implies a stern, strict dealing with sin and self; allowing no conscious hypocrisy or insincerity; no compromise with known sin; no excuse or vindication for wrongdoing; no condoning of sins such as temper, irritability, worry or depression on the ground of physical causes or domestic circumstances. It compels us to face things just as they are and call them by their right names. He who is the truth encompasses our whole being, making every part true, beginning with the inward character, and ending with the outward conduct.

"Stand—having the breastplate of righteousness"

Satan comes to us as accuser and tempter, so God provides for us the breastplate of righteousness.

I Cor. 1:3. "Christ is made unto us *righteousness.*"

4:24. "Put on the new man which is *created in righteousness.*"

"*Having on.*"—Righteousness is not a day a week luxury, but a seven days a week necessity, if we are to resist Satan's temptations. "*Wear integrity* as your coat of mail." "*The breastplate*"—covering the vital organs where a wound would be fatal. "*Of rightousness.*" Being right because adjusted to God's will, and doing right because acting according to God's Word. This breastplate of righteousness is ours when we live according to the pattern of Christ and the precepts of the Word in our relationship to men. We can then stand before Satan's accusations with a good conscience and without self-reproach. We can also stand before his temptations without yielding. But there must be no flaw in the breastplate in the form of permitted wrong habit or practice. In all things, large and small, there must be strictest integrity up to our knowledge of God's Word and ways. A lustful desire allowed to rest in the heart can result in adultery; a love of money can lead to theft or to dishonesty in securing or handling funds. "Nothing exposes a saint in conflict more readily than a bad conscience in his ways."

"Stand—your feet shod with the preparation of the gospel of peace"

We have seen how Satan is the destroyer of peace between man and God and the instigator of discord between men: how also he will rob the saint of the peace of God through all kinds of inward distress of spirit, mind and heart, that he might hinder him from being the messenger of peace. But Christ our peace is our protection against all such attacks.

2:14. "For *he is our peace.*"

John 14:27. *"My peace I give unto you. . . .* Let not your heart be troubled, neither let it be afraid."

"Your feet shod."—For progress in our daily walk or for protection in our warfare we need to be well shod. No warrior would think of entering a battle in dancing slippers. If you ever noticed a soldier's shoes you know they are substantial and suitable for any kind of road, weather, or hardship. *"With the preparation of the gospel of peace."* God has told us we would have temptations, trials, testings, so we must be prepared to stand the strain of slippery paths of temptation and of the stony hills of adversity and affliction. Only the peace of God is sufficient for the heart in the midst of life's losses, infirmities and tragedies. As we walk through this disordered world there are a thousand things to bruise and wound us, but "the peace of God that passeth all understanding shall keep your hearts and minds through Christ Jesus."

Stand—*"above all taking up the shield of faith, wherewith ye shall be able to quench all the fiery darts of the evil one."*

Satan's very first work with man was to create doubt of God Himself and then of His love, in order that man might be separated from God. On the manward side faith is the first necessity, for it is the cable that links us with Christ and keeps us united with Him. But even this faith is not our own; it is the gift of God, and is the creation of Jesus Christ.

2:8. "By grace ye are saved through *faith; and that not of yourselves; it is the gift of God.*"

Heb. 12:2. "Looking unto *Jesus, the author and finisher of our faith.*"

"Above all."—All other parts of the armour are put on or taken

by faith, so faith really equips one for warfare. *"Taking up"*—as a gift, faith must be appropriated, as are all other gifts, and then used. Faith is not faith unless it is at work. True faith is always active. *"The shield of faith."* In olden times the shield protected all parts, and had to be movable so as to repel attacks from any quarter. Faith has but one value for a warrior. It connects him with the Victor, the all-powerful, all-sufficient Lord, whose victory over Satan is his victory. *"Wherewith ye shall be able to quench all the fiery darts of the evil one."* Oh, how many of Satan's darts are fire-tipped, hellish balls of fire with but one purpose—to produce distress of mind, depression of spirit, disappointment in our relationships or in our work or in ourselves. *"Of the evil one."* It is sometimes hard for the child of God to distinguish between a dart from Satan and discipline from God. The Lord tests, but He never tortures. The Lord's discipline is for the purpose of making us a partaker of His holiness, while Satan's dart is to make us a partner in his hellishness. *"Able to quench."*—The shield in olden times was made of skins and saturated with water. As the fiery darts of the enemy came against it, they were quenched. As we daily take our shield of faith, that enables us to rest fully upon the faithfulness of God, the finished work of Christ and the fulness of the Spirit, we shall be able to quench every fiery dart of Satan.

Stand—*"and take the helmet of salvation"*

Satan wages a real battle for the possession, control and use of the mind of the saint. He tries in every possible way to corrupt or confuse it through his false teachings and teachers. The Christian has but one safeguard against his attacks.

I Cor. 2:16. "We have *the mind of Christ.*"

Phil. 2:5. *"Let this mind be in you,* which was also in Christ Jesus."

4:23. *"Being renewed in the spirit of your mind."*

"Take the helmet,"—the covering for the head. There is tremendous need of protecting the mind of the Christian, for Satan finds an undiscerning mind a ready prey to deception and delusion and an undisciplined mind an easy mark for his defiling thoughts and suggestions. *"Of salvation."* This is the great all-inclusive gospel word that gathers into itself the exceeding riches of God's grace, and then gives out those riches in election, predestination, adoption, acceptance, redemption, enlightenment, inheritance, sealing and security, as we have found out in Ephesians. Salvation covers the whole range of the work of God, the Father, Son and Spirit in creating a

saint out of a sinner and in making him an heir of God and joint-heir with Christ.

The experimental knowledge of full salvation in Christ is absolutely essential for the Christian warrior, for if he has any doubt of his own salvation, how can he confidently meet the foe, or how can he effectually win a sinner to Christ? And in these days of manifold Satanic counterfeits, how can he discern the false from the true?

Stand—"and take the sword of the Spirit, which is the word of God"

Five pieces of armour were given for our defence against Satanic attacks upon us. But God provides one piece for offensive, aggressive warfare, that we may be able to deal death-blows to the enemy, and gather spoils from the battlefield.

"Take the sword of the Spirit," which God Himself defines "which is the word of God." The sword is God's own utterance given to us in His written Word, inspired by the Spirit, revealed to us by the Spirit (1:17, 18), used by the Spirit in us to sanctify and cleanse (5:20), and then wielded by the Spirit through us to defeat the devil (6:17).

The word of God was the one weapon used by Jesus in the wilderness when, as the Representative Man, He won not only His victory, but ours too, over the devil. Each of Satan's three attacks was met with a sword of the Spirit,—"It is written," and three times Satan was repulsed. Only as we use this mighty weapon with intelligence and skill will we be able to withstand Satan successfully. This will require of us a constant, systematic study of God's Word, that our sword may be easily and quickly unsheathed, and that just the needed part of it may be used at the right time and in the right way.

With such power, position and protection ours, should not our battlecry ever be "able to stand" and our battle song "The Lord hath given me the victory."

7. PRAYER WARRIORS

6:18. "Praying always with all prayer and supplication in the Spirit, and watching thereunto with all perseverance and supplication for all saints."

6:18 is not a mere postscript to 6:10-17. In the wars of earth many a battle has been lost by the sagging in spirit of a section of the army which, giving up in defeat, has allowed the enemy to break through and win. How, then, is the spirit of an overcomer to be habitually maintained in the individual, and how is the spiritual morale of the whole army of Christ to be kept in effectual fighting trim? Then, if the victory of the wrestler is dependent upon the power, position and protection provided in Christ, how is his connection with the Lord to be maintained unbroken? Still further, if the Lord has given the Christian wrestler power over all the power of the enemy to bind him and spoil him of his goods, how is that power to be released and made operative? The answer is clear:

$$\text{Stand Praying} \left\{ \begin{array}{l} \text{always} \\ \text{with all prayer} \\ \text{in the Spirit} \\ \text{and watching} \end{array} \right\} \text{For all saints}$$

The Potent Wrestler is a Prayer Warrior

"Stand *praying*."—Subjectively prayer is the admission of utter ignorance and impotence. We neither know what to do, nor have the power to do; therefore we pray. Objectively, it is the expression of supernatural wisdom and power. We have been told what to do and given power to do it. The spirit of the prayer warrior is a strange paradox; Christward it is one of conscious weakness seeking strength: Satanward it is one of conscious strength expressed in victory. This dual attitude is both the cause and the effect of prayer. The Christian warrior has absolutely nothing in himself with which to meet such a foe or to win out in such a conflict. Standing alone before Satan and his hosts, he would tremble in fear and flee in defeat. He gladly acknowledges the truth of His royal Commander's words, "Apart from me ye can do nothing." But the wrestler has everything in Christ. His one necessity, then, is to keep in constant communication with his Lord. Unbroken communion through prayer with our Captain-Conqueror-Christ is the only ground of assurance of habitual victory over Satan.

"Praying *always*" is to have the spirit in such unbroken communion with the Lord that all things, at all times, in all places, may be carried to Him in the upward look and inward attitude, even if no words are spoken. It implies also the outstretched hand of complete dependence both on ordinary days and in sudden crises. But preparedness against Satan's wiles requires the wisdom and strength that only comes through definitely-stated times set apart for prayer. Many Christians in different parts of the world are setting aside a special day each month on which they give themselves in prayer for world-wide evangelization and revival within the Church.

Satan fears nothing as he fears a saint who knows how to prevail with God in prayer and release the omnipotent power of God against him. So he will use every devise to keep us from praying. He will cause physical fatigue and lethargy; unfit us mentally for prayer through the cares and burdens of the home and of business; and destroy our power in prayer through doubt, discouragement and depression. So when we least feel like praying is the time we most need to pray, for Satan already has gained a foothold in us.

"With all prayer." Might not "all prayer" have several meanings? Praying on all occasions, in a prayer group, in prayer meeting, in public worship, even where God's people are gathered together socially, prayer is befitting. Praying in all places; in one's own closet with the shut door, at the family altar each morning, in the Bible class, or devotional meeting. Praying at all times; in prosperity as well as adversity; in sickness or health; morning, noon and night, as the Psalmist prayed. Praying for all things in our personal life, home, business, work, that no loophole may be left for Satan to enter and to work. Everything needs to be covered by prayer. How often we could say what one friend recently wrote me, "For the enemy has attacked in such a surprising way and we were so unprepared to meet the onslaught." *"And supplication."*—Going beyond our own needs and withstanding Satan's attacks on others by specific petition. Prayer should be focused on some special need or danger of one of God's saints, as the prayer of the Church for Peter when he was in prison.

"In the Spirit." As carnal weapons do not prevail in spiritual warfare, neither will prayer that is in the flesh have any power. There may be a form of prayer without reality; even a use of all the accepted terms of prayer warfare, but without point or power. Prayer to be effectual in warfare needs to start with God, who sees the whole battlefield, who knows the devil's plan of campaign, who decides the place and part of every wrestler, and who directs the movement of the entire army of the Lord with the definite objective of carrying out His eternal purpose. God Himself must give us the prayer to pray. It must come straight from His heart to ours with a deep sense of conviction, urgency and assurance. This is the work of the Holy Spirit. We do not see Satan's hidden ambush, his ingeniously concealed snare. But the all-wise, ever-watchful Spirit sees every danger and pitfall, and will so inspire prayer within us that we are forewarned and forearmed. How can we ever remember all the things for which we know we should pray? We cannot, but the Holy Spirit will bring them to our remembrance, and we should never dis-

regard any impulse of the Spirit to pray. The Holy Spirit praying in us will determine both the character and the content of our prayer. Prayer in the Spirit must be Spirit-inspired, Spirit-inwrought, Spirit-taught, Spirit-directed, and Spirit-energized.

"And watching thereunto." The prayer warrior must be vigilant; permitting no laziness or self-indulgence that unfits for prayer; guarding his time so that even odd moments may be requisitioned for prayer, and definitely planning his daily schedule so that suitable time may be given to prayer; watchful for everything that feeds and fosters the prayer life, and on guard against anything that enfeebles or hinders it. *"Thereunto."* Through the Word know God's purpose both for the Church and the world; then watch the trend of events and praise as you see God's eternal purpose being fulfilled, and pray as you observe Satan's efforts to thwart it.

"With all perseverance."—Hold on and hold out, not fainting through fatigue, not yielding to discouragement because of delayed answer, not being deflected by pressure of other things. But persevere in faith until victory comes.

"For all saints."—We are members one of another, bound together in Christ in a union so real that if one member suffers, all the members suffer, therefore the members should have the same care one for another (I Cor. 12:25, 26). The whole body of Christ suffers defeat to the degree that the individual members are defeated and the victory of the Church over the Satanic foe is dependent upon the victory of every Christian. Herein lies the responsibility of each saint for all saints. Not all Christians are appropriating their wealth in Christ, or walking worthily of their high calling, or standing victoriously against Satan. Many are grieving the Spirit by still walking according to the world and the flesh, thereby giving place to the devil. So few are enlightened by the Spirit (1:17); praying in the Spirit (6:18); strenghtened by the Spirit (3:16); and filled with the Spirit (5:18). Wherein does the blame lie for the weakness of the Church? Does not each saint share the blame in so far as he has failed to pray for all saints?

So much of narrowness, selfishness and exclusiveness characterizes our prayers. We pray for our own local church and for our own denominational home and foreign mission work, but what of the many other hundreds of battalions of Christian soldiers under a different name and leadership, but all part of the Lord's host? Battles may be won here and there, but the war will be lost unless there is advance along all sectors of the fighting line. There are new recruits to be found; wounded comrades to be cared for; thinned-out ranks to be filled; officers to be trained; funds for carrying on the warfare to be provided, and only as each prays for all can all this be done. One wonders what measure of new life and power would come into the Church if every saint faithfully offered for all saints the two inspired prayers of Ephesians.

6:19, 20. "And *for me*, that utterance may be given unto me, that I may open my mouth boldly, to make known the mystery of the gospel, . . . for which I am an ambassador in bonds, that therein I may speak boldly as I ought to speak."

"*And for me*."—Paul was Christ's chief-of-staff of the human forces of that early Church. Therefore he was the mark for Satan's most vicious attacks. Satan had succeeded in putting him in prison, and thought he had put him out of the conflict, but the dauntless old warrior binds the enemy with prayer, who had bound him only with chains, and in that very prison wins new spoils for his Lord.

Though undaunted, he was not self-confident. He needed strength and courage to preach the gospel boldly and to faithfully fulfil his duties as an ambassador of Christ. To this end he craves the help through prayer of other saints. Oh, what need there is to-day for this very petition for ambassadors of Christ, both on the mission field and at home! It is becoming increasingly hard for loyal messengers of Christ to proclaim boldly the gospel of a perfect salvation through the Saviour. Many are persecuted and imprisoned for the gospel's sake, even as Paul was, and they are saying to us, "Pray *for me*."

There is no retiring list in God's army. He may shift the position of some of his old wrestlers and, because of their rich experience, gained in years of active service on the front firing line, place them with His prayer reserves. He needs prayer warriors to-day almost more than anything else, so, if He has given you the honour to be one, let it give you unbounded joy.

A tremendous responsibility rests upon the prayer warrior, both Christward, Churchward and Satanward, upon which we may only briefly touch. But the subject deserves most careful and prayerful study. Christward, it involves fullest co-operation with the Lord in the carrying out of the Father's eternal purpose in and through Him. This requires a knowledge of the Father's will in regard to the Church and the world as revealed in His Word, that we may know what within the work of the Church to-day is under the direction of the Lord Himself through the Spirit's guidance, and what is the worldly wisdom and policy of human leadership, largely misguided through false prophets and teachers. Only so can we intelligently work, pray and give for the Lord's work. By co-operation with our Lord in prayer we can fight in all parts of the battlefield, and penetrate to the furthest reaches of the enemy's territory.

Our responsibility Churchward is great and manifold. From God's Word we need to know the teaching regarding the Church as the Body of Christ; to recognize not merely doctrinally but practically our oneness with all saints of whatever colour, race, country or status, and to so live, work and pray that the whole Body of Christ is lifted to life on that highest plane, "far above all," and maintained in that position in victory over Satan.

Satanward our responsibility is tremendously great, very far beyond what the vast majority of Christians have ever known or been willing to accept. Let Christ tell us what it is:

Matt. 12:29. "Or else how can one enter into a strong man's house, and spoil his goods, *except he first bind the strong man?* and then he will spoil his house."

Luke 10:19. R.V. "Behold, *I have given you authority . . .* over all the power of the enemy."

Have not most of us tried to spoil Satan of his goods before binding him? Have we not been ignorant of the authority given us and, when we did know of it, shrunk from fear to exercise it? Consequently, Satan has bound us (Lk. 13:16), instead of our binding him, and hindered us instead of our hindering him. The Lord would have His warrior know and experience this binding power of prayer in His name and use it in the defeat of Satan. God needs to-day prayer warriors who have learned the secret of exercising their God-given authority in prayer, and who will direct it against the most strategic efforts of the evil one, so that he has no power to close doors to the gospel; to compel Christians to worship at his shrines; to expel missionaries from the mission fields; to stop funds and other supplies for God's work; to send out his own ministers and false teachers to the mission field or into the pulpits of evangelical churches at home; to forestall the work of revival and the giving of the message of full salvation; to stir up trouble and strife in the church and the mission station; to wear out the saints in spirit, soul or body; to blind Christians to the truth of our Lord's return and so hinder the work of the completion and the purifying of Christ's Body; to hasten the ultimate triumph of Christ and the fulfilment of God's eternal purpose.

Dear fellow-Christian, are you a prayer-warrior? If not, will you offer yourself to Christ to-day to become one as His Spirit teaches and trains you?

The Apostle Paul, himself a tried and trusted warrior, by two crisp commands warns of two vulnerable spots which open to Satan the way of victory through crippling the Christian in spiritual warfare. Then by a third he exhorts every Christian to perfect his preparedness for warfare.

Giving Place to the Devil

4:27. "Neither give place to the devil."

Giving place to the Devil gives Satan headquarters in Christ's camp. It provides him a base from which to conduct his campaign. *Giving place to the devil* makes a part of Christ's army an ally of His arch-enemy, for the devil will not wrestle against himself. *Giving place to the devil* lessens the man-power of the Lord's host and surrenders to Satan spiritual resources which belong only to the Captain of our salvation. It compels Christ to go out to war handicapped. It weakens the warring power of omnipotence. It diminishes the working force of the supernatural. *Giving place to the devil* divides allegiance and puts traitors and deserters into the army of the Lord.

So the devil is ceaselessly busy seeking to gain some place in the life of every Christian wrestler. He will start with a very small place, anything so long as he gains a foothold. He knows our weak spot. He comes up on our blind side. He breaks through where the crust is thinnest. He bides his time until he can take us unawares. He tempts at our most susceptible points. He works wilily, archdeceiver that he is, to beguile us into making a league with him. To the truly spiritual warrior he comes most often as a veritable angel of light, even ensnaring some by claiming to be an envoy from God. He uses any method, however clever or cruel, to gain access, and does his best to disguise his approach. What he seeks to gain is a "place" to begin his activities, that he may undermine the Christian warrior's morale and render him incapable of fighting, that he may ultimately gain control and use him as his own accomplice.

Grieving the Holy Spirit

4:30. "Grieve not the Holy Spirit of God."

One who might shrink with horror and fear from giving place to the devil may, nevertheless, be making his victory in the heavenlies possible by grieving the Holy Spirit.

The Holy Spirit dwells within us to reproduce within us the victorious life of the glorified Christ that we may be enabled "to stand" and to release through us His supernatural power that we may be empowered "to withstand." Whatever restrains or restricts the Holy Spirit from carrying out His work to His utmost capacity, plays into Satan's hands to defeat Christ.

Then what is it in us that grieves the Holy Spirit? Naturally anything *un*holy. Whatever in us that is contrary to what He is, grieves Him. He is the Spirit of truth, faith, grace, wisdom, power, love, discipline, holiness, so anything that is *un*truthful, *un*believing, *un*gracious, *un*wise, *un*fruitful, *un*loving, *un*controlled, *un*holy, grieves the Spirit of God. Therefore sin of any nature or degree, whether open or secret, whether in flesh or spirit, whether gross or refined, grieves the Holy Spirit.

Being Filled with the Spirit

5:18. *"Be filled with the Spirit."*

This is the slogan of the victorious wrestler. It is the Spirit-filled warrior, and only he, who overcomes and overthrows the satanic hosts.

"Filled" with the Spirit's wisdom (1:17), he discerns the wiles of the devil (6:11). *"Filled"* with the Spirit power (3:16), he stands against them. *"Filled"* with all the Spirit's fullness (3:19), he is supernaturally equipped to engage in this warfare between the supernatural forces of good and evil and is supernaturally strengthened to come off victor.

6:13. "Wherefore take unto you the whole armour of God, that ye may be able to stand your ground in the day of battle, and, *having fought to the end, remain victors on the field."*

THE AFTERGLOW

LOOKING back over the Grand Canyon of Scripture four great truths suffuse a glory light over it like an afterglow. Interwoven and interpenetrated, they reveal the Trinity at work linking eternity with time, heaven with earth, glory with grace, God with man, the Saviour with the sinner, Christ with the Church.

The Purpose of the Father

Antidating creation was the eternal purpose of God determining, conditioning and relating all things of creation and salvation in their origin and their end. With God there were no surprises and no emergencies. The Word made flesh was not an after thought of God. The purpose of the Father stretches from the eternal past over the millenniums of time to the eternal future. This eternal purpose encompasses God's relationship to men, both sinners and saints; to angelic beings, both evil and good; and to Satan and his hosts. It centres in His Son for whom in the eternal ages of the past He chose a company of saints to be His Body and His Bride who would be in Him, become like Him and be with Him now and through all the ages upon ages to come.

The Person of the Son

One luminous Person fills and floods the Grand Canyon of Scripture with heavenly glory light—the Person of the God-man, our Lord Jesus Christ. The Jesus of history is not in view here. The Saviour of the gospels has gone from the Cross to the Throne and is seated there at the Father's right hand. The light that suffuses the Grand Canyon of Scripture is the glory of the crowned Victor; of the holy Head of the Church in whom dwelleth all the fulness of the Godhead bodily; and of the One to whom the Lordship over all things in heaven and upon earth is given.

The Position of the Christian in Christ

In Christ—how simple the words! How superb the truth! All Christians, of whom the Church consists, made one with the glorified

Christ so that His position is their position; His possessions their possession; His privileges their privileges; His power their power; His plenitude their plenitude.

"In Christ"—then "Into Christ in all things."

The Power of the Spirit

The outworking of the Father's purpose is in the Son. The inworking is by His Spirit. Access to the unsearchable riches in Christ and the appropriation of them is made possible only by the mighty power of the Holy Spirit. The fulness of God the Father made available in the fulness of the Son is made actual through the fulness of the Spirit.

"Be ye filled with the Spirit."

Printed in the United States of America

The SOVEREIGN ETERNAL PURPOSE of GOD regarding THE CHURCH	"According to the purpose of Him WHO "According to the ETERNAL PURPOSE "THE CHURCH which is His body, THE FU "For we are MEMBERS OF HIS BODY"		
	Calling 1^{3-14} / Prayer-Revelation 1^{15-23}	Creation 2^{1-10} / Conciliation 2^{11-18} / Construction 2^{19-22}	Constitutio...
GOD	"CHILDREN"1^5	"HOUSEHOLD"2^{19}	"FAM
CHRIST	"Chosen"1^4	"Created" 2^{10} "Reconciled"2^{16} "Builded Together"2^{22}	"Fellow "Fellow "Fellow
HOLY SPIRIT	"SEALING"1^{13}	ACCESS 2^{18}	STRE
CHURCH	IN THE HEAVENLIES IN CHRIST		

"In Whom we have obtained an inheritan

IN CHRIST

WEALTH — RICHES OF GRACE / RICHES OF CHRIST / RICHES OF GLORY

DOCTRINAL — REVELATION — K

Put on the new man 4^{24}

That ye may be filled unto all the fulnes

LIKE CHRIST

Till we all come unto a perfect man, unto

That He might present it to Himself a glo

That in the ages to come He might show the e

Outline Chart — Epistle to the Ephesians by Ruth Paxson

	Prayer— Realization 3$^{13-21}$	Character 4$^{1-16}$	Conduct 4^{17}-6^9	Conflict 6$^{10-18}$
o		"For we are MEMBERS OF ONE ANOTHER" 4^{25}		
" 3^{15}		"FOLLOWERS" 5^1		"WRESTLERS" 6^{12}
rs" mbers" 3^6 takers"		"Fitly joined" 4^{16}	"Walk not" "Walk" 4^{17}	"Stand" 6^{13} "Withstand"
TH 3^{16}		UNITY 4^3	FULNESS 5^{18}	PRAYER 6^{18}
			ON EARTH BEFORE MEN	IN WARFARE WITH SATAN
' 1^{11}		The riches of the glory of His inheritance in us 1^{18}		
3 6		WALK	IN UNITY 4$^{1-16}$ IN HOLINESS 4$^{17-30}$ IN LOVE 4^{31}-5^2 IN LIGHT 5$^{3-14}$ IN WISDOM 5$^{15-17}$ IN PRAISE 5$^{18-20}$ IN HARMONY 5^{21}-6^9	6$^{10-18}$ WARFARE Wrestle against Able to Stand Withstand
OW		EXPERIMENTAL — REALIZATION — BE		
		Grieve not the Holy Spirit 4^{30}		Neither give place to the devil 4^{27}
f God 3^{19}		Be filled with the Spirit 5^{18}		
he measure of the stature of the fulness of Christ 4^{13}				
us Church, not having spot or wrinkle or any such thing 5^{27}				
eeding riches of His grace in His kindness toward us through Christ Jesus 2^7				